The PowerBuilder Construction Kit

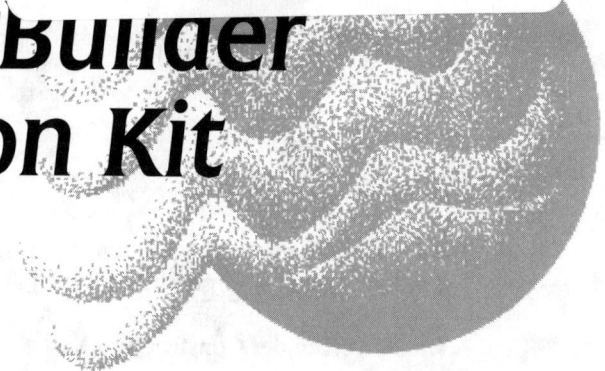

L. John Ribar
Steven Nameroff

Osborne **McGraw-Hill**

Berkeley New York St. Louis San Francisco
Auckland Bogotá Hamburg London Madrid
Mexico City Milan Montreal New Delhi Panama City
Paris São Paulo Singapore Sydney Tokyo Toronto

Osborne **McGraw-Hill**
2600 Tenth Street
Berkeley, California 94710
U.S.A.

For information on software, translations, or book distributors outside of the U.S.A., please write to Osborne **McGraw-Hill** at the above address.

The PowerBuilder Construction Kit

34567890 DOC 998765

ISBN 0-07-882079-0

Publisher
Lawrence Levitsky

Acquisitions Editor
Jeffrey Pepper

Project Editor
Mark Karmendy

Copy Editor
Kathryn Hashimoto

Computer Designer
Rhys Elliot

Illustrator
Marla Shelasky

Series Design
Jani Beckwith

Quality Control Specialist
Joe Scuderi

About the Authors...

L. John Ribar is a programmer and the author of several acclaimed books on C programming, including **BYTE's Windows Programmer's Cookbook**, **C DiskTutor**, and **FORTRAN Programming for Windows**. Ribar is the president of Picasso Software Group, a software development firm in York, Pennsylvania, specializing in the creation of custom applications and programming tools.

Steven Nameroff is the author of **QuickBASIC: The Complete Reference**, and co-author of **WordPerfect 6: The Complete Reference** and **Turbo Pascal 7: The Complete Reference**. Steve works as a consultant for Rational Software Corporation, specializing in complex software development using object-oriented methodologies.

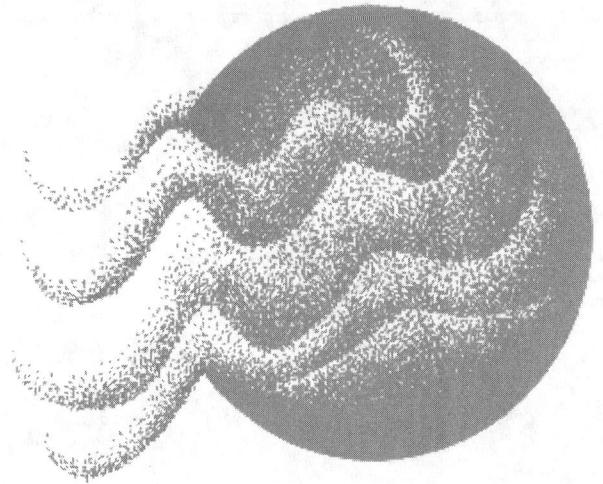

Contents At A Glance

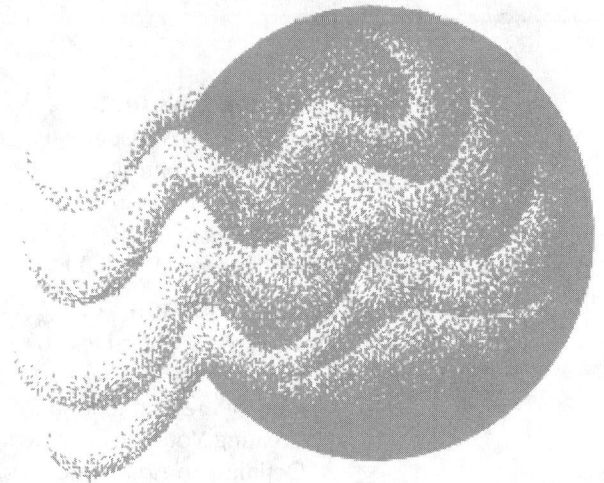

Contents

Acknowledgments

This has been a really interesting journey. A year ago I started my own full-time venture in the software development world, after running it on the side for a dozen years, and holding down full-time jobs in software design and development. Being out on your own changes the entire perspective on time ("management of" and "lack of") and real life!

Along came my good friend and editor Jeff Pepper, who helped immensely by letting me continue to write for Osborne/McGraw-Hill, in fact by giving me several projects in quick succession. This is the last of those books to be completed, and the one that took the most effort (physical, mental, verbal, and boy do I have sore wrists), probably from everyone. Why? Because about the time this book got going, the business did too.

Jeff, together with Ann Wilson, form a great editing team that deserves a lot of the credit for getting this work completed. Many thanks also to Steve Nameroff, who came in as a pinch hitter and had just a wonderful day at bat!

Thanks also to Greg Keesey and Mark Lindsay, two guys who have waited more patiently for the end of this project than anyone thought possible.

As always, I dearly thank my wife Deborah, and the kids (Louis, Jamie, Michael, and Leah) for putting up so much with my frequent absence. I think Deb pulled more hair out than I did on this one!

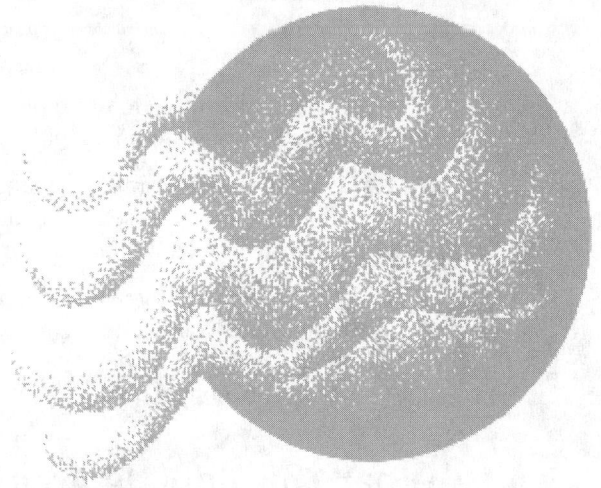

Introduction

Welcome to a new generation of application development tools. Are you a programmer? You don't need to be one to use PowerBuilder. Are you a manager of programmers? Maybe you can start showing off with your own applications now. But who is this book for? And what will this book do for you?

Who Should Read This Book

There are several categories that you might fit into, making this book the perfect choice for you.

- You want to get a good client-server database tool, and aren't sure which one to use. This book will give you the basics of PowerBuilder, showing you the simplicity with which applications can be built, and the power that is available through the script language, should you want to expand that far later.

- You just bought PowerBuilder, and aren't sure where to start in all the documentation you got. Start here, and get the overall view first. Then, if you need more details, look into the manuals that came with your software.

- Your company uses PowerBuilder, but you haven't yet. You don't want to try learning from the software manuals, but think a good background would help you in future projects, or in dealing with others who will be using the software on a regular basis.

■ You are a programming manager, looking for a quick method of generating client-server database applications without tying up valuable (and expensive) programmers all the time.

■ You are a programmer, looking for an overview of just how these new tools work. You want to learn something about the scripting language for future reference, or have just started a new project, and want a good product overview before getting into the actual programming.

What This Book Is About

First, the book provides an overview at the functionality that is available with PowerBuilder 4.0, the newest incarnation of the Powersoft application development environment. You will learn how to design your application, how to develop the database, and how to create a real application, including menus, dialog boxes, and reports.

Second, you'll find out what other support is available as part of the PowerBuilder Enterprise series, that you will need to complete your project. This includes help files, debugging, creating a project file, and using libraries to allow you (and your associates) to share the work you have done.

Third, you'll learn about the PowerScript language, a simple language you can start learning to enhance your PowerBuilder applications. The appendix gives you a quick reference to all the functions that are available once you start using scripts. Don't worry, though; this is something you can ease into gradually to start, and build up to later as your needs and capabilities (or courage) grow.

We still need programmers. After all, they are the ones that brought you the magic of PowerBuilder in the first place. But with tools like this, you can build the first versions of programs, seeing exactly how the menus and dialog boxes work, how the data is to be entered and displayed, and what capabilities you will give your end user.

Then, if you need more help, you can explain graphically what you expect, using the tools in the PowerBuilder series, and even start with a program that works. See how quickly your programmers will be asking more questions. How did you do that? That would have taken me a lot longer! Can you show me that Power stuff?

Here is an outline of how the book will proceed.

In Chapter 1, you will learn about the Powersoft offerings, and about the concepts of client-server technologies. You'll get deeper into client-server database concepts in Chapter 2.

Chapter 3 continues with a discussion of Windows programming and the use of Object-Oriented Technology. These topics are very important in utilizing PowerBuilder to its fullest. In Chapter 4, you'll start learning the details of PowerBuilder by building your first application objects.

Then, in Chapters 5 through 8, you'll start to design and develop your application database, organizing it with menus, toolbars, DataWindows, radio buttons, and list and dialog boxes.

Chapter 9 introduces you to the terminology and the language of PowerScript, then lets you see how scripts, functions, variables, and attributes work together to complete the implementation of an application.

Chapter 10 lets you experiment with more advanced data windows, window objects, and window controls to add some sophistication to the look of your applications.

In Chapter 11 you learn about the process of adding help for your application's users. In Chapter 12, the use and creation of libraries are discussed, two very important topics for reusing the objects and code you develop in each project. In Chapter 13, you learn to create the final application, and how to prepare to distribute it to your users. You'll learn about debugging your application (removing any possible defects) in Chapter 14.

Chapter 15 shows you another product, which works in concert with PowerBuilder. ER*win*/ERX for PowerBuilder adds extensive database design capabilities to your development environment, and is fully integrated with the PowerBuilder environment.

Finally, the appendix is full of information about the functions that are available in your PowerScripts. These scripts are how you add even more power to your application, often without the need for a programmer.

Let's get started. Turn the page to Chapter 1.

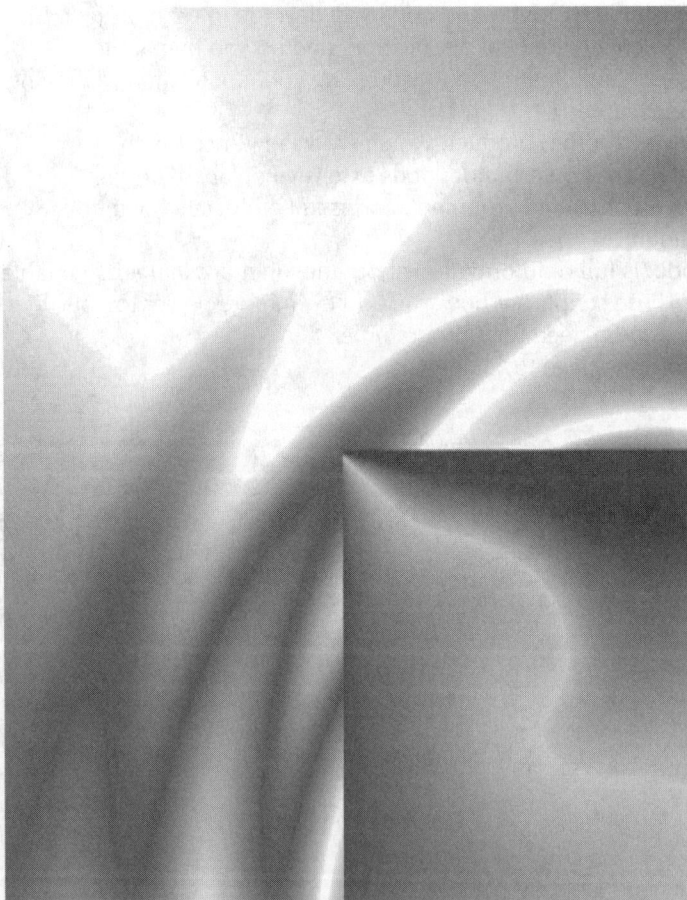

CHAPTER 1

Getting to Know Your Tools

Welcome to the PowerBuilder Construction Kit. You are about to learn how to create your own database applications and Windows programs. Imagine that only a few years ago, programming was done exclusively in Windows by specially trained C-language programmers, who had to work very hard to produce even the simplest program.

Times have changed, and PowerBuilder is a part of that wave of the future. In this chapter, you'll be introduced to the toolkit you have available in the Powersoft Enterprise. In Chapter 2, "Data Basics", you will get an introduction to database design. In later chapters, you'll learn more about all these tools through building an actual application or two.

PowerBuilder Enterprise

PowerBuilder, from Powersoft Corporation, is one of a new generation of application development tools. These tools enable non-programmers to create their own applications in a simplified manner, often without the aid of programming talent. This is a major shift in how programs are built. Previously, you might have had to wait months or years for the program you needed or the specific feature your existing software needed.

Powersoft provides you with a whole bag of tools to aid in your application construction tasks. Several different levels of software are available.

- PowerBuilder is a package that is useful in creating new applications. It is an object-oriented development tool for producing client-server database applications. It forms the basis of the Enterprise package, which will be covered throughout this book, and which contains all the other tools mentioned here.

- PowerMaker is a personal tool (that is, one that is not geared for full-time programmers) that uses a form-based approach useful in creating reports, queries, and graphs to view business information using an existing database.

- PowerViewer is a personal tool used for viewing information through queries and reports, utilizing databases and forms created by others.

- WATCOM SQL Database is a local, single-user database management package, integrated into the Powersoft Enterprise, that allows you to develop your own applications and test client-server applications without needing access to the actual data source. WATCOM SQL is also available in multiuser editions.

- PowerBuilder Enterprise is the complete package of tools. It includes the functionality of all the tools listed above, and more. It is the basis of this book.

To get started, let's review the Enterprise painters, the tools you use to graphically create (hence the name "painter") the many portions of your new application.

Painters Galore

The *painters* are the separate programs within PowerBuilder that allow you to create (or paint) each portion of your application. They are called painters because of their visual nature and interface (see Figure 1-1). While these painters will be covered in depth in later chapters, a brief overview here will give you a better overall feel for what is available.

All of the painters are available from the opening PowerBuilder screen by simply selecting one of the PowerBar buttons (shown below). Each of the buttons corresponds to a specific painter.

Application Painter

The Application painter is used to create your overall application. It includes the hierarchy of the application, showing everything from the icon that will be used down to the scripts (programming code) used to perform each of the specific functions. Don't worry, you don't need to be a programmer to write scripts—you'll learn how in this book.

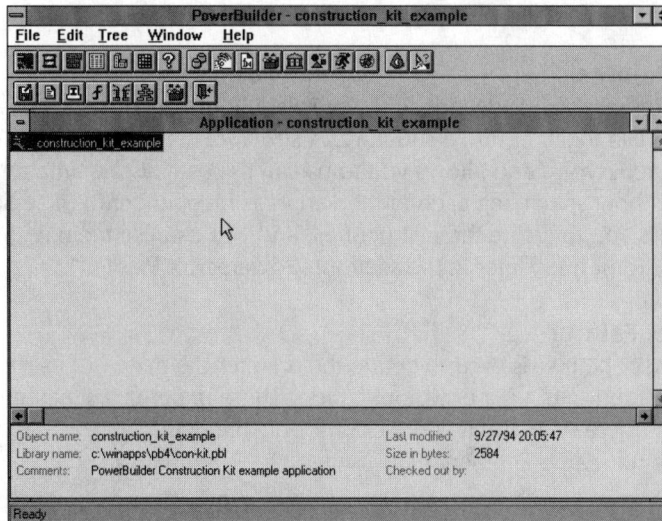

FIGURE 1-1.   *The Application painter allows you to graphically generate a new program*

Window Painter

Once you have defined an outline for your application in the Application painter, you define the specific windows in the Window painter. These windows are the method used to interface with the user of your program, and they may include such things as buttons, scrolling lists, radio buttons and check boxes, and DataWindows (described later in the section, "DataWindow Painter").

Menu Painter

To move around within your new application, you will want to define one or more menus. Each item in a menu can be used to call a script or move about within the windows and other objects you have defined. The Menu painter also allows you to create *toolbars,* a type of graphical menu that uses small buttons (with an icon on each to define what the button will do) to interface with your user. This allows the more common functions to be selected by picture, rather than through multiple menu selections.

DataWindow Painter

A DataWindow is a special type of object that is used in PowerBuilder applications. DataWindows are smart; they know how to do what is necessary to display information from your database. Depending on your application, you may never have to write any code at all to access, display, and report on the information in your database.

Structure Painter

If you plan to write scripts dealing with your data, it is sometimes simpler to package the data together into a structure. A *structure* maintains several variables, often of different types, and allows you to use all the data at one time and to keep it organized without specifying each of the variables independently. The Structure painter allows you to create these structures, and you can use them within your PowerScripts (described later in the section, "PowerScript Painter").

Preferences Painter

The Preferences painter is used to define the preferences that your user desires during the execution of your new application. These preferences may include the *data source* (where your application looks for data), default libraries, and window setup preferences, among others.

Database Painter

The Database painter is used to define your data requirements. It is the basis upon which your entire application is defined. In the Database painter, you design your data files, the *keys* (which define the sorting order for the data), and how the data files are related to each other. Once this is defined, your other objects will use the design.

In Chapter 2, "Data Basics", you'll learn more about how a database is defined. Later, in Chapter 16, "Using ER*win* to Design Databases Visually", you'll learn about another tool called ER*win*/ERX, from Logic Works, which works with the Enterprise series to design your database graphically.

Query Painter

Since you will probably not want to look at all of your data all of the time, you will want to define some queries to get specific information from your database. These queries are simple to define when you use the Query painter. Simply select the fields of information you wish to view and which records are important, and the Query painter generates the requisite SQL code.

Report Painter

The Report Painter allows you to graphically design reports for your data. You can easily lay out the page header, column heading, and data, as well as build totals and subtotals where you feel they are appropriate.

PowerScript Painter

As you become more knowledgeable with the workings of PowerBuilder, you will probably want to add even more functionality into your applications. For the functions that you just can't find, you will use the PowerScript painter. This tool allows you to write scripts (similar to programming code) that can be used throughout your application.

Function Painter

As you begin to write scripts for your applications, you may realize that you are writing a similar function over and over for each new application. The Function painter allows you to package these functions for reuse, so you can keep them available for each new program, without rewriting anything.

Library Painter

The Library painter is a development team's answer to code management in a PowerBuilder environment. The library concept involves the requirement that only one developer at a time should be able to change source code. The Library painter allows code to be checked out by a developer, and then checked back in when any changes are complete. In addition, the version of a specific object or script is maintained for each application you design.

By the way, a library can contain more that just scripts. Any object you design that you feel will be useful in other applications can be stored in a library; these objects can include DataWindows, menus, and structures.

User Object Painter

The User Object painter creates objects for use in PowerBuilder from existing Windows control objects. This painter includes the ability to use some VBX controls (as used in Visual Basic applications).

A Blueprint for Success

Okay, now you have an idea of what types of tools are available in the PowerBuilder Enterprise. But what now? How do you create your first application? It's not as difficult as you might think. In fact, according to Powersoft, there are just ten steps to the process.

1. Create the application object. Use the Application painter to create the application object. This is the container into which all your other objects and designs will be placed.

2. Design the user interface. For this step, you will make use of the Window and Menu painters, adding these objects into your application as they are completed. In addition, advanced users will utilize the User Object painter for non-Powersoft Windows controls and VBX files.

3. Define the behavior of the objects you've created. For this, you will use the PowerScript painter, writing the scripts that are needed to make each button and menu item work as you desire.

4. Add data to the application. There are two steps to this process. First, you may need to design a database using the Database painter. Or, you may need to find out more about the existing database your program will utilize. In either case, your next step is to define how you wish to view and access the data, using the DataWindow painter, possibly placing your resultant DataWindows into your user interface windows.

5. Generate reports, using the Report painter. (This step is only necessary if you want to have reports available.) Generate some reports, which your user can view on the screen or on the printer (depending on how you set it all up).

6. Add help to your application. (Again, this may be optional, but you might as well make the program look professional, if you're doing it at all.) Adding help also reduces the number of phone calls you'll get from the users when they aren't sure how something is supposed to work. Use the PowerScript painter again to generate the help.

7. Use the Library painter to use and track the various objects you are creating or that you are using from previous applications. With the Library painter, you can better manage these reusable objects for all the people at your site.

8. Debug your application using the Debugger. Bugs? Without programmers? It may never happen, but if you find a function or menu item acting odd, try using the Debugger to find out what is happening. Perhaps it is a simple misspelling or other minor flaw. The debugger is a tool that allows you to go through your application step by step, looking for any problems.

9. Deliver the application to the user. Using the Application painter, you can make all the final adjustments required for the application to be released, bringing together all the work that you have done.

10. Documentation. You may not be a programmer, you may not be used to writing, and you may not want to document your new application. But if you don't, you'll have more phone calls, and you'll have trouble remembering why you did things the way you did. Save yourself the headaches and write a document that describes how the application works, what database files (or sources) are used, what the different menu items should do, how to install and run the program, etc.

This is not the only outline for application development. But it is simple to understand and easy to follow. In this book, you'll see this ten-step plan put into action, and you'll also see some places where your own ingenuity will come in handy.

One more thing before you start. What exactly are you trying to create?

A Goal in Sight: The Client-Server Model

For many years, databases were maintained on large mainframe computers. No one really knew how they worked, and flexibility was not common.

This scenario has changed over the years. Bigger database systems have become more flexible, and many database systems have arrived at the personal computer level. The question is how to use these tools together.

Originally, PC database tools only allowed a single user to use a database file. If you wanted a report or you wanted to look up some information, you had to call the person who had the data. Then networks arrived, and database files could be shared between several users.

The next evolution is the client-server database. In a *client-server* environment, one computer acts as the database *server*, and all those wishing access to the information are the *clients*. The server does nothing but manage the database. Clients send requests for information (*queries*) to the server, and then receive an answer with the appropriate data. This is a very powerful solution, allowing a specialized piece of software to maintain the data, while allowing anyone to have access through remote commands.

PowerBuilder Enterprise is a client-server development tool. You will be creating a database (the server), but you will mostly be generating user (client) applications to access that database. The database can be the WATCOM SQL database included with the Enterprise package, or one of many other options.

But enough of the overview. Let's start learning about databases themselves.

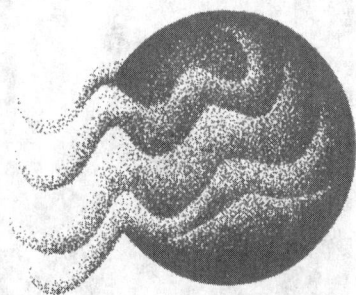

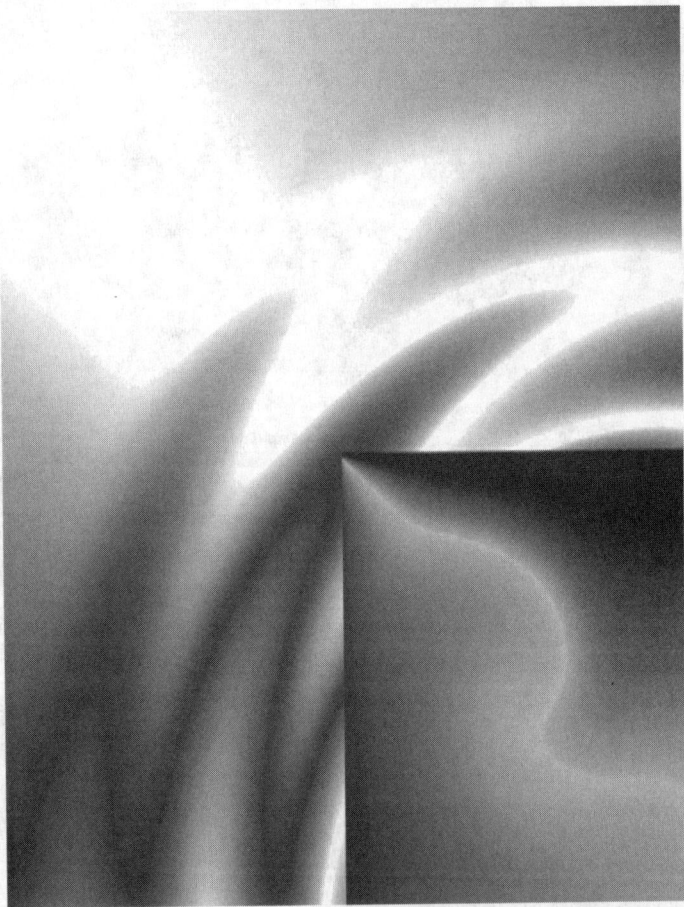

CHAPTER 2

Data Basics

Before we get into building PowerBuilder systems, there are a few techniques you will need to learn. In this chapter, you'll learn about database technology, and in Chapter 3, "The Working Environment," we'll cover object-oriented technology. If you are already familiar with these technologies, feel free to skip ahead to Chapter 4, "Laying a Foundation."

Early Life Databases

You were probably introduced to database technology at a very young age. If you (or a friend, or brother or sister) had a baseball card collection, your collection can be considered a database. How were your cards organized? Perhaps they were kept in order by the card number on the back of each card. Or, maybe you kept them in order alphabetically, by team and then by the player's name within each team.

Of course, what happened the second year you were collecting? Now there were two cards for most players. The card numbering was duplicated. Did you keep the cards together by year, by team, or aphabetically by player?

Believe it or not, all of these questions are related to database techniques. Before we get into a better explanation, lets look at some basic database terminology and concepts.

Terms of the Trade

An *application* is any project or system for which you have responsibility. This can be an accounting system, a construction cost-tracking system, or a point-of-sale system for a video store. An application can also refer to a computer program that handles the data for you. If you are in an office environment now, your application might be stored in a filing cabinet, as shown in the illustration below.

A *database* is a collection of information. It is all the information you need to maintain for a given application. For instance, for an accounting application, you will need to keep information about accounts payable (people you owe money to), accounts receivable (people who owe you money), and accounts (how you organize the money that flows in and out of your business). All of this information put together is the database. In your current office, a database might be considered a drawer in your filing cabinet, as shown here:

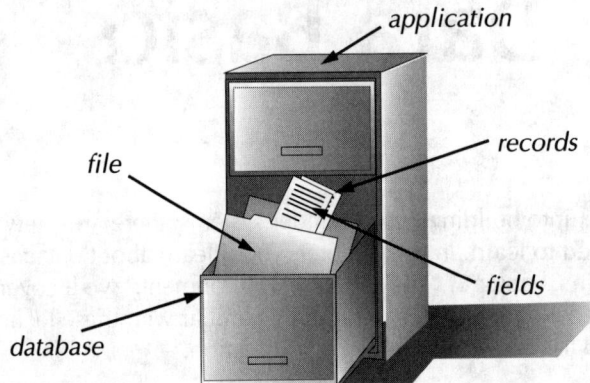

Continuing this analogy, your database is composed of files. *Files*, which are also known as *tables* in some circles, are the groups of information that your database contains. If we talk about the accounting system again, you may have a file for accounts receivable information, another for accounts payable, and a third for client information. (Of course, there will be a lot more files involved in an accounting system, but this is just an illustration.) Using the filing cabinet example, the files might be the specific folders within each drawer (i.e., one for Accounts Payable, one for Clients, etc.).

Within each file are one or more *records*. Each record has the same format as others in the same file, but the information in each one is different. For instance, a personnel record contains information about an employee: name, address, social security number, salary, withholdings, etc. But, although the format of the information for each employee is the same, the information kept for each is different (that is, different names, different addresses, etc.). In the filing cabinet, a record is a single piece of paper within a filing folder.

Each piece of information in a record is called a *field* (or *column* in some circles). If your database system uses files, it will probably use fields. If it uses the term "tables," fields will probably be referred to as "columns." Each field is a specific piece of information (employee name, address, salary, etc.).

Back to the Story

With a better feel for the database terms, lets see how the baseball card collection is really a database application.

The database is the set of all the cards that you owned. You may have kept files for each team, each year, or whatever method you used to divide and sort your cards.

Each record in the file is a single card. And of course the fields are the pieces of information stored on each card (player's name, team, statistics, etc.).

Armed with this information, and these many years of database experience, you are ready to start learning more about database design, and how databases are managed on computers.

Automating the Database

One of the problems with the baseball card collection was that it took a lot of time if you wanted to reorganize the cards. If you had all the cards in order alphabetically, there was no way to tell if you had all the cards in the set. Therefore, you had two options.

First, you could physically put the cards in numeric order. Then, if any cards were missing, you would see those cards missing from the pile. Then you'd probably keep a list of the missing cards, and check them off as you got them at a later time.

A second method would be to use a checklist. Many baseball card series came with one or more checklist cards, which list all the available cards, by number. Here, you would go through all the cards in your collection, in whatever order you kept them, and mark the cards off on the checklist as they are found.

On a computer, this process is greatly simplified through the use of *index files*, or *indices*. In a data file, the information is stored once, usually in the order it is placed into the database. Index files are then used to find things in different sortations. Here is how it works (look at Figure 2-1 for a quick visual aid):

■ The data is stored in a data file, in the order that it was entered.

■ Index files are created to maintain one or more sorted listings of the data.

■ Each index file only contains the index value (also known as the key value), and a pointer to the associated record in the data file. The index value is the field that is being sorted.

■ When a new record is added into the file, each of the index files is updated, even sorted if necessary. The data record itself is just added to the end of the data file.

Index files are very important in the design of database systems. If you only have a few records in your file, an index may seem like a lot of overhead. But if you have thousands of records, they are your only means for finding information quickly. Without an index, you would have to search through each and every record to find a specific one. With an index, you can quickly find the desired value in the index (which is sorted), and then read the correct record from the data file for the rest of the information that you need.

Now this may all seem a little confusing, but there's more. Not only do you need to use all these different files, you need to design them right, so you don't

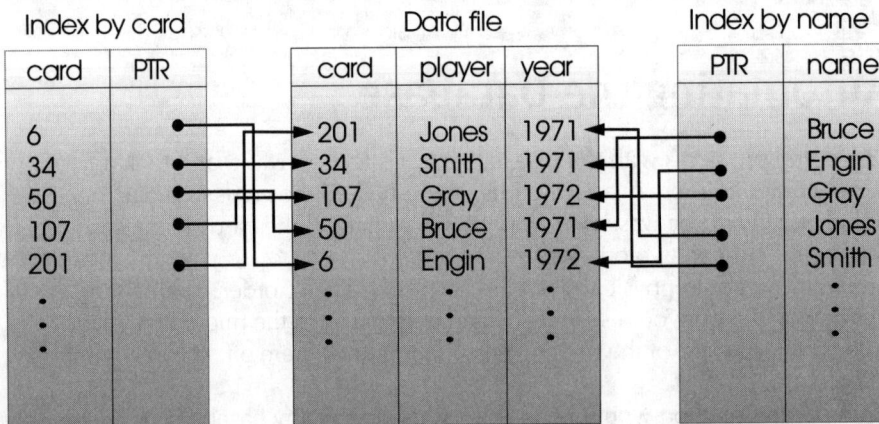

FIGURE 2-1.   *A sample database*

waste space, add dangerous replication or redundancy in data, or slow down the speed of the programs you are using. So, let's proceed with a little database design training.

Designing the Database

Database design is not a simple subject. In fact, there are dozens (or maybe scores) of books written about database design. Often, organizations have one or more people who are designated and trained as database administrators, and much of their training is in database design strategies and techniques. So if you feel that you need to know more than what we discuss next, look for a database administrator at your organization, or look for a good book about database design; one of the best known authors you might look for is C. J. Date. His books have been used in training classes and colleges for many years, and he is very thorough and understandable.

But let's get back to our own mini-course in database design. As you design a database, you need to look at all the information that you need to store, and then start to break it down into separate files, records, and fields.

As you do this, remember a few rules:

1. Try not to replicate data more than once. For instance, if you have a person's address in more than one place, then you will have to change it in all the different places each time the person moves.

2. Try to group information that is similar together. For instance, combining all the personnel information together makes sense, but adding the addresses of each division of your company doesn't make sense for the same file; it is not related to personnel records.

3. If you will be using the same information in more than one place, consider making a separate file to hold the information. For instance, suppose your company uses a handful of insurance carriers for your employees. You don't want to maintain the insurance company's address in each employee's record! Instead, come up with a short code for each insurance company, and put the code for the correct carrier in each employee record. Create a separate file for the insurance carriers; each record will have the code you defined, along with the name and address of the carrier. This is the beginning of a *relational database*, where a small code in the employee record is *related* to a complete record of information in the insurance carrier file.

4. If at all possible, don't waste space by leaving room for unnecessary information. Instead, store this information in a separate file, and use some sort of lookup to retrieve the information when it is available.

Let's design a database for the baseball card example.

Determine the Information to Keep

The first thing you need to do when designing a database is to determine the information that is to be stored. After that you can start to organize it.

For the baseball card database, there are several pieces of information that will be found on each card, and only once per card:

- The year of the card
- The number on the card
- The company that made the card
- The type of card (player, pitcher, manager, team, checklist, etc.)
- The team
- The player's name (if it is a player or pitcher card)
- The location where the card is being stored
- The state of the card (mint, excellent shape, average shape, or needs replacement)

This information will occur only once on each card, and will help to identify the card. However, there is also information in some cards that may occur several times. For instance, player type cards will have the

- Year,
- Team,
- Games played,
- Hits,
- Home runs,
- Runs batted in, and
- Batting percentage

for each year the player has been playing (or at least for the most current 4 or 5 years). Of course, this information is only for player cards. Pitcher cards might have the following information for the years they have been playing:

- Year
- Team
- Innings pitched
- Wins
- Losses
- Saves
- Earned run average

Team and manager cards are different even more. They might have wins and losses listed for recent years.

Now our task is to determine how to store all of this information in several files without repeating any data in more than one place, if possible, and wasting space, i.e. leaving room for information that is not always required.

In the next section, we'll make our first pass at the design.

Break the Information into Files

Your first inclination might be to create separate files for each type of card. For instance, the file for players might have the following fields:

- The year of the card
- The number on the card
- The company that made the card
- The type of the card (player, pitcher, manager, team, checklist, etc.)
- The team
- The player's name (if it is a player or pitcher card)
- The location where the card is being stored
- The condition of the card (mint, excellent, average, or needs replacement)
- The year, team, games played, hits, home runs, runs batted in, and batting percentage for the most current year played
- The year, team, games played, hits, home runs, runs batted in, and batting percentage for the previous year

■ The year, team, games played, hits, home runs, runs batted in, and batting percentage for two years ago

■ The year, team, games played, hits, home runs, runs batted in, and batting percentage for three years ago

Already, though, you may see a problem. What if the player has only been playing for one year? You've wasted three years of storage space. And what if they've played seven years? There isn't enough space to store everything. Therefore, let's try another way.

First, we'll create a file to store the base information, available for every card. This file could be called BASECARD, and would contain the fields shown below. Notice that we are starting to get ready for the computerized version by assigning short, yet descriptive names to each of the fields.

■ CARD_YEAR: The year of the card

■ CARD_ID: The number on the card

■ MFGR: The company that made the card

■ CARD_TYPE: The type of card (player, pitcher, manager, team, checklist, etc.)

■ TEAM_ID: The team

■ PLAYER_NAME: The player's name (if it is a player or pitcher card)

■ LOCATION: The location where the card is being stored

■ CARD_STATE: The condition of the card (mint, excellent, average, or needs replacement)

There will be one record in this file for each card that you own. To store the other information on the cards, we will create a few other files.

The next file we need, which will be called PLAYER, will maintain the information that is only shown on player cards. There will be one record in this file for each year of data shown on a card. The following fields will be used in this file:

■ CARD_YEAR: The year the card was made

■ CARD_ID: The number on the card

■ STAT_YEAR: The year for which the statistics were gathered

■ TEAM_ID: The team that the player was with in the given year

■ GAMES: The games played during the given year

- HITS: The number of hits during the given year

- HOME_RUNS: The number of home runs hit during the year

- RBI: The runs batted in during the year

- PCT: The batting percentage for the year

In a similar manner, the PITCHER file will maintain fields specific to pitcher type cards. Again, there will be one record in this file for each year of data shown on a pitcher's card.

- CARD_YEAR: The year the card was made

- CARD_ID: The number on the card

- STAT_YEAR: The year for which the statistics were gathered

- TEAM_ID: The team for which the pitcher pitched

- INNINGS: The number of innings pitched during the given year

- WINS: The number of wins during the given year

- LOSSES: The number of losses during the given year

- SAVES: The number of saved games during the given year

- ERA: The earned run average for the given year

You may notice two fields at the top of each of these special files, namely CARD_YEAR and CARD_ID. In the next section, you'll see how these are used to relate the files together.

Relate the Files to Each Other

If we want to break the information up into multiple files, there needs to be some way to find the information again if we need it. For instance, once we look at a BASECARD record, how do we find the specific statistics that were on that card?

In the examples shown above, the fields CARD_YEAR and CARD_ID are used to relate the files together. Once you have found the BASECARD you want, look at the CARD_TYPE. If it is a player-type card, look in the PLAYER file for all the records with the same CARD_YEAR and CARD_ID as the BASECARD record. In this way, there can be any number of statistics years gathered, without duplication or waste of space.

In a similar way, the CARD_YEAR and CARD_ID fields are used in the PITCHER file to look up pitcher statistics that were found on a specific base card.

Moving On

In this chapter, you learned some of the basics of database design. Some of it may seem like common sense. However, if you don't feel like you have all of it under your belt yet, don't fear. As you continue through the book, you will get a great deal of practice designing your own databases.

If you feel that more training would help you become comfortable with what you've learned thus far, I'd suggest talking with your company's database administrator for some tips. Or, look for a book by database expert C. J. Date—he has quite a few available.

In the next chapter, we'll start learning about object-oriented techniques. Once you have mastered OOT and databases, you'll be ready to dive into PowerBuilder.

CHAPTER 3

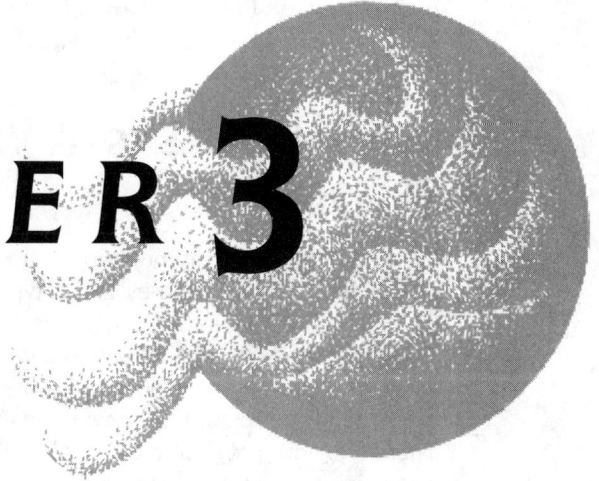

The Working Environment

Microsoft Windows was designed to be a simple-to-use, easy-to-understand graphical user interface for the masses. With each revision, Windows gets closer to this goal. Already, it doesn't take advanced "C" language programmers to produce useful applications. And once taught the basics, a Windows user can make fairly good progress with almost any Windows application.

In this chapter, you will learn more about this environment, in which PowerBuilder runs. This will help you create applications that a user can better understand. This will also greatly reduce the amount of time you'll need to spend training and supporting the thousands of people using your programs. In addition, you'll learn about object-oriented programming, a technique embedded in PowerBuilder that simplifies the reuse of programming components.

In addition, because PowerBuilder is also available on other platforms (such as UNIX, Windows NT, and the Apple Macintosh), you can develop an application under Windows that can be used by people on other operating systems. This is a rare power for a programmer to wield.

Windows Basics—A Visual Perspective

Currently, the most common type of user interface is the *Graphical User Interface,* or GUI (pronounced "goo-ey"). This type of interface was made popular by the Apple Lisa and Macintosh computers, but it now spans a multitude of platforms. These include Microsoft Windows and Windows NT, IBM OS/2 Presentation Manager, NeXTstep, and several UNIX variants (Motif, OpenLook, etc.).

A GUI is a program itself, which handles all input from and output to the user. Therefore, your program must be able to receive messages from the GUI, recognizing when one or more GUI commands have occurred. These commands might include menu selections, moving or sizing windows, or drawing within a window. In every case, your program must know how to handle the message.

This activity is quite different from that of non-GUI programs, in which a programmer dictates the order in which a program is executed. With GUIs, you never know when a user will move a window, or change its size. Even in the midst of printing a report, the user might decide to cancel it and start a different task. So your programs must be much more aware of all the things that *might* happen, and they must include a plan for anything the user might do.

This type of programming is called *event-driven* programming: the program is driven, or caused to act, by external events. These events usually come from the user, but they may also come from the GUI program, a serial port, or another program that is running at the same time.

Luckily, a package like PowerBuilder is knowledgeable about the events that may occur. You can specify how each event will be handled, if you want, but much of the interaction will be handled by the defaults built into PowerBuilder applications.

Here is an example of a program written for Microsoft Windows, back before the tools you have now in PowerBuilder were available. Naturally, this program would not actually do much, but it does illustrate how difficult it used to be to implement event-driven programming.

```
/*

   Simple Windows Program to say Hello.

*/
```

```
#include <windows.h>

/* Prototypes */
LONG FAR PASCAL EventHandler( HWND, UINT,
                        WPARAM, LPARAM);


/* Global variables */
char szProgramName[] = "Hello";

/*
   The WinMain() function is required in every Windows
   program. It replaces the main() function found in
   normal C programs. WinMain() defines the way that
   the program should look, and then goes into a loop,
   which receives messages from Windows and processes
   them.
*/
int PASCAL WinMain( HINSTANCE hInst, HINSTANCE pInst,
         LPSTR lpszCommandLine, int nCommandShow );
{
   HWND hWnd;
   MSG  lpMsg;
   WNDCLASS wcMyApp;

   if (!pInst)
   {
      wcMyApp.lpszClassName = szProgramName;
      wcMyApp.hInstance = hInst;
      wcMyApp.lpfnWndProc = EventHandler;
      wcMyApp.hCursor = LoadCursor(NULL,IDC_ARROW);
      wcMyApp.hIcon = NULL;
      wcMyApp.lpszMenuName = NULL;
      wcMyApp.hbrBackground = GetStockObject(WHITE_BRUSH);
      wcMyApp.style = CS_HREDRAW ¦ CS_VREDRAW;
      wcMyApp.cbClsExtra = 0;
      wcMyApp.cbWndExtra = 0;
      if (!RegisterClass( &wcMyApp ))
         return FALSE;
   }
   hWnd = CreateWindow( szProgramName, "Hello There!",
                WS_OVERLAPPEDWINDOW, CW_USEDEFAULT,
          CW_USEDEFAULT, CW_USEDEFAULT, CW_USEDEFAULT,
```

```
                 (HWND)NULL, (HMENU)NULL, (HANDLE)hInst,
                                          (LPSTR)NULL );
    ShowWindow( hWnd, nCommandShow );
    UpdateWindow( hWnd );

    /* Here is the main processing loop. */
    while ( GetMessage( &lpMsg, NULL, NULL, NULL) )
    {
        TranslateMessage( &lpMsg );
        DispatchMessage( &lpMsg );
    }

    return ( lpMsg.wParam );
}


/*
    Here is the meat of the program, where the events
    that occur will be handled. If this were a larger
    program, with more features, there would be many
    more entries in the switch statement below!
*/
LONG PAR PASCAL EventHandler( HWND hWnd, UINT msg,
                  WPARAM wParam, LPARAM lParam )

{
    PAINTSTRUCT ps;
    HDC hdc;

    switch (msg)
    {
        case WM_PAINT:
            hdc = BeginPaint( hWnd, &ps );
            /* this is where you would put commands
                to place text or graphics into your
                window */
            ValidateRect( hWnd, NULL );
            EndPaint( hWnd, &ps );
            break;
        case WM_DESTROY:
            PostQuitMessage(0);
            break;
        default:
            /* If this program does not handle a specific
```

```
      event (or message), pass it to the default
      Windows message handler, as shown here. */
   return( DefWindowProc( hWnd, msg,
                    wParam, lParam ));
  }

  return (0L);
}
```

You may realize that the code segment above is rather difficult (or impossible) to understand. That is why some programmers who *did* understand it came up with tools for the rest of us, in the form of PowerBuilder, Visual Basic, and others.

Common Controls

Even though you won't need the knowledge to write programs like the one above, you will need to understand how the user interfaces are created, and you'll need to know the user interface elements, often called *controls,* that are used to control the execution of your program. Some of the more common controls you will use in PowerBuilder applications include command buttons, radio buttons, check boxes, edit and list boxes with scroll bars, which are all illustrated here:

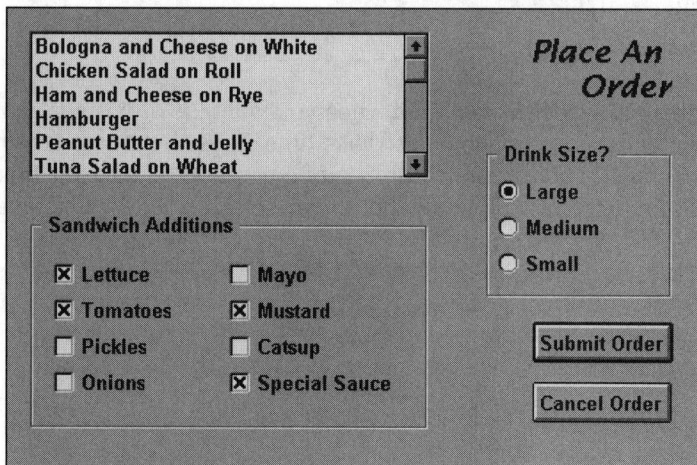

Each of these controls is shown on the Windows screen as a small drawing, often reflecting the object in the real world that the control is trying to emulate. In the sections that follow, you'll see how each of these controls look.

Command Buttons

A command button (shown below) is used to start or end an action. For instance, very often in Windows, you will be shown a small window, containing some text and a button that says "OK". If you press this button, it means that you have read, or at least acknowledged, the message that was displayed.

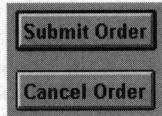

In this illustration, there are two buttons (Submit Order and Cancel Order). You may notice a darker line around the Submit Order button. This implies that the button is the *default* button, the one that will be selected when you press ENTER, unless you do something to change the default. By supplying the user with a default button, you can help them know what to do next in your application.

Command buttons are very common in Windows programs. In fact, buttons show up in many places. For instance, a button bar can be added to your program, allowing the user to press a button to start a function rather than selecting it from a menu. This makes running your application much more customized and intuitive—the user can learn how to press a button much more quickly than determining which path of menu selections must be followed to start the same function without a button.

Radio Buttons

Radio buttons (shown below) are used when you want the user to make a selection, and only one of the choices can be used at a time. These buttons get their name from your car radio: you can only push one of the station buttons at a time. How could you listen to the radio if two stations were selected at the same time?

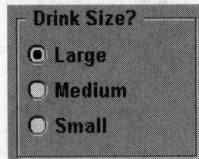

In the illustration above, you are shown the size options for a soft drink. Naturally, only one can be selected for a given drink order. In this example, notice that the Large option is already selected (the circle is filled in); this is the default selection. When you define radio buttons in PowerBuilder, you can provide the user with default selections, saving them from making too many choices at once.

Check Boxes

While radio buttons allow only a single selection, check boxes provide you with multiple choice selections, as shown in the following illustration. Like radio buttons, check boxes can have a default value (on or off). For instance, when you view a report, you might default to also having the report printed.

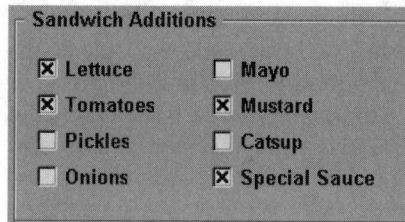

```
┌─ Sandwich Additions ──────────────────────┐
│                                            │
│   ☒ Lettuce        ☐ Mayo                  │
│   ☒ Tomatoes       ☒ Mustard               │
│   ☐ Pickles        ☐ Catsup                │
│   ☐ Onions         ☒ Special Sauce         │
│                                            │
└────────────────────────────────────────────┘
```

This type of control is used when the user can select one or more choices, or even no choices, from a list of options. In the illustration above, you can easily see how a sandwich might be made with nothing, or everything, or any combination in between, using the check boxes given.

List Boxes and Scroll Bars

A list box is simply a list of choices the user may choose from. A list box is used when you do not know all the choices that will be available when you are creating the application. The choices can be added by your application as it runs or might be read in from a database file. For instance, in the illustration below, the restaurant owner might want to change the selection of sandwiches without forcing the application to be reprogrammed.

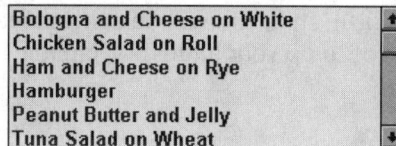

```
┌──────────────────────────────────┬──┐
│ Bologna and Cheese on White      │▲ │
│ Chicken Salad on Roll            │▓ │
│ Ham and Cheese on Rye            │▓ │
│ Hamburger                        │  │
│ Peanut Butter and Jelly          │  │
│ Tuna Salad on Wheat              │▼ │
└──────────────────────────────────┴──┘
```

If there are too many selections to fit in the list box, a scroll bar appears on the right side of the box (as shown above). Using the scroll bar arrows, the user can scroll through and then select choices that are currently off the screen.

List boxes with scroll bars are very common in database applications. It is common to show all the valid options from one database in a list box when you are trying to relate two database files together; for instance, a user might pick their local city and state from a list, rather than typing it in, saving keystrokes and possibly preventing errors.

Object-Oriented Programming

While Windows was designed to make the user's life simpler, object-oriented programming is a type of development that promises to make a programmer's job easier. Object-oriented programming (OOP) has been around for a number of years, but only recently have tools been made available for the average programmer, and even more recently have tools for non-programmers become available. And while OOP is a wonderful tool, it requires a basic change in thought patterns. Using OOP means learning to design your programs around the objects involved (that is, around the individual subroutines), instead of focusing on a global knowledge of the entire process.

If you are a beginning programmer, you are actually at a great advantage here. If you don't have a lot of experience with more traditional methods of program development, then you haven't developed any rigid ideas or habits that might prevent you from approaching newer methods, such as object-oriented programming, with an open mind.

What are objects? Objects are the things you deal with each day in real life. They are not something designed just for programmers. Take a moment and think of the objects you are using as you read this book: the book is an object, as is the chair you are sitting in; so is your house, the can of diet soda sitting next to you, and the lamp shining on this page.

Relating these objects to programming involves a change in thought patterns from more traditional structured programming concepts. Previously, programmers thought about data and about functions that would process data. With OOP, a programmer must define everything in terms of the object at hand: how the object will act, what data it knows about itself, and how it reacts with objects around it. Once you make this paradigm shift, you will be able to create reusable objects that will greatly simplify and speed up your future programming.

Concepts of OOP

There are three key concepts that an object-oriented language or environment must support: encapsulation, inheritance, and polymorphism.

Encapsulation

Encapsulation, also known as data hiding, is the ability to gather, and optionally hide, the data within an object. Many people own or use a television set—but they probably don't open the set and poke around the insides of it too often. It probably has a sticker that warns "Only Qualified Technicians Should Open This Television for Service." This is a type of encapsulation.

People can use their TV without knowing what is inside of it. The set may use tubes, resisters, or digital signal processing, but as long as the on/off button works, the user probably doesn't know or care what is inside. Everything the TV needs in order to operate, though, is contained within its plastic confines.

In programming, objects are also self-contained. The user has to know how to use them, but their internal operations, or how they work, are only important to you, the original developer. Objects are made up of two parts, data and methods. *Data* is the information available to the object (its current state). *Methods* are commands that the object understands. For instance, a TV knows how to be turned on and off. And it has several functions it can perform, as shown in Figure 3-1.

Within an object, the data and methods can be private or public. In our television example, private information includes the transistors that are installed in the TV, the details of how the power supply is connected to the circuit board, and so on; public information includes the current channel selected, the on/off command, and so on. The *private* information is used by the object to maintain its current state of processing, and it is not available to other objects. The *public* information is used by other objects to give commands to the object in question, or to determine its current state.

You may notice in the television object above that the actual data is not accessible outside the object; it is all in the private section of the class definition. Why? You don't want anyone changing this information without using the right methods (pun intended). This would be like going inside the TV and manually changing the channel; the display on the front of the set would then be incorrect. Encapsulation is not just for hiding data—it is also for protecting data! As you can see in the sample code above, you the programmer need to supply methods for setting and checking the current value of each data element in use. In this way, *you* define how the data can be changed.

Inheritance

One of the great benefits of object-oriented programming is its ability to reuse the code and objects created in previous programs. Inheritance is the method by which much of this recycling occurs. Inheritance means that data and methods from one class of objects can be passed on to a new class, without the need for redefining all of the information. Consider the following example.

In grade school, you may have played a game called "20 Questions." In this game, the goal is to discover what object is in someone else's mind. Often, the first question is something like, "Is it animal, vegetable, or mineral?" While this is a simplified classification of all the objects in the world, let's start with these as our "base classes," from which all other objects will inherit traits.

Players generally know that these base classes have some common characteristics. Animals are alive, they can move, they have offspring. Vegetables, on the other hand, cannot move, and they live at least partially underground.

```
Television object

    ┌──────────────────────────────────────────────┐
    │ Private Information                            │
    │                                                │
    │   These data elements are not even known       │
    │   outside of the television:                   │
    │   • Tubes                                       │
    │   • Wires                                       │
    │   • Transistors                                 │
    │                                                │
    │   These data elements are maintained inside    │
    │   the television, but can be changed and       │
    │   viewed using the public methods:             │
    │   • Current Channel                             │
    │   • Volume Level                                │
    │   • Tint Level                                  │
    │   • Contrast Level                              │
    └──────────────────────────────────────────────┘

    ┌──────────────────────────────────────────────┐
    │ Public Information                             │
    │                                                │
    │   These are the methods used to make changes:  │
    │   • Turn On                                     │
    │   • Turn Off                                    │
    │   • Change Channel                              │
    │   • Change Volume                               │
    │   • Change Tint                                 │
    │   • Change Contrast                             │
    │                                                │
    │   This method is used to display current settings: │
    │   • Display Current Info                        │
    │                                                │
    │   Methods used to request specific information: │
    │   • What Is Channel                             │
    │   • What Is Volume Level                         │
    │   • What Is Tint Level                           │
    │   • What Is Contrast Level                       │
    └──────────────────────────────────────────────┘
```

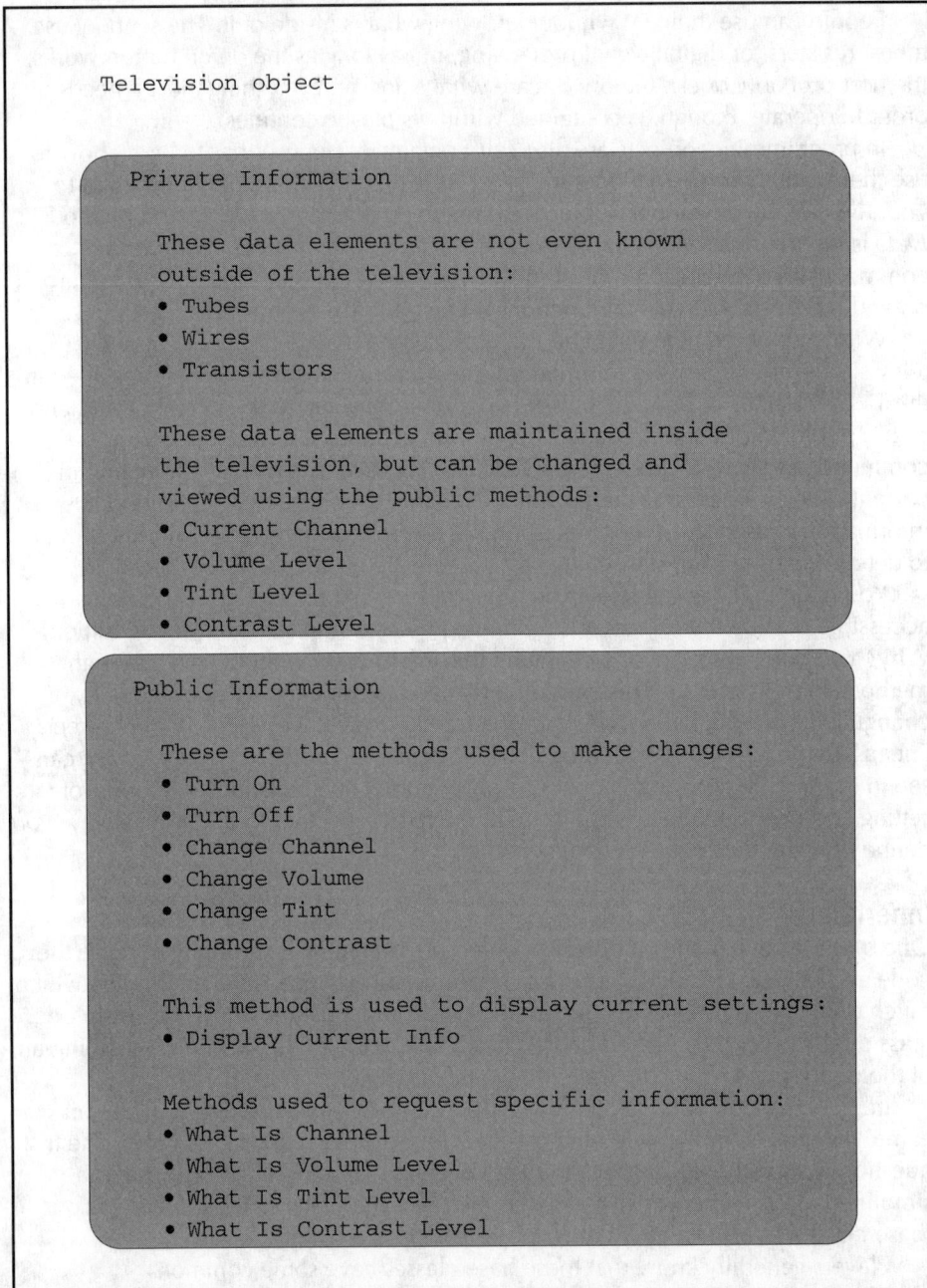

FIGURE 3-1.   *The data (information) and methods (processes) within a television set*

Minerals are not alive, cannot move, and do not bear young. Let's say the object in mind belongs to the animal class. You know some basic characteristics about all animals, so the goal of your next question is to find the "subclass" of the object. For instance, some animals have two legs, some have four, and others move on their bellies; so you find out that the animal is a quadruped.

Inheritance allows you to break knowledge down one step at a time and to know that characteristics of the parent class still exist for the subclasses. You know that your object has four legs, because the "quadruped" class has that characteristic. In addition, you know that it is alive, can move, and can have offspring, because those characteristics are inherited from the "animal" class. After a few more questions, you are able to determine that the object is a kitten.

A specific kitten is called an *instance* of the kitten class. It has all the characteristics of a standard kitten, which makes it like all other kittens. You know, for example, that it has fur, eyes, and paws. As an instance, you can give actual values to each of the characteristics. Not only does your kitten have fur (as do all kittens), but the color of its hair is gray (its own value). Your kitten has eyes (as do all kittens), with the specific color of blue (its own value).

Polymorphism

One of the most common misconceptions of OOP is the real meaning of the term polymorphism. Many newcomers to OOP interpet this word to mean the ability to give similar methods the same name, such as Chair.GetColor and Kitten.GetColor. However, just because these two methods have the same name and perform a (somewhat) similar function does not mean they are polymorphic. The ability to use the same name in more than one place is certainly no breakthrough in software engineering.

So what is polymorphism? Well, to have polymorphism you must start with inheritance. Let's imagine a fairly typical example: There is a Window class, and there is a DialogBox class that inherits from Window. The Window class defines a method called Close, which DialogBox inherits, but modifies it slightly. Therefore, there is a Window.Close and DialogBox.Close—two methods from different classes with the same name. So how is this example different from the GetColor example?

Suppose a window can contain several child objects, which may be either windows or dialog boxes. Suppose further that you want to explicitly close all child objects when the parent window is closed. Without polymorphism you would have to previously determine the type of each child object to call the proper Close method. With polymorphism you can simply call ChildObject.Close, and the language (or environment) will determine which Close method to call *at run time*! Now there's the real power of polymorphism.

PowerBuilder Awaits

You may be wondering why you needed to learn about Windows user interface objects and about object-oriented programming. You'll find out starting in the next chapter. You see, PowerBuilder is an object-oriented development for Windows. It all fits together.

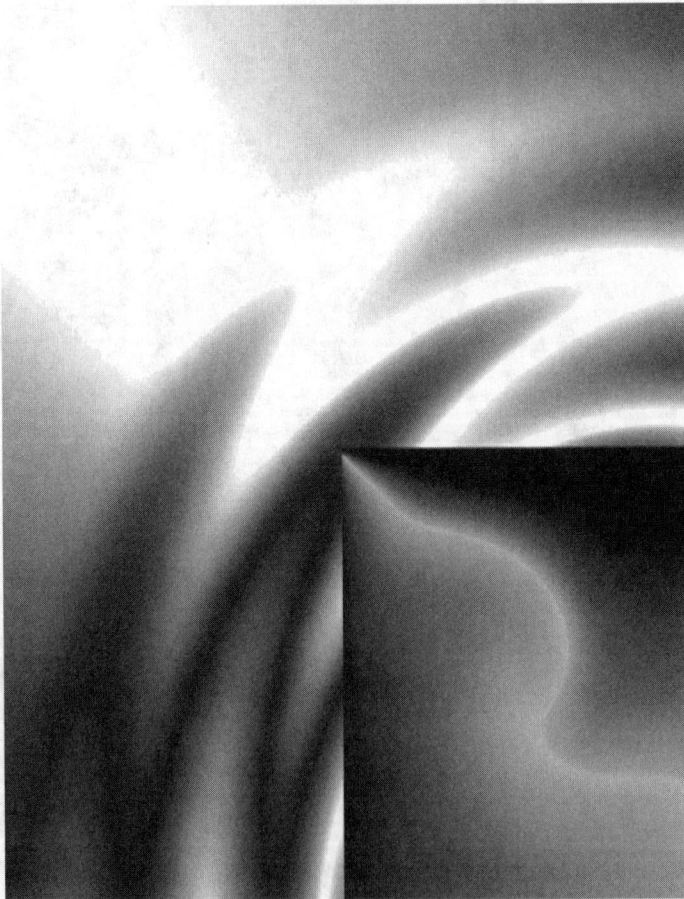

CHAPTER 4

Laying a Foundation

Before you start developing an application in PowerBuilder, spend a little time deciding exactly what the application is supposed to do. What data files will be involved? Where do the files exist? Who will be using the application? What functions or features will they require? Are there reports that will be required? What is the best way to organize all the requirements you have?

These may seem like a lot of questions, and many of the applications you use now may not answer them the way that you would like. But if you are ready to begin developing applications with PowerBuilder, you first need to know how to design them.

In this chapter, I'll introduce you to some software design guidelines. Then, you'll use PowerBuilder's Application painter to develop the shell of your first application.

Introduction to Program Design

The process of writing a program involves much more than typing in code and watching it run. Programming also involves planning, *modularizing* your program (breaking it into smaller pieces), writing the code, testing, and documentation. Following a good design process allows you to write the program with a minimum number of changes. Not following any design process might result in a program that won't do what is expected and that you'll need to rewrite.

The following steps are suggested as a strategy for developing any non-trivial program (one that consists of more than a few functions, or more than a page or two of code). This sequence of steps is based on some of the more common development methodologies now in use. A detailed discussion of these methodologies is beyond the scope of this book; however, the guidelines here should get you started.

1. **Determine the purpose of the program.** Think of all the options that will be required. What will the inputs be? What processing is involved? What outputs will be required?

   For example, a program to calculate loan payments requires input values (length of the loan, amount of the loan, interest rate), processing (calculating the loan payment amount), and output (a printed report showing the input information, the calculations performed on that information, and the final result—a schedule of loan payments).

2. **Write down the decisions made in step 1.** If you're writing a small program for your own use, then just put this information in the comment at the beginning of the file. If the program is for someone else, write this information down and let them agree that the purpose is correct.

   NOTE
   Step 2 may seem like overkill, because you've already determined in the first step what the program is to do. However, writing out the established goals of the program, in detail, often helps you work out any problems before it is too late. A written framework lets you show your client (or clarify for yourself) exactly what the program will do before the code is written. This is the best time to determine any changes necessary in the design or to find any errors and correct them. In addition, an outline of goals gives you a reference during development, helping you stay focused on what the final program requires.

3. **Decide what functions should be performed.** These will usually include input functions, output (or reporting) functions, and functions to perform each of the processing steps. Once the necessary functions have been determined, you can assign and develop separate pieces of the program, called *routines,* to handle each function. In PowerBuilder, these separate routines might be scripts, menu options, windows, or one of many other controls. This process is called modularizing your program.

   In general, modularizing your program involves determining the main functions that need to be performed, and then breaking each function down into the steps that are required for its completion. If any of these steps seem complicated or unclear, they should be broken down even further. Once you are finished, each of the routines in your program should only be performing a single step of the entire process.

4. **Design the connections between the main program and the separate routines.** The Application painter will help you to create a "road map" of the final program. Then, you will define menus to help guide the user through the processes.

5. **Define each object you will require (menus, windows, etc.), and write any necessary scripts in small modules.** Test each object as it is finished. Each one should relate to a function that you detailed in step 3.

6. **Put the objects into the application as they are developed, and try the program out as it is completed.** This is the debugging stage, where you locate and correct any errors in your program. For instance, you may find that the input information does not produce the expected results. You will need to determine the problem: the input may not have been entered correctly, the processing routines may include flawed calculations, or the output routines may be printing the wrong data.

7. **Determine whether the program fulfills the original plan.** If so, pat yourself on the back and go on to step 8. If not, you need to go back and trace—or repeat—the earlier stages of the development process, as early as step 3. Your goal here is to find out where changes need to be made to bring the program into agreement with the original plan.

8. **Complete the documentation.** Even if this program is not for anyone but yourself, you need to record how the program was designed so that you can continue to *maintain* it (program maintenance involves correcting any bugs that may arise and making future enhancements). Your documentation should include all the diagrams you developed during the programming process, as well as the original discussion of program requirements (from step 2).

9. **Take a break!** *Then* start the next project. This break time allows you to learn from each project, and it also helps prevent burnout. Trying to do too much too fast can make even the best programmers less productive.

Many good books are available today that cover, often in great detail, how to handle a programming project. The steps just described are a combination of several methods, and they will work well with most projects. Extremely large projects may require additional planning before the actual code is written and more exhaustive testing before the program is finished. In these cases, you may want to follow one of the complete software development methodologies used in the programming industry.

Following a formal methodology may seem like just a lot of extra work, but the time invested in producing and documenting a good design is always appreciated during the actual implementation stage. The extra steps imposed by an established methodology often result in less time spent drawing and editing objects, and writing and rewriting program code, to match changing requirements.

Application Painter

PowerBuilder offers a powerful tool, the Application painter, which you will learn about in this chapter. This tool automatically builds much of your database application. Once you learn how this painter works, you will be able to quickly generate your own applications.

In Powersoft terminology, an *application* is a collection of objects that are packaged together into an executable program, delivered to your end user. An *application object* is one of these objects, the one used to contain all the other objects you will create (windows, menus, scripts, data windows, and so forth). Let's start by creating our first application and its related application object.

Parts of the Application Painter

The Application painter is the PowerBuilder tool that is used to create and populate the application object. The application object contains all the objects that go into creating your application.

To begin, open a PowerBuilder session. The Application painter is selected by pressing the button shown here in the PowerBar toolbar. You will immediately be put into the Application painter. If you have not used this painter, it will bring up the example application that is provided. Otherwise, it will bring up the previous application you worked with. Assuming you have already created an example application for use with this book, your screen might look like Figure 4-1.

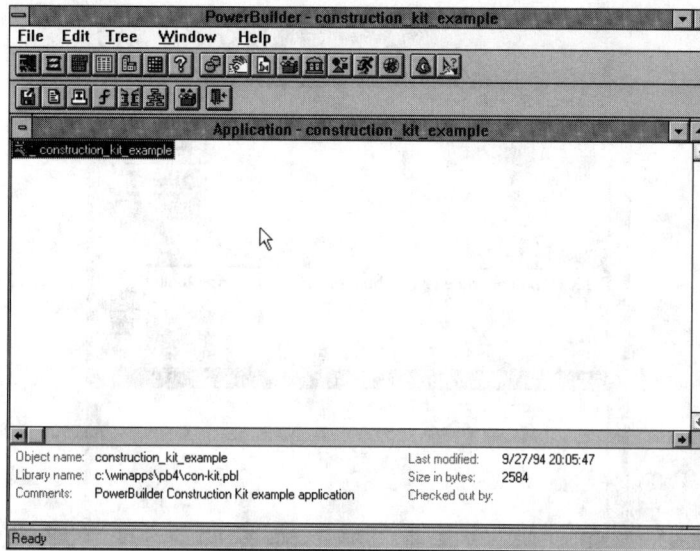

FIGURE 4-1. *Application painter brings up the previous project you were using*

You don't see much here at first, but this is where you build all the parts of your application. This is a hierarchical view, similar to an outline. If you double-click on any item in the outline, it will display or hide the items that reside beneath it (if any exist, of course). You may also open and close the outline using the plus and minus keys on the keyboard.

Let's create our own application and begin our programming experience.

Creating Your First Application

If you have not yet started the Application painter, start it now. Once you see the painter (similar to that shown in Figure 4-1), select New from the File menu.

Immediately, you will be asked to select the file name that will be used for your new application. Then you are shown a Save Application dialog box, as shown in Figure 4-2. In this dialog box, you will first define the name of the application. This can be any name you select, and it will be displayed in the top line of your application outline. You then add any comments that you want saved with the application, and finally choose the name of the library into which the application will be stored. In Figure 4-2, you'll notice that these three items have already been filled.

This is all it takes to define the raw outline of your application. Next, you'll need to start adding the innards of your program. But first, PowerBuilder helps you

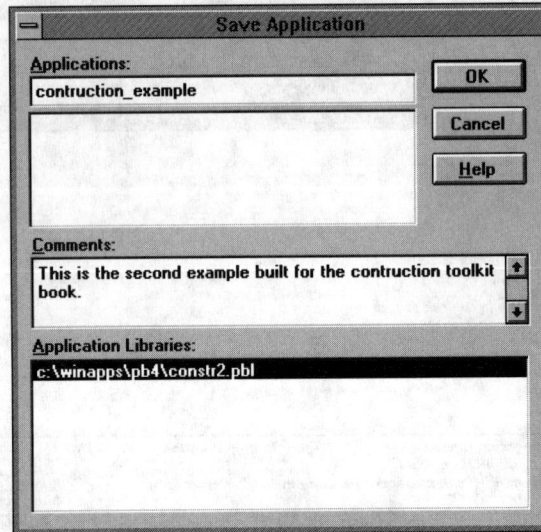

FIGURE 4-2.   *When you begin creating your application, you'll need to answer the questions in this dialog box; this information is saved with your application*

get started. After you have defined your application's description, you are presented with this dialog box:

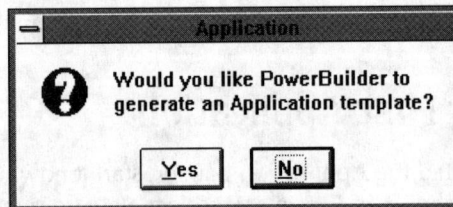

By answering Yes to this question, PowerBuilder starts building a template, or framework, for you, adding simple menus for file handling (open, close, print, etc.), for help, and for window manipulation (once a window has been opened).

These are all standard functions expected of a Windows application and also of applications in other GUI standards, so it is very handy to have them prewritten (see Figure 4-3). Once this has been done, your hierarchy, or outline, will look more impressive; compare Figure 4-3 to Figure 4-1.

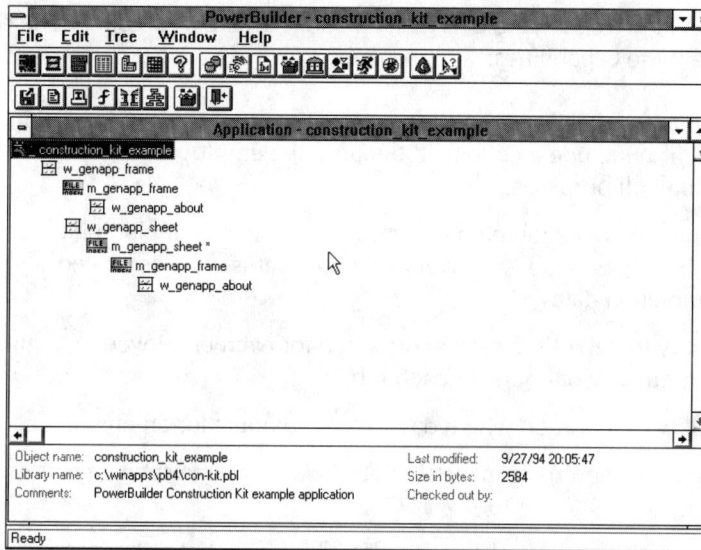

FIGURE 4-3.   *The template application has a lot of functionality built in*

You may notice that each item in the outline has a small icon on the left side. This icon is used to tell you what type of object is represented (e.g., window, data window, menu, and so forth).

Before we go any further, though, let's define an application to work with throughout the rest of the book. This will let you see all the objects as they are created for an actual application, rather than just the theoretical use of each object.

Defining an Application for This Book

If you recall from earlier in this chapter, you should always design the application and its objects before you start to run off into coding (or painting) heaven. So before we continue to build an application in this book, let's decide what it should do.

In order to make an example worthwhile, it needs to be useful, and it needs to have requirements for the different types of objects available in PowerBuilder. For this book, a Time Accounting application will be created.

Time Accounting is the process of tracking each employee's time with respect to various jobs. You are probably familiar with time cards, and may even (relunctantly) fill one out each week. As we develop an automated time accounting system, we will strive to make it as general and reusable as possible. The program should have these capabilities:

- Ability to enter employee information, such as name, department, etc. We will also include a code that identifies the employee as hourly or salaried, for payroll purposes.

- Ability to create job names within job categories, including placeholders for how long a job will take, its current status, plus estimated start and completion dates.

- Ability to enter time card information for each employee for a given date, with number of hours for each job.

- Ability to report on which dates have no hours for an employee.

- Ability to report summary of a job, including time spent versus estimated time.

- Ability to create graphs and reports showing what percentage of each employee time is spent doing each job category.

- Online help, to assist the beginning user utilitizing the application.

- A toolbar with buttons for the common functions.

Starting the Book Application

To get started, let's create the application object for Time Accounting, the application we are producing in this book. Follow these steps:

1. Start PowerBuilder.

2. Select the Application painter from the PowerBar.

3. Select New from the File menu.

4. Enter the name of your new application (time_accounting).

5. Enter a description and other pertinent information for the application (see Figure 4-4).

6. Allow PowerBuilder to create a basic application for you.

7. View the application in the outline hierarchy (see Figure 4-5).

8. Get ready for the next chapter, and the creation of all the objects we'll need to complete the application.

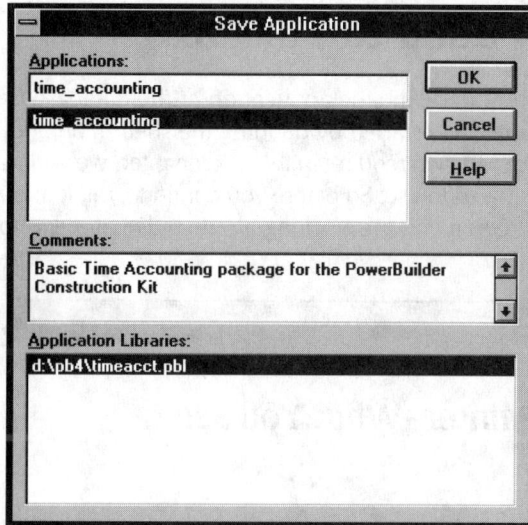

FIGURE 4-4. *Define the time_accounting application in the Application painter*

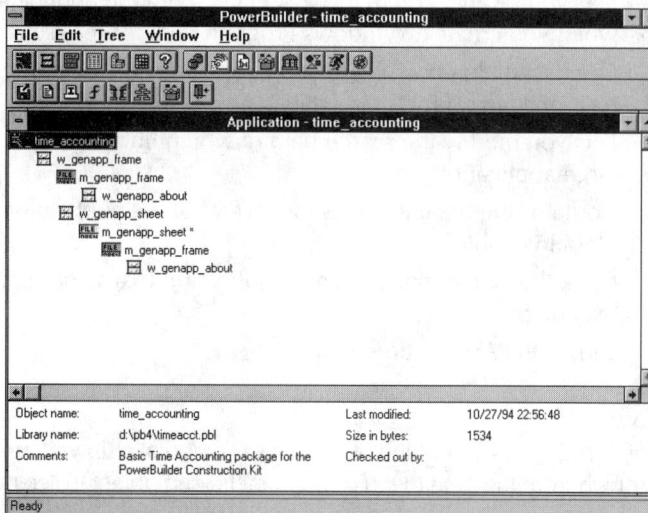

FIGURE 4-5. *The time_accounting application starts to take shape*

Starting to Build the Insides

The choice of whether to define the application or the database first is sometimes difficult. In this chapter, we started by defining the shell of an application, and later we'll fill it with the objects we require. In the next chapter, we will start by developing the database that we need to use. So before you continue, think about the information you might want to keep if you are tracking all the bills you need to pay.

Application Painter—What You See

PainterBar Icons

Open   Lets you open an existing application or create a new one; fortunately, PowerBuilder remembers the last application you opened, so you don't need this one very often.

Script   Click this icon to modify the Open script for the application, which is where many objects get initialized.

Icon   Lets you set the icon that is associated with the application, for when you create a Windows Program Item for the executable.

Fonts   Opens a dialog box where you can change the default fonts for text, headings, labels, and data.

LibList   Lets you modify the search path of which libraries to use to build a large application.

VarTypes   Contains the default values for several of the application-wide global variables.

CreateExe   Click this one to convert your application to a stand-alone executable.

Return   Closes the Application painter.

Main Window
In the center of the screen is an outline of the objects that make up your application. Use Expand Branch from the Tree menu or double-click an object to see more detail.

Summary Area
As you move through the main window, the summary area will provide more information about each object, such as the library that contains it and when it was last modified.

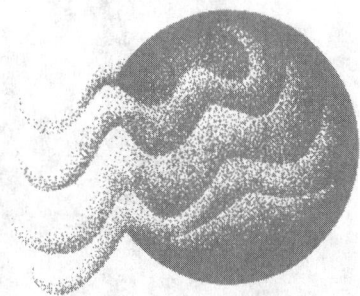

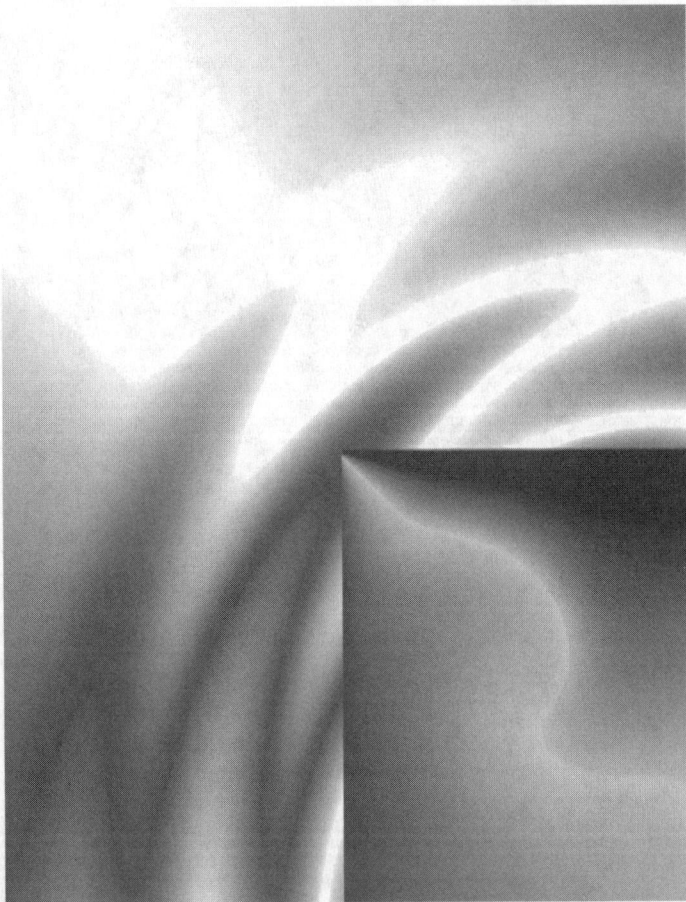

CHAPTER 5

Building Your Database

In Chapter 4, "Laying a Foundation," you created the application object that will house all the other objects to be created throughout this book. In this chapter, you'll create possibly the most important of these objects: the database.

One of the strengths of PowerBuilder is that it can be used with many different database programs. The single-user WATCOM SQL database comes with the PowerBuilder Enterprise, but you are free to use any ODBC (Object DataBase Connectivity) compliant database. The databases with ODBC drivers are increasing all the time and now include, among others, Paradox, Access, dBASE, FoxBase, and more.

ODBC is not the only game in town for PowerBuilder, though. There is also direct support (or *native* drivers) for some of the more common SQL databases (Oracle, Sybase, Microsoft SQL Server, and others), all of which do not require the ODBC interface.

Now you know that the data you want to keep can be put in almost any database manager. But how is the database designed, and why is the design so important to the success of your application? In this and future chapters, we'll start to build some databases, and you'll see why their proper design is of such great necessity.

Basics of Database Painting

The first step in designing your database is to start PowerBuilder, if it is not already running, and load your application. Remember that if you are using the same application over and over, PowerBuilder will bring it up for you automatically.

Once the application is opened, bring up the Database painter. This painter is selected from the PowerBar by pressing the icon shown here. At this point, you are ready to start the definition of your database (unless the database already exists, in which case you can move to the "Create New Tables" section later in this chapter).

Create a New Database

In order to create a new database, you will need to specify some information in the Create Local Database dialog box, as shown here:

The first item of information you need to specify is the name of the database. Remember, this is not the name of a specific table or data file but the name of the entire database for your application. So in this case, the name Timeacct was selected.

You next specify the User ID and password that will be used with this new database. By default, the User ID will be DBA (short for DataBase Administrator). This is normally reserved for the person who will have the responsibility and access for managing the database. The password is SQL by default (referring to the fact that the WATCOM database is SQL-based, I'm sure), but you will only see three asterisks since the password is hidden. If you'd like to create your own name and password for access to the database, enter them at this time.

Finally, you specify the startup command for the database server. If you are using the WATCOM server, which is the default, the command is

```
db32w -d %d
```

The %d will be replaced with the actual database file name when the server is started. If you are using another local database (other than WATCOM), there will probably be a different startup command.

At this point, there is no data in your database. In fact, there are not even any tables into which you can place data, or any specification on how the data will look. That is covered in the next section, so keep reading.

Database Painter—What You See

PainterBar Icons

Open	Brings up the Alter Table dialog box. If the table is already in the main window, you can right-click the table header and choose Definition.
New	Lets you create a new table in the database. To create a completely new database, choose Create Database from the File menu.
Index	Steps you through the creation of an SQL CREATE INDEX statement.
View	Steps you through the creation of an SQL CREATE VIEW statement.
Preview	Lets you view, add, change, and delete the actual data stored in the database.
Admin	Takes you to the Database Administration painter, where you can create and execute SQL statements that are semantically correct.
Drop	Completely removes a table from the database. You can also right-click the table header and choose Drop Table.
Arrange	Rearranges the tables in the main window using an auto-layout algorithm. Occasionally your manual arrangement will look better.

Main Window

In the center of the screen is an arrangement of the tables (you wish to visualize) which make up the database. The primary keys of each table are shown with a P key. The foreign keys are shown with an F, and an arrow is drawn to show the relationship between the tables.

Create New Tables

Once you have created a database, you may begin to add the tables, or specific data files, into the database. The tables, remember, are the places into which the actual data will be placed. Before you start creating tables, you need to be sure what is going to be in each of the tables. Let's do a little design work.

Time Card Entry Table

We can do the tables in any order, so we'll pick the Time Card Entry table first, as shown in Figure 5-1. This table maintains all time card entries for all the employees in the database. What do we need to store? Well, we at least need a representation of the employee, the date, the job worked on, and how many hours were applied to that job. We also add a sequence number to make sure that each record is unique.

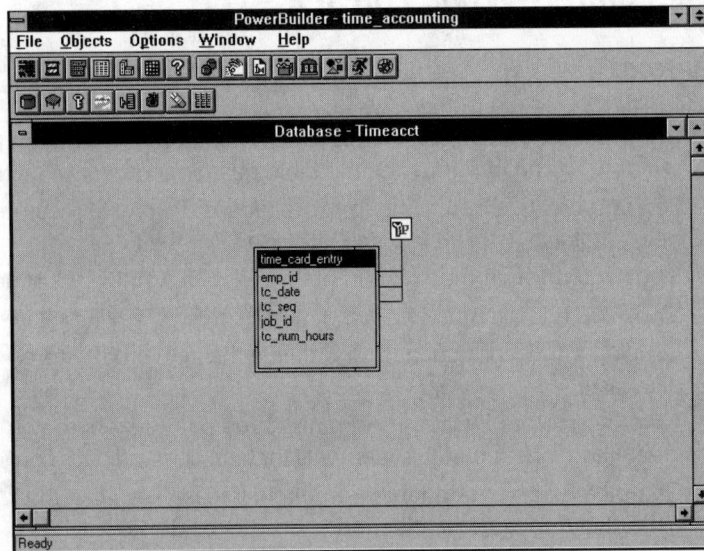

FIGURE 5-1. *This is how the Time Card Entry table will look when completed*

To get started, bring up the Create Table dialog box, shown here:

You'll notice that the fields in the table have already been entered. In the next section, I'll tell you what was required to build this table. Before you start adding fields, though, you need to give the table a name; in this example, the name selected was **time_card_entry**.

Entering Fields

For each field, there are five pieces of information that may be required:

- **Name:** This is the name of the field. It should describe what the field will be used for, such as name, address, salary, etc.

- **Type:** This is the type of information that will be kept in the field. The different options for the type are discussed below.

- **Width:** This is the width of the field, the number of characters that will be saved in the database.

- **Dec:** This is only used with real number types, and it specifies the number of decimal places that will be stored for the number. For instance, monetary units are generally stored with two decimal places (representing cents), while a weight might require only one decimal place of accuracy.

■ **Null:** This is generally set to No, meaning that there should not be any null (or empty) fields. This makes it necessary for all the information about a vendor, for instance, to be entered before the vendor record is actually sent to the database. If you don't need information in a specific field for every record, set this to Yes instead, and null (empty) values will be allowed.

As I mentioned earlier, if you look at the illustration above you'll notice that the fields for the Time Card Entry table have already been entered. Several of the field names start with the characters **tc_**. This is not required, but as you build more and more database tables, you can use this type of prefix to remind you which fields belong to which tables.

There are several types of fields that we could use in a database, as described in Table 5-1. These field types are different for each database that you might use; Table 5-1 shows the types available with the WATCOM server (these data types are fairly common for most databases, but the names might change from implementation to implementation).

Once you have built the fields in the Create Table dialog box, go back to each of the fields and look at the extended attribute information that is available at the bottom of the dialog box.

Adding Extended Attributes

As far as a database is concerned, the information you have already given is enough to create a data file. But since PowerBuilder will be helping with the creation of your entire application, you can specify more information about each field in the Extended Attributes area of the dialog box.

Format Attribute This attribute is used to describe how the field will be displayed any time it is used. This is true not only for screen displays but also for printed information.

Edit Attribute This attribute describes how the entry of the field should be controlled. For instance, you may want to specify dates in American or in European format.

Valid Attribute This attribute allows you to specify a rule that will make sure that the field contains a valid value. For instance, an age over 200 or less than 0 would not be appropriate. Neither would a starting date of 1/1/80 be valid for a company that began operations in 1994.

Justify Attribute You may specify the justification of the field using the Justify attribute, selecting left, right, or centered display of your data.

DESIGNATION	WHAT IT STANDS FOR	HOW IT IS USED
char	character string	Used for names, addresses, or any item that will contain textual components. Usually used when you know the length of the data that will be stored (for instance, most street addresses are about the same length).
varchar	variable length character string	This type is used when there will be a great variance between the longest and shortest strings being stored. For instance, if you are storing notes about certain vendors, many vendors might have no note, while others may have pages and pages of notes. Using a varchar data type, only the required amount of space will be used.
numeric	numbers	This is used for storing any numeric data, such as dollar amounts, ages, weights, etc.
integer and short integer	counting numbers	These are numbers for which there is not a decimal portion. The integer types are a subset of the numeric type. Short integer and integer are different only in the size of numbers that can be stored.
float and double	floating point numbers	This field type is specifically for numbers where a decimal portion will be stored. Float and double are only different in the size of numbers and resolution which may be stored.
binary	binary data	This field type can be used to store any other kind of information. It is called binary because there is no attempt made to fit the data into a certain type (numeric, char, etc.). Rather, the pure binary data is stored. This is useful for digital information (sound, pictures, etc.).
date, time, and timestamp	date, time, and timestamp	These field types are used to maintain date and time information without the requirements for any special formatting on your part as the programmer.

TABLE 5-1.   *Valid Field Types for PowerBuilder Tables*

Height and Width Attributes   You can also specify the height and width of the input area for this field by setting the Height and Width attributes. Remember that the font and screen resolution will have a lot to do with the sizes you will need; PowerBuilder will fill in default values that will work in most cases.

Header Attribute   This attribute is the information that you want printed above the column in which this field is displayed in a report.

Label Attribute   This attribute is similar to the Header attribute but is used for dialog boxes. By default, the information in the Header and Label fields is the same as the field name, but feel free to be creative. You can see the labels in Figure 5-2; they have been left as default values, which are not greatly descriptive.

Finally, you can specify a comment about the field in the Comment attribute. This is not used for any processing, but it can be used in documentation.

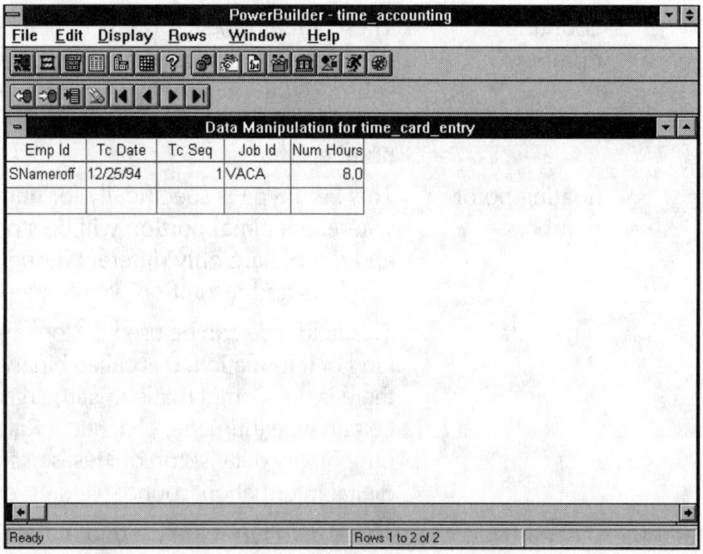

FIGURE 5-2.   *Data Manipulation screen showing labels for the Time Card Entry table*

Table Attributes

The previous discussion centered on the Extended Attributes than can be set up for each field in a table. There are also several attributes that can be selected for the entire table, including the font, a comment, and the keys.

As you might expect, the Font... button in the Create Table dialog box is used to specify the font that will be used for the table. You may select the font, the size, and the style (bold, italic, normal) for the data itself, as well as for the headings and labels. This exercise is left for you to try, as it is very similar to changing fonts in other Windows applications. Keys, however, require a bit more explanation.

Using the Primary and Foreign Keys

When you create a data table, you need to select the field or fields that will define the *primary key*. This is the minimal amount of information that is required to make each record unique. For instance, in the vendors table, the vendor identification is different for each vendor, so it can be used as the primary key.

In some cases, you will need to use a multipart key. Consider a name and address list. If you used only the last name as a key, there might be duplicates. Maybe you could use the last name and first name as a combined, or multipart, key.

A *foreign key* is a field that contains a value in one table that can be used to look up a record in another table. For instance, if you used a two-character abbreviation to store state names in your address list, you could look up the state names in a state table. In this case, the abbreviation would be the primary key in the state table, while the abbreviation in the address table is a foreign key.

Primary Key Selection　　With this background in mind, it becomes simple to pick a primary key for the vendors table. Press the Primary... button in the Create Table dialog box, and you will be presented with the following question:

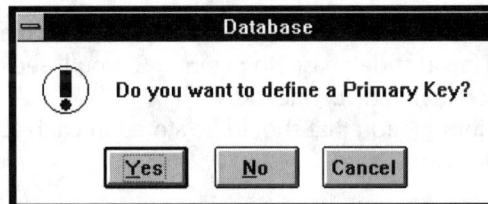

Answer Yes, and you will move into the Primary Key Definition dialog box.

For the Time Card table, the primary key will be made up of just the tc_id (time card identification) field. If you click the field name in the Table Columns list, it will appear in the Key Columns area, as shown below.

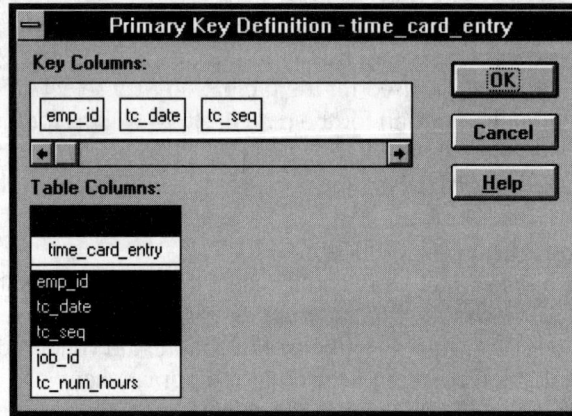

If you need to create a multipart key, you would simply select the additional column or columns you need, and they would also move into the Key Columns area.

Press the OK button, and you are finished creating the primary key.

Connecting to Foreign Keys   With only one data table defined, you cannot create a foreign key; after all, there are no other tables you can connect to. For now, assume that it is very similar to creating a primary key, except that you have to specify the primary key of *another* table, the one to which you will connect.

Adding the Other Tables

Now that you have seen a table created, take a few minutes to try creating the rest of the tables in our Timeacct database. In Figure 5-3, you'll see all the tables, with their primary and secondary key connections.

Following is the information that should be stored in each table and what the table will be used for.

employee
This table is used to maintain all information pertinent to each employee. This includes name, id (possibly username), department, plus some indication on whether the employee is hourly or salaried, and whether overtime is paid. This data will be included in the emp_wage_key field. The primary key is the employee id.

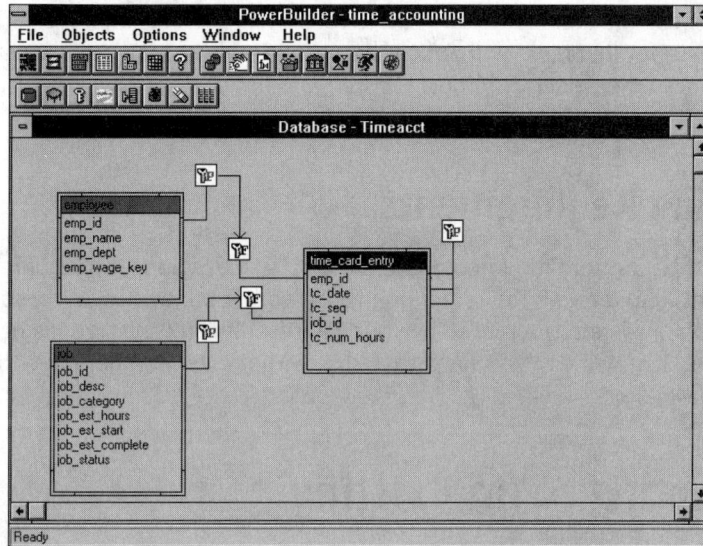

FIGURE 5-3. *Here is the entire Timeacct database, in drawing format*

job

This table stores information about each job. A job can be a specific job like creating a product or consulting at a customer site, or it can be an ongoing job, like hardware maintenance or customer support. How detailed you want to get on the job descriptions is up to you. Each job has an identifier, a category (to assist with summary reports), and a status, such as In Progress, or Late. The table also includes optional fields for estimated start and stop dates, and estimated hours to complete the job.

Creating Foreign Keys

A foreign key establishes a relationship between two tables. It lets you reference the primary key of a table in another table, so that you don't need to duplicate information anywhere. In the Time Accounting application, the Time Card Entry has two foreign keys: The first is the employee id, which gives it access to the rest of the details about an employee. The second is the job id, which lets it access the details of a job.

To create a foreign key, open the table that contains the reference; in this case, the Time Card Entry table. Choose the Foreign key icon, and then choose New. You should then be in the Foreign Key Definition dialog box. On the right side of the box, choose the table that you want to reference, such as Employee. The primary key(s) for that table will appear below the table name. Then select the same field from the Select Columns: section, and finally name the key (usually the same name as the field).

Verifying Requirements

Now would be a great time to compare the database design to your original requirements. Go through the requirements list and visualize how the information or report you need can be retrieved by your database. If you can't satisfy a particular requirement, it may mean you need to add a field or even another table to your database.

Connecting to an Existing Database

You spent a lot of time setting up your own database in the previous sections. Will this always be the case? No. Sometimes it will be much simpler, and often it will be more difficult. Remember that database design is the topic of many four-year college degrees, and it takes a bit of know-how, luck, training, or experience to get one just right. That is why many companies have a *DBA*, or database administrator. The DBA should have all the background, training, and experience to help you along.

In many situations, you will not be allowed to create your own database. In fact, you will need to connect to a database that already exists. In this section, you'll see how easily this can be done.

Using the Database Profile

It is very simple to connect to another database. Simply select the Database Profile button from the PowerBar while you are working in the Database painter. You will be provided with a list of available databases from which you may make a selection.

If you haven't done so already, you should at some point connect to the Powersoft demonstration database. There are numerous examples of database design, as well as all facets of PowerBuilder construction.

If you wish to connect to a database that is not yet set up in PowerBuilder, select the New button, and then specify the following information:

■ **Profile Name:** Whatever you would like to call this database profile (a profile is required for each database that you use).

- **DBMS:** This is the type of database connection you will attempt. It may be ODBC (for any of the many ODBC database types), or one of the direct connections (ORACLE, Sybase, etc.).

- **User ID:** Your username on the database in question. If you do not have a username or password, you may need to speak with your DBA before continuing.

- **Password:** If you need a password to gain access to the database, enter it here.

- **Database Name:** Here is where you actually select the database file you wish to connect with. You are only shown the files that seem to match the DBMS type you selected.

Press OK, and you're on your way to working with an existing database, in only minutes!

Now Use the Data

In this chapter, you've started building your database, and you learned how to connect to a database that already exists. Once you have the database created or opened, you can look at any tables quickly with the Objects Data Manipulation menu selection. You can view the data in a grid or in a tabular or freeform layout.

But these are not ideal screens to use. They have no personality. In the next few chapters, you will add an application with pizzazz to manipulate the tables you've just created. Or, if you are using an existing database, you will begin doing things only a programmer used to be able to do!

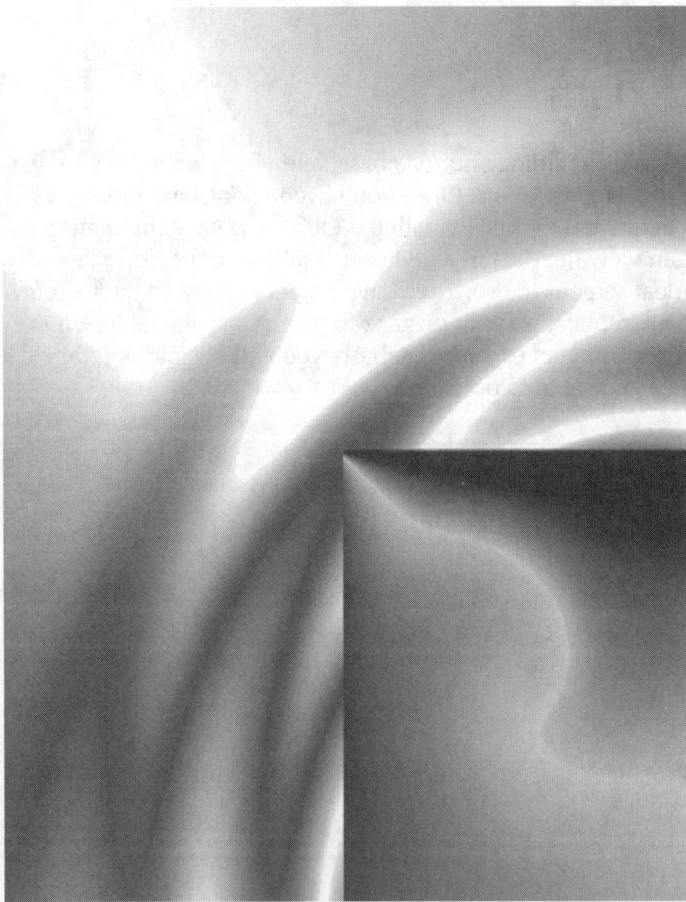

CHAPTER 6

Organizing with Menus and Toolbars

When you start developing an application by designing the database, as we did in Chapter 5, "Building Your Database," you are working with one of the lowest levels of a PowerBuilder application. Starting at the bottom works best when you have a keen understanding of the details of the program. If you are developing a program in uncharted territory, however, you are better off starting at the top—the menu. If your knowledge of the application is somewhere in between, you will benefit by using a "sandwich" development process: Do the top and bottom first, then work your way to the middle.

The advantage of the sandwich approach is that you reduce the risk of discovering missing pieces of the application late in the development life cycle. For example, suppose you design the database, then the data windows, then the reports, and then you finally work on the menus. When you get to the menu you realize that you are missing a key feature and must make a change to the database. This in turn will force you to change the data window and reports, too. If you attack the problem from both ends, you're less likely to have to redo multiple parts of the application.

Enough of the methodology soapbox—let's build a menu!

Starting with the Generated Menu

One of the nicest features of PowerBuilder is the *template application*, the optional application that PowerBuilder can create for you. (You used it in Chapter 4, "Laying a Foundation.") Did you realize that you can actually run this application? Try it—click on the "running man" icon, shown here:

PowerBuilder reduces the development environment to an icon, and you see the screen shown in Figure 6-1.

MDI Menus

Chapter 8, "Designing Windows and Dialog Boxes," will cover MDI (Multiple Document Interface) in more detail, but a quick discussion of menus as they apply to MDI applications is appropriate here. For now you only need to understand that an MDI application consists of a frame and one or more sheets. A *frame* is the main MDI window; a *sheet* is a window that can exist only within the frame. The term MDI implies that a frame can control multiple sheets. The sheets cannot display menus inside their boundaries; they can only override the menu displayed by the frame. When you run your application, you see the sheet menu when a sheet is open, and you see the frame menu when all the sheets are closed.

Menus attached to MDI sheets inherit from the menus attached to the MDI frame. This explains why the sheet menu includes the Update and Report menus, even though you didn't explicitly add them to the sheet menu. The sheet menu also selected the Shift Over/Down option for the Help menu, which forced the sheet menus (Edit and Window) to appear in front of the Help menu.

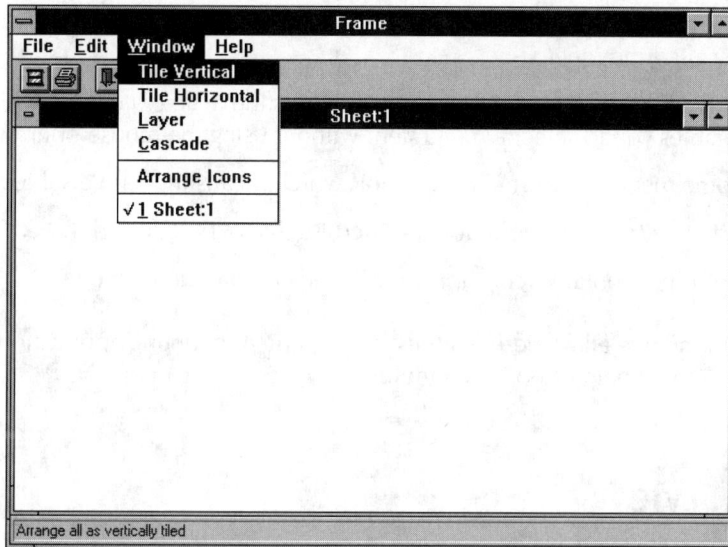

FIGURE 6-1.   *The template application runs without any programmer*
intervention

The Time Accounting application does not need a different menu when a sheet is opened, so you can disable it now if you like. Follow these steps:

1. From the Application painter, select the entry called w_genapp_sheet and press ENTER. Or, click the Window painter icon, and select the same entry from the list.

2. Choose Window Style from the Design menu.

3. Click the check box called Menu to disassociate the menu from the sheet.

4. Click OK, save your work, and close the painter.

When you rerun the application, the extra menus and toolbar icons will no longer appear.

Trying Out the Menu

The template application is much more than an empty screen with a menu. It is an MDI frame that lets you create multiple sheets, arrange them, and even print them (although they are blank).

Take a closer look at the menu using the arrow keys. Notice these advanced features:

- The status bar shows a brief description of the highlighted menu item—this is called *microhelp*.

- The underlined letter in each menu item is the *accelerator* key, which enables you to select a menu item without using the mouse or arrow keys.

- Some menu items are gray in color, which means they are disabled.

- A few items have shortcut keys listed, such as CTRL-P for Print.

- A toolbar contains icons for some of the popular menu choices.

We will include all of these features in the Time Accounting application, and PowerBuilder will help us do it in minutes.

Menu Style

One of the keys to developing a Windows application successfully is the ability to adhere to the style of a Windows application. Notice how quickly you can determine all the capabilities of the template application. You can create multiple sheets, tile them, move them, minimize them. The secret is that this application has the look and feel of most other applications.

The menu style is also Windows-compliant. The first two pull-down menus are usually File and Edit, and the last two are often Window and Help. When you modify these menus to work for your application, try to make sure you keep with the Windows style. You might try developing your menu, then having friends try it out to see how quickly they understand the menu items you have created.

Modifying the Menu

Rather than starting from scratch, it makes more sense to modify the generated template. Close the running application if you haven't done so already. If the Application painter is active, locate the m_genapp_frame menu, select it, and press ENTER. If not, click the Menu painter icon, and select the same menu from the list in the Select Menu dialog box. Either way, you should see the Menu painter similar to Figure 6-2. Actually, this figure shows part of the completed File pull-down menu, but we'll get to that shortly.

Menu Painter—What You See

PainterBar Icons

Insert   Inserts a menu item just above the current location (shown by the pointed finger).
Move   Moves a menu item up or down in the current pull-down menu.
Delete   Removes a menu item.
Next Level   Click this to create and display a cascaded menu, or to display an existing one.
Prior Level Returns from a cascaded menu.
Script   This icon takes you to the PowerScript painter, where you define what action to take when the user chooses a menu item.
Run   Runs the current application (not just the menu).
Debug   Debugs the current application.

Main Window
The left side of the main window contains the definitions of each of the pull-down menus. Use this side to add, move, or delete menus and menu items. The right side contains the details of the current selected menu item (the one with the finger pointed at it). Use the right side to modify individual menu items.

Preview Window
When you choose Preview from the Design menu, PowerBuilder displays the current menu in a frame. In this window you can browse through the menu items to make sure they have the look you intended. Choosing any item will have no effect on the window—you must Close from the control menu (or press CTRL-F4).

The best place to start is with the pull-down menu names—that's the top row across the menu bar. The template contains two menus: File and Help.

NOTE
You may have noticed the running application had four pull-down menus, including Edit and Window. These menus are part of the MDI sheet menu. If you close the sheet while running the application, you'll see the MDI frame menu.

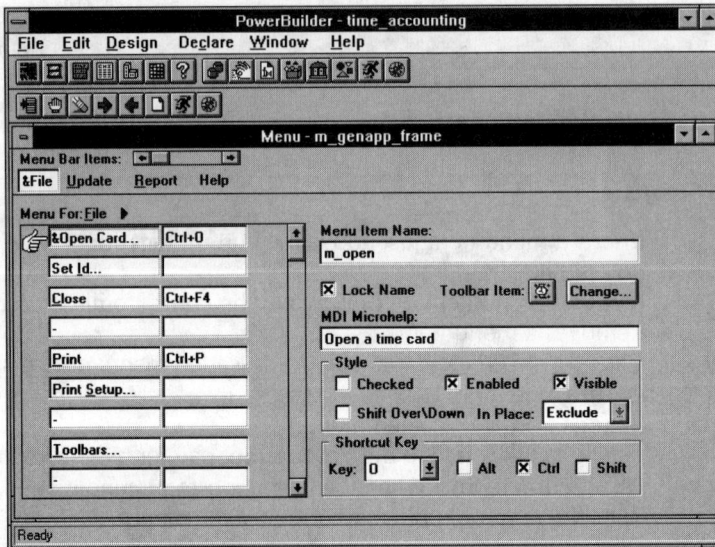

FIGURE 6-2. *The Menu painter helps you create complex menus with ease*

To insert a new pull-down menu, click on Help in the Menu Bar Items section of the window, then click the Insert icon. PowerBuilder will create a blank pull-down menu, like the one in Figure 6-3. Enter the name of the new menu, in this case Update. Follow the same steps again to create an empty menu called Report.

Defining Menu Items

Once you have defined the menus, you can move on to each of the items in those menus. For Time Accounting, when users want to enter time card information, we should let them specify a card by date without being concerned with whether a card for those days already existed. Therefore we don't need both New and Open in the File menu.

Because there is information in the New script we want to keep, change New to "Open Card..." by clicking on the menu item and inserting the required characters. Then delete Open by clicking on the word "Open" and clicking the Delete icon. Next, we want to insert a new item before Close, so click on Close, click the Insert icon, and type **Set Id...** in the appropriate space. The meaning of this option will become clear in later chapters. We can change the microhelp text for these items as well with the MDI edit box.

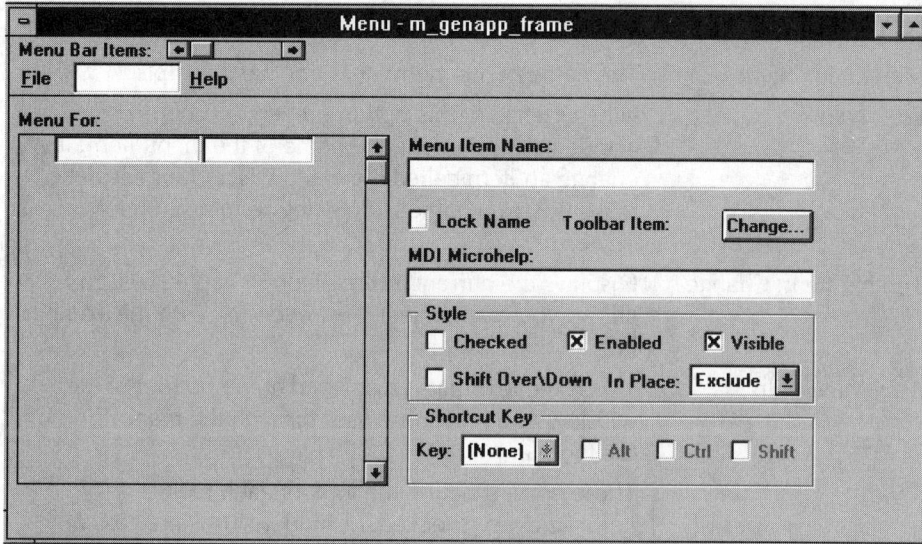

FIGURE 6-3. *Inserting a new pull-down menu using the Menu painter*

For the Update menu, you must start from scratch. Click on the menu name near the top of the window. Now click on the first input area in the Menu For group. Enter **Jobs...** as the name of the first menu item, then click the down arrow and enter **Employees...** as the name of the second menu item. You may add MDI Microhelp as well if you wish.

With that much done, save your work and run the application. PowerBuilder has included enough default values to make your new menu items appear. Nothing happens when you choose one of these items, but you'll need to be patient for a while.

Menu Item Options

When you are satisfied with the look of the menu, you can start adding more detail to each menu item. There's no need to deal with options before the menu is right, since you might delete or rearrange menu items. When you are ready to set your own menu options, use the summaries given in Table 6-1 as a guide. Many of these options are covered in greater detail in later sections of this chapter.

OPTION	DESCRIPTION
Menu Item Name	The name of the menu item, for use in scripts
Lock Name	When checked, this option prevents you from accidentally changing the name of the menu item. If you change an item called Delete to Discard for aesthetic reasons, you won't obsolete any scripts that refer to m_delete.
Toolbar Item, Change	Displays the current toolbar icon, if applicable, and allows you to change it. See "Working with the Toolbar" later in this chapter.
MDI Microhelp	This is the text that is displayed at the bottom of the window as the user browses through the menus or the toolbar.
Style	These options define the look of each menu item—grayed, checked, or hidden. They are typically changed during the execution of the program as a result of some other activity. For example, report functions might be grayed out when no database is open.
Shortcut Key	Here is where you define shortcut key combinations. See the section entitled "Accelerators and Shortcuts."

TABLE 6-1.   *Options for PowerBuilder Menu Items*

One other option available in the Menu painter is the ability to add separators. A *separator* is a line that runs across the menu to help you distinguish among groups of menu items. To add a separator to a menu, insert a new item, and enter a hyphen (-) as the name of the item.

Accelerators and Shortcuts

Two features of menus in Windows are particularly helpful in letting you keep your hands on the keyboard: accelerators and shortcuts. *Accelerators* are the underlined characters in the menu item that you press to choose the item instead of finding it with the mouse or arrow keys. *Shortcuts* are key combinations, usually function keys or CTRL key combinations, that let you choose a menu item without even pulling down the menu.

To select the accelerator for a menu name or menu item, place an ampersand (&) just before the accelerator character. For example, "&Update" will make the U the accelerator for the Update menu. Try to choose the letter that the user would most likely associate with the menu item. Also, double-check your accelerator choices to be sure you have no duplicates.

For the shortcut keys, the Menu painter supplies a group that includes a list box and three check boxes. Suppose you want to set CTRL-F4 as the shortcut for Close from the File menu. Click on File, then Close. In the Key: list box, select F4 from the list. Finally, check the CTRL box.

Remember, you are trying to develop applications that users will be able to use with little or no help from you. With this in mind, try to use similar accelerators that other Windows programs use, and avoid using popular accelerators for functions other than their expected one. This table lists several common accelerators:

ACCELERATOR	FUNCTION
CTRL-C	Copy to clipboard
CTRL-F	Find (search for text)
CTRL-O	Open
CTRL-P	Print
CTRL-V	Paste from clipboard
CTRL-X	Cut to clipboard
CTRL-F4	Close window

Cascaded Menus

A *cascaded* menu is a menu within another menu. You can recognize a cascaded menu by the right arrow (▶) symbol at the right of the menu item. When you click on the item, a submenu appears, and you select one of those items. Cascaded menus are used primarily in the following situations:

■ The menu is too large to fit all available options on a single pull-down.

■ Many of the menu items belong in the same category.

■ The items being cascaded are not used as often as the non-cascaded menu items.

Remember, cascaded menus add extra work for the users, so include them only when necessary.

The Time Accounting program uses cascaded menus in the Report menu, so that we can add new reports in the various categories and still maintain the general feel of the menu system (and it demonstrates cascaded menus). The menu items for the Report menu are "&Personal" and "&Department." Both are cascaded. To cascade the Personal menu, click the word Personal, then click the Next Level icon. Enter **&Missing Cards...** and **&Category Summary**. As you can see in Figure 6-4, the Menu For line shows both Report and Personal to help you see where you are. To return to the main menu items, click Prior Level.

Working with the Toolbar

As mentioned previously, the application template includes a toolbar and icons for several of the menu items. Control of the toolbar is done with the Menu painter. Which menu items get toolbar icons is totally up to you, but consider this advice: Add icons only for those menu items that will be used on a regular basis, and be sure to use icons that help the user remember which actions are associated with them.

Let's associate the Open Card command with a toolbar icon. In the Menu painter, click on that menu item and choose the Change button on the right side of the window. From the Toolbar Item dialog box, choose Change Picture. PowerBuilder will take you to the Select Toolbar Item Picture dialog box, shown in Figure 6-5. This dialog box lets you choose from the many PowerBuilder pictures, or from any bitmap. Time cards are related to time, so we'll use the AddWatch! picture. Click AddWatch! in the Stock Pictures list box and choose OK.

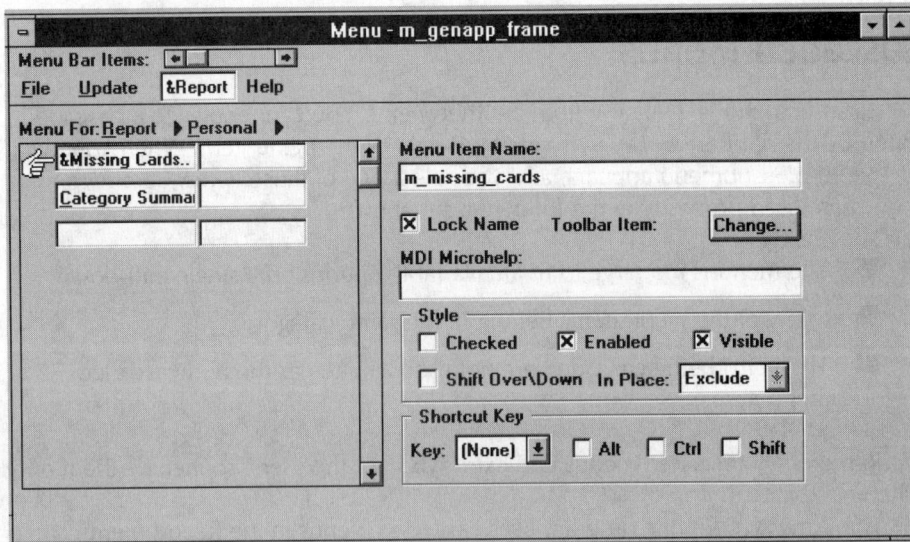

FIGURE 6-4.   *Adding a cascaded menu to the Time Accounting frame menu*

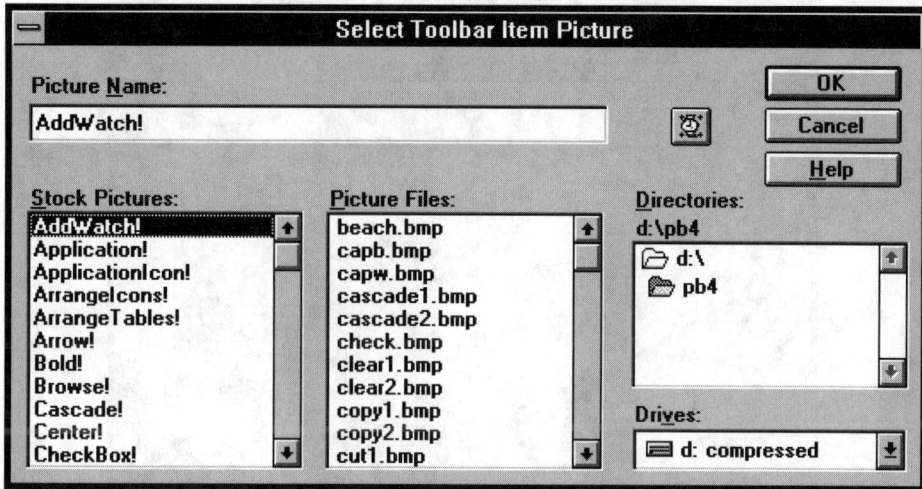

FIGURE 6-5. *Selecting an icon for the toolbar*

When you have selected an icon, you will return to the Toolbar Item dialog box, depicted here:

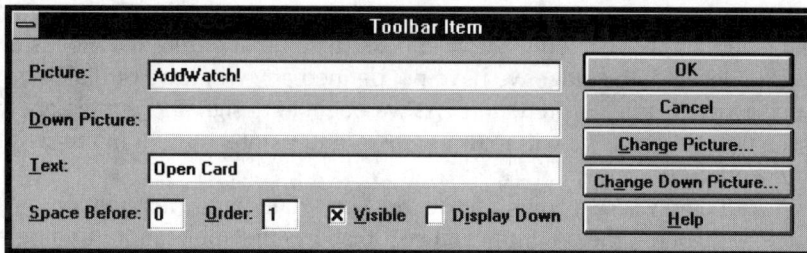

The Down Picture is the bitmap that is displayed when the user presses the icon button. In rare cases you may want to leave the button "down" and change the picture. The Text string is what is displayed as the user passes the mouse over the icon, usually in a yellow box. Space Before lets you group the icons in a meaningful way. Finally, the Order input area lets you determine the left-to-right order of the icons.

For the Time Accounting application, we have associated icons for File | Open Card (Watch!), Update | Jobs (Move!), and Update | Employees (Custom077!).

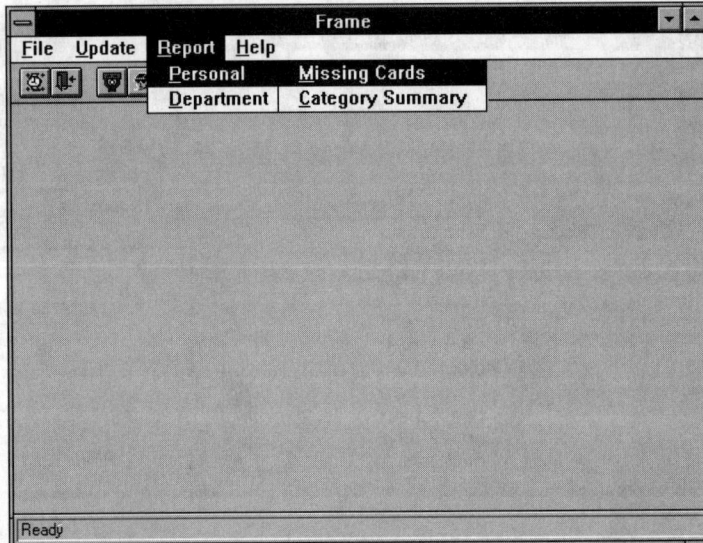

FIGURE 6-6. *The running application as it stands so far*

What About the Scripts?

At this point the design of the main menu is complete. If you have used
PowerBuilder before, you might be asking, "What about the scripts?" The *scripts*
define the actions taken when the user chooses a command from the menus or
toolbar. However, at this stage we have not defined any windows or dialog boxes,
so editing scripts would be premature. As we begin to design and implement the
rest of the user interface we will return to the Menu painter and fill in the scripts as
they are needed.

Even with empty scripts, plus a few scripts provided by the application
template, you can run the program. Figure 6-6 shows the application running after
choosing Close from the File menu to get rid of the MDI sheet, which we haven't
modified yet.

Making the Menus Useful

This chapter taught you how to design a menu, but none of the menu commands
have any actions associated with them. As we continue our "sandwich" method of
development, we will go back to the bottom of the architecture and bring the
database to life with a data window.

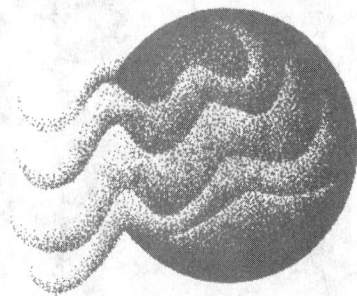

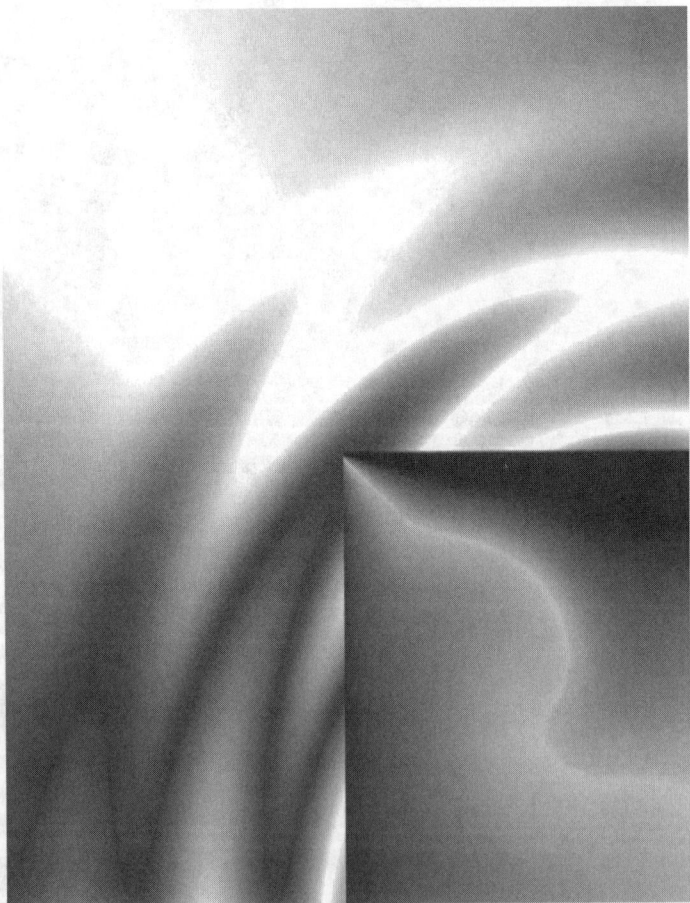

CHAPTER 7

Interacting with
the Data

In Chapter 5, "Building Your Database," you learned how to create a database as a series of tables. Unfortunately, the best way to store data is not necessarily the best way to present it. Some fields are stored as single characters but would be better understood by users if they were displayed as radio buttons. Other fields, such as sequence numbers, are necessary to create primary keys, but should be controlled by the program, not the user. This chapter will introduce you to the DataWindow painter, which lets you create amazing views of the database tables without any programming.

When you have finished this chapter you will understand how to present database information in a DataWindow, but you still won't see it when you run the application. You'll need the information in the next few chapters as well. Don't despair—it will all come together much faster than if you tried to do it with any traditional programming environment.

Creating a DataWindow

The DataWindow painter is one of the most versatile painters in PowerBuilder, and it therefore can be the most overwhelming. The key to mastering this painter is to learn enough options to let you get your job done, without trying to determine how every option and style works.

When you try to create a DataWindow, you'll see firsthand how complex this painter can be. Click the DataWindow painter icon, and you will see the set of pictures shown in Figure 7-1. A little math will tell you that there are up to 54 possible combinations of data sources and presentation styles. The next two sections will give you a brief summary of these options, but will concentrate on the few that are most commonly used.

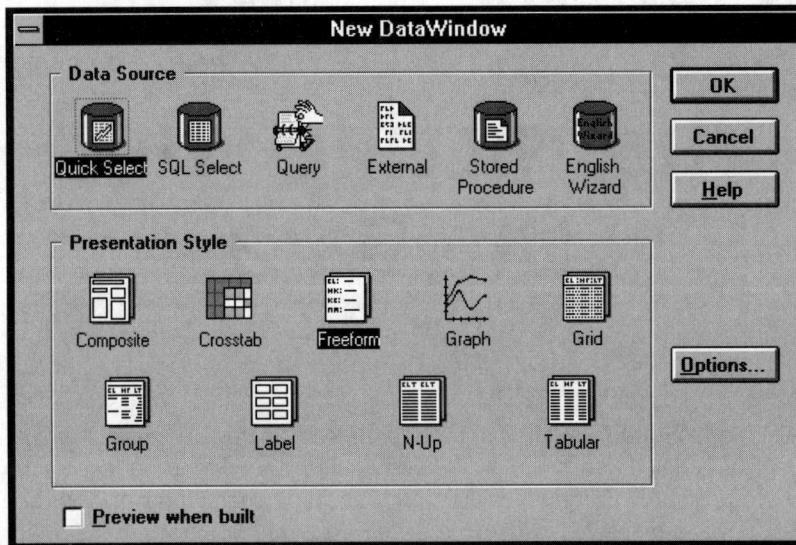

FIGURE 7-1.   *There are a plethora of options when creating a new DataWindow*

Data Sources

The data source options determine not only which tables in your database will be used for the DataWindow, if any, but also which records in those tables. Table 7-1 provides a summary of the sources available with PowerBuilder. As you can see, several of them provide different ways of creating the same DataWindows. For instance, for typical single-table display, you can use Quick Select to choose the table and column, SQL Select if you are comfortable with SQL syntax, or English Wizard if you prefer English-like syntax. All three eventually generate the same SQL SELECT statement.

If you are retrieving data from the database, try Quick Select first. It is the data source that lets you visualize the retrieval the best. If you can't seem to get exactly the information you need, then investigate one of the other options.

DATA SOURCE NAME	DESCRIPTION
Quick Select	The simplest way to choose data. A single dialog box lets you choose a table and a series of columns in that table. The only limitation is that it cannot support different columns from unrelated tables.
SQL Select	Selects data from the database based on an SQL SELECT statement. PowerBuilder creates a series of option tabs that make it easier to define the statement.
Query	Selects data from the database based on a predefined query. Or, lets you create a query using the Query painter.
External	This option is the only one that lets you get data from a source other than a database.
Stored Procedure	Selects data based on a procedure stored in the databases. Not all databases support stored procedures.
English Wizard	Selects data from the database based on a structured English statement that is then translated into an SQL SELECT statement.

TABLE 7-1. *Data Sources for the DataWindow painter*

When you choose Quick Select as the data source and click OK, you will see the dialog box depicted in Figure 7-2. The box itself provides easy-to-understand directions for selecting the table and columns you desire. The selection and sorting criteria at the bottom of the window can be ignored for now—you can add or change these options easily from the DataWindow painter itself. If you add a bunch of special criteria before you see the DataWindow, and then decide you don't like the window, you've wasted effort needlessly.

Presentation Styles

The presentation style determines how much data will appear on the screen and how it will look (at least before you customize it). Before you can pick a style you must envision the window you are trying to create. Do you see one record at a time, or several? Do you see the information in straightforward rows and columns, or a little more specialized? Once you have answers to these questions, use the descriptions in Table 7-2 to help you determine the best presentation style.

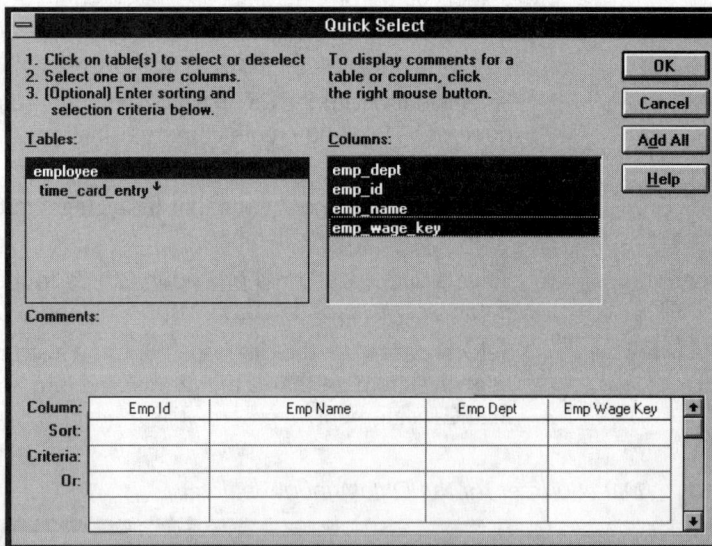

FIGURE 7-2. *The Quick Select dialog box provides instructions as easy as 1-2-3*

PRESENTATION STYLE	DESCRIPTION
Composite	Combines other DataWindows to create a single composite report.
Crosstab	Displays multiple records in spreadsheet format, with totals or calculations for both rows and columns.
Freeform	Displays a single record in the window, but lets you manipulate how that record is presented. This style is best used when users would not want to view more than one record at a time.
Graph	Displays database information as a graph.
Grid	Displays multiple records in a specific row-column format, with very few customizations allowed. This style is best used when you need to view more than one record at time and are not particularly concerned with aesthetics.
Group	Displays multiple records in specific groups in report format, with full customization supported. This style is best used when the user considers the data by group, such as department, category, date, etc.
Label	Displays multiple records in label format, suitable for printing.
N-Up	Displays multiple records in multiple columns. Unfortunately, the data goes in order across the screen, instead of down.
Tabular	Displays multiple records like a table, with full customization supported. This style is best used when you need to view more than one record at a time, and you want the user interface to look professional.

TABLE 7-2.   *Presentation Styles for DataWindows*

Designing a Freeform DataWindow

Now that you have a little background in the types of DataWindows, let's select a particular window from the Time Accounting application. The Employee table in the database keeps track of pertinent information for each person in the company. In a perfect corporation, there would only be one place for all employee information, for payroll, insurance, mailings, and even org charts. This scenario becomes unlikely as the company, and the number of software applications, grows. However, it is important that you design each database for reuse so that other applications can use the same data.

The employee data has the following characteristics:

- There can be many fields in each record (although there aren't yet), probably too many to fit straight across on one line of the screen.

- Users don't need to see other records for comparison when updating or adding an employee.

With these characteristics, it makes the most sense to use the freeform presentation style. To create the initial employee DataWindow, follow these steps:

1. Choose the DataWindow icon from the PowerBar.

2. Choose New to create a new DataWindow.

3. Select Quick Select and Freeform presentation style

4. Click on the Employee table.

5. When the column names appear, select all the columns in the order you want them to appear. (We chose this order: emp_id, emp_name, emp_dept, emp_wage_key.)

6. Click OK. You should see the DataWindow shown in Figure 7-3.

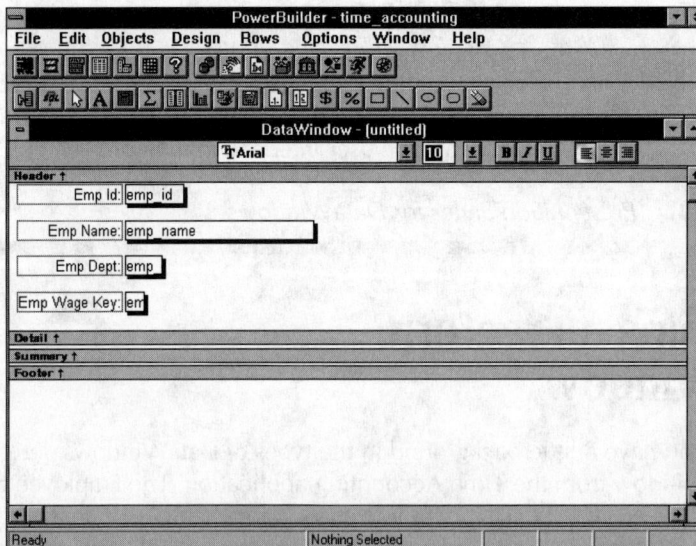

FIGURE 7-3. *The employee DataWindow with the default presentation style*

The labels and field widths are both taken from the definition of the database given in Chapter 5, "Building Your Database." If you are unsatisfied with these, you may want to return to the Database painter and make your modifications there; otherwise, you might end up making the same changes in DataWindows multiple times.

DataWindow Painter–What You See

PainterBar Icons

Preview
Displays the DataWindow as you have designed it, with the actual data from the database. In some cases you can modify the database in this window.

Select
Lets you modify the selection you made when you first created the DataWindow. This command displays a Select painter where you can change the column, sort order, and so on.

Selection
Lets you select an object or set of objects to modify.

Text
Click this icon to add text to the DataWindow.

Compute
When you click the Compute icon, then click a location in the DataWindow, PowerBuilder will display the Computed Field Definition dialog box, where you can define the function for a computed field without programming.

Sum
To calculate a sum, select a column in the window and click this icon. A computed sum will be created in the summary band.

Column
If you deleted a column in a DataWindow and you click this icon, PowerBuilder will re-create the deleted column.

Graph
Creates a graph. See Chapter 10 for more information.

Nested Report
Use this command to nest another report that you've already defined into the current one, thus turning your window into a composite presentation style.

Picture
Inserts a bitmap into the DataWindow.

Page Computed Field
Inserts a page number field in the DataWindow, usually in the header or footer bands.

Today's Date
Inserts a field for today's date.

Currency Format
Converts the selected field to a currency format, based on the current language.

Percent Format
Multiplies the selected field by 100 and adds a percent sign (%).

Rectangle, Line, Oval, Round Rectangle
Lets you draw a shape as part of the DataWindow.

Delete
Deletes the selected field.

Main Window
Once you have chosen a DataWindow, the main window will normally be broken up into *bands*, or sections, such as Header, Detail, Summary, and Footer. These sections let you customize the appearance of the DataWindow or report.

Preview Window
When you choose Preview from the Design menu, PowerBuilder applies the current SQL selection and displays the resulting data using the DataWindow format. In certain formats you can modify the data in the database with this window.

Without doing any more work, you can see how this window will look in your application using the actual data from your database (if you have any). Choose Preview from the Design menu, and you will see the DataWindow with the first entry in your database. You can use the toolbar icons to help you insert new records, delete records, change records, then update the database.

Changing Edit Styles

The simplest of DataWindows leaves every field as a text edit box, where the user is forced to enter strings for all values. With PowerBuilder, however, you can easily modify the way the data is displayed and edited to make it easier on the user. An *edit style* is a method of displaying data in a different way than it is stored in the database.

Which type of edit style should you use? Well, it depends on the number of possibilities the data field can have. Use this table as a rough guideline:

NUMBER OF POSSIBILITIES	RECOMMENDED STYLE
2	Check box
3-6	Radio buttons
6-20	List box or drop-down DataWindow
More than 20	Text edit, possibly with additional formatting to help the user enter data properly

Most of the styles should be familiar to you. A *drop-down* DataWindow is a powerful mechanism that lets you retrieve data values from the database so that the user can select one. This feature allows you to change the set of possibilities without making any changes to the PowerBuilder library. *Spin controls* are the small up and down arrows that you normally see next to numeric fields, which let you increase or decrease a number without typing in the number.

Adding Radio Buttons

In the Employee table in the Time Accounting database, there is a field called emp_wage_key that gives an indication of how the employee gets paid. In the database, this field is stored as a single character. Since there are only a few values, however, you can use a radio button style to make reading and updating easier for the users.

To convert the wage key to radio buttons, select the emp_wage_key field. Then right-click to display the pop-up menu. Choose the Edit Styles cascade menu, then Radio Buttons. The main window of the dialog box contains two columns called Display Value and Data Value. In the Display Value column enter the labels of the radio buttons. In the Data Value column, enter the character that will be stored in the database that corresponds to that display value. Then click Add. Figure 7-4 shows the final radio button contents for emp_wage_key.

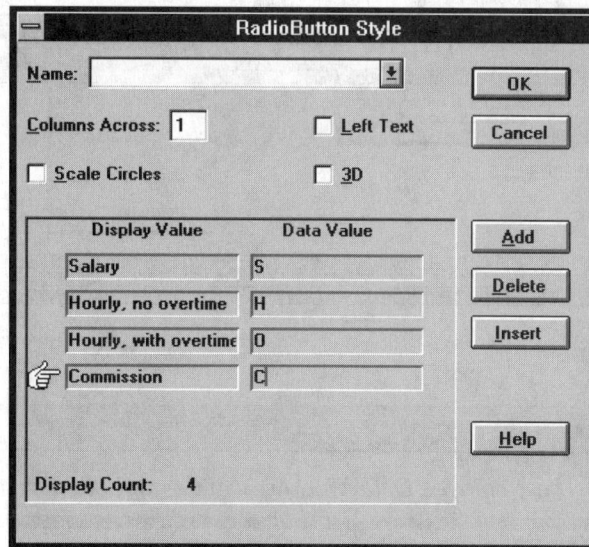

FIGURE 7-4. *Converting a field to a radio button group*

When you return to the DataWindow painter, the emp_wage_key field will be changed to radio buttons, but the field size will still be the same. To expand the field so you can see all the options, drag the field to the right side of the screen, then drag the corners until the field is large enough. Finally, move the field label next to the radio button group. The final window should look like Figure 7-5.

Designing a Grid DataWindow

The Jobs table in the Time Accounting application also requires a DataWindow for database maintenance. This table differs from the Employee table in that a user is much more likely to want to see related jobs when adding or changing a job. Therefore it is important that the DataWindow include multiple rows of the table. We'll use the grid presentation format, since we're not trying to do any fancy calculations or formats (although the grid is certainly versatile enough to do plenty of formatting).

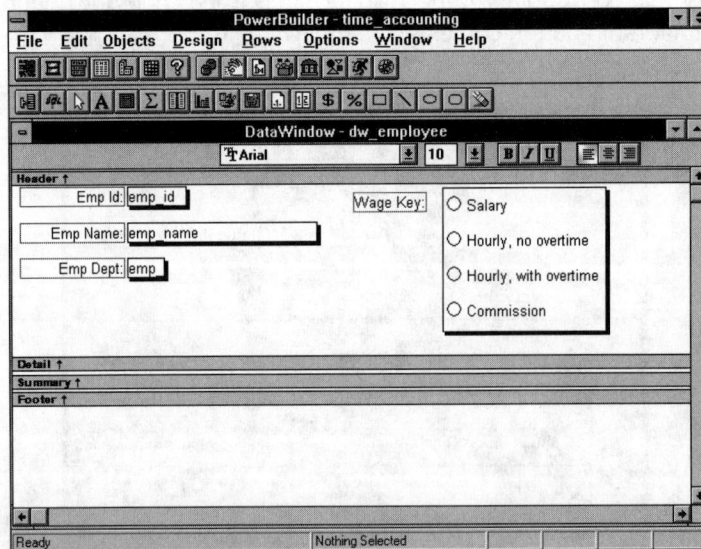

FIGURE 7-5. *The employee DataWindow with the radio button style added*

To create the Jobs grid, follow these steps:

1. In the DataWindow painter, choose New from the File menu.

2. Choose the Quick Select data source and the Grid presentation style.

3. In the Quick Select dialog box, choose the Jobs table; then click each field in the table in the order you want them.

After the disk whirls and spins, you should see a grid in the DataWindow like Figure 7-6. Feel free to change column headings and column widths to suit your tastes.

Adding a List Box

The second column in the Jobs window is Category. Let's assume that all categories are known and are stable. We will use a single character to store the category in

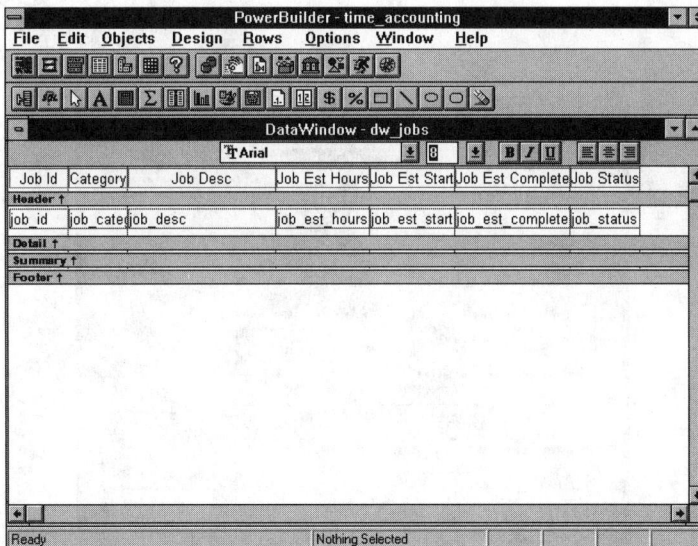

FIGURE 7-6. *The grid design for the Jobs table created by PowerBuilder*

the database, but we want to display meaningful names for the user. There are too many options to use radio buttons, so it makes more sense to create a list box.

Select the job_category field, right-click to get the pop-up menu, and choose Edit Styles and DropDownListBox. In this dialog box, shown in Figure 7-7, you can add pairs of values the same as you did for radio buttons.

When you have added all the necessary values, click OK and you will return to the DataWindow. To verify that the list box works properly, choose Preview from the Design menu. Once you add data to the database, your screen should be similar to Figure 7-8.

Cleaning Up Display Formats

You can use formats to make your displays more consistent. For instance, the start and stop dates in the Jobs table are stored as dates, but displayed the way the user entered them. To make them look the same, click the job_est_start field, and choose Format from the pop-up menu. Set the date format using m's, d's, and y's like you see in Figure 7-9. You can use the Test button to verify the format. Then click OK. Do the same for the job_est_complete field.

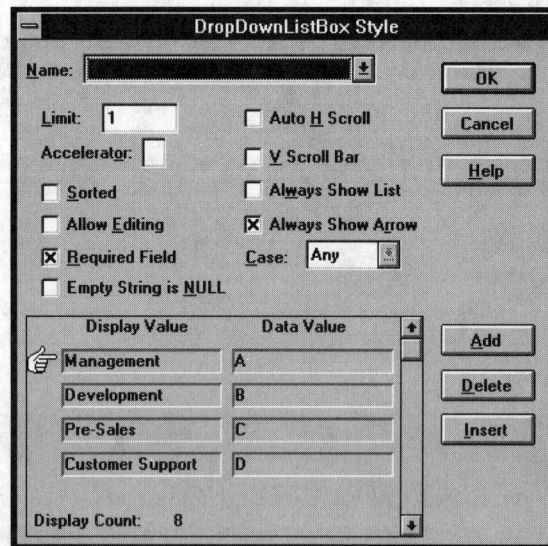

FIGURE 7-7. *Creating a list box with special values*

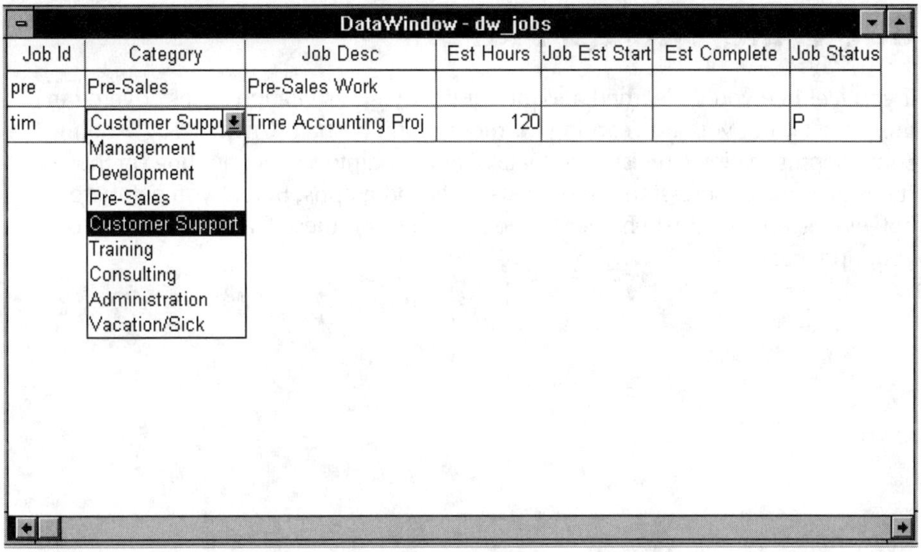

FIGURE 7-8. *Modifying a Category field in the Preview window using the list box*

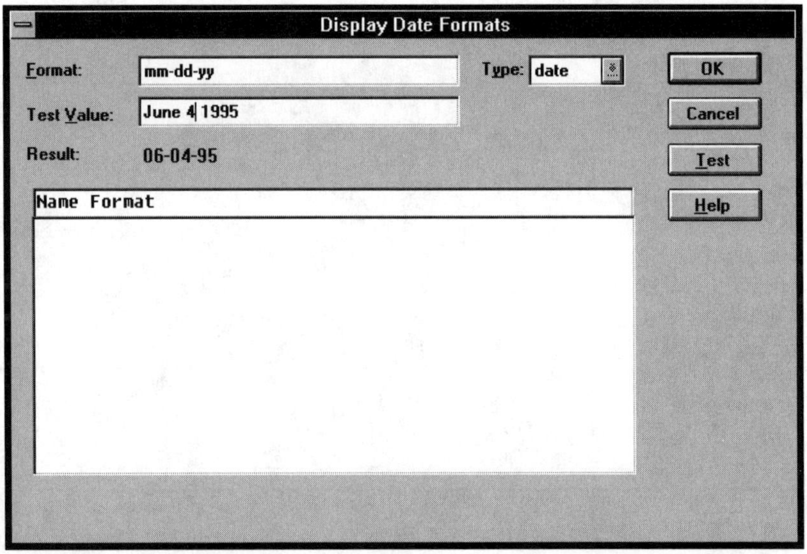

FIGURE 7-9. *Specifying a display format for start and complete dates*

But Wait, There's More!

If you feel like you've learned a lot about the two presentation styles covered in this chapter, but you are yearning for more, don't despair. Chapter 10, "Adding Some Sophistication," revisits the DataWindow painter, concentrating on those styles that make professional-looking reports and graphs. Before you get there, however, study the next chapter to see how to insert these DataWindows into your application.

CHAPTER **8**

Designing Windows
and Dialog Boxes

The fundamental element of a Windows application is the window. So why have we waited this long to discuss designing windows in PowerBuilder? Two reasons: First, the template application creates windows for you that you can use and manipulate easily. Second, windows take the most time to develop. As you work through the design of your application, your ideas and requirements will change. If you do the windows towards the end of the design you will have less chance of wasted effort and rework. This chapter will show you how to modify the windows created by PowerBuilder as well as how to create a window from scratch.

It is important to distinguish between a DataWindow and a window object, or simply a window. A *DataWindow* is a view of your database, whereas a *window* is an object that appears on your screen. You can include DataWindow as part of a window, as you will see in this chapter.

As you read this chapter, consider the terms "window" and "dialog box" as being almost interchangeable. A dialog box is usually just a special case of a window, but with PowerBuilder you can customize windows so easily that windows and dialog boxes become indistinguishable.

Starting with the Simplest of Windows

The template application comes with three predefined windows: one for the MDI frame, one for an MDI sheet, and one called w_genapp_about. The third window is the window that will appear when the user chooses About from the Help menu. If this window is unfamiliar to you, run the application and display it from there.

To customize this simple window for the Time Accounting application, click the Window icon from the PowerBar, and choose the window called w_genapp_about. You should see the screen shown in Figure 8-1. Click on the text area, and change the text to **Copyright 1995, Me**. Now let's change the title of the window to include the name of the application: Move the cursor to a blank area in the white part of the window, right-click to display the pop-up menu, and choose Title. Change the title to **About Time Accounting**.

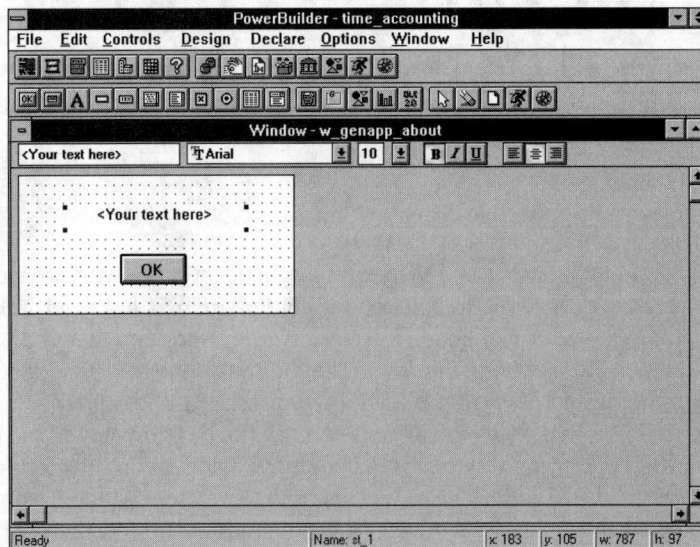

FIGURE 8-1.   *The Window painter showing a very simple window*

Adding a New Control

Chapter 3, "The Working Environment," introduced you to the concept of *controls*. The About window contains two controls, a static text control that now contains a copyright notice and a command button named OK that returns you to the application. The Window painter supports all of the controls found in common Windows applications; these controls are summarized in Table 8-1.

CONTROL TYPE	FUNCTION
CommandButton	A pushbutton with text written on it
PictureButton	A pushbutton with an icon and possibly text on it
Static Text	A string that cannot be changed by the user (but can be changed during program execution by a script)
SingleLineEdit	An area where the user can enter a single line of text, usually enclosed by a box
EditMask	A single-line edit area where the user is forced to enter data in a specific format
MultiLineEdit	An area where the user can enter text that spans more than one line
ListBox	A textual list that remains visible in the window
CheckBox	A small square that the user can click between checked (an X) and not checked (blank)
RadioButton	A set of circles where the user must choose one and only one option
DataWindow	A control that displays a DataWindow object created in the DataWindow painter
DropDownListBox	A textual list that remains hidden except when the user clicks the down arrow
Picture	A bitmap, usually for information or aesthetics only
GroupBox	A rectangle that contains a set of controls with similar functions (or some other grouping mechanism)
UserObject	A user-defined control that is some combination of the PowerBuilder controls
Graph	A pictorial representation of data
OLE2.0	A control that serves as a link to another OLE 2.0 object, such as a spreadsheet

TABLE 8-1. *Controls Supported by the Window Painter*

Window Painter—What You See

PainterBar Icons
CommandButton, PictureButton, Static Text, SingleLineEdit, EditMask, MultiLineEdit, ListBox, CheckBox, RadioButton, DataWindow, DropDownListBox, Picture, GroupBox, UserObject, Graph, OLE2.0 are the Window painter control types. When you click in the data area of the window after clicking one of these icons, you will create a new control.

Selection	Lets you select multiple controls.
Delete	Deletes the selected control.
Script	Displays the script associated with the most common event for that control. If the icon is white, no script is defined. If the icon looks like it's been written on, a script has been defined.
Run	Runs the application (same as the icon in the PowerBar).
Debug	Debugs the application (same as the icon in the PowerBar).

Main Window
The main window displays the layout of the window and lets you add, change, move, or delete controls.

Preview Window
When you choose Preview from the Design menu, PowerBuilder displays the window as it will appear in the application. You can test data entry in this window, but none of the scripts will run.

Now suppose you want to provide version information, which is customary in a Help About window. Since the static text can only hold one line, you'll need to add another static text control. Follow these steps:

1. Click the Static Text icon (the big A).

2. Click in the white part of the window between the Time Accounting Program line and the OK button. A new static text control will appear with the word "none".

3. Change the text of the control to read **Version 1.0**. Drag the upper text control up a little, and move the new text field so that it looks centered.

4. To check your work, choose Preview from the Design menu. You should see a window like this one:

```
┌─────────────────────────────────────────┐
│ ▬         About Time Accounting           │
├─────────────────────────────────────────┤
│                                           │
│            Copyright 1995, Me             │
│               Version 1.0                 │
│                                           │
│              ┌───────────┐                │
│              │    OK     │                │
│              └───────────┘                │
│                                           │
└─────────────────────────────────────────┘
```

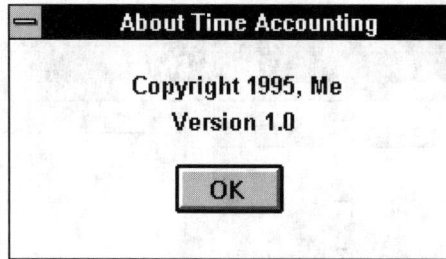

When you are in the preview window, you will be tempted to click the OK button. You can, but it will have no effect. To close the window you must chose Close from the control menu, or press CTRL-W. In order to verify whether the OK button works, you need to run the application and choose About from the Help menu.

Creating a Simple Window from Nothing

Lest you feel like the template application gave you too much of a head start, let's create a window from scratch. Assuming the Window painter is still active, choose New from the File menu. Unlike most other painters, the Window painter takes you directly to the painter without having to select any options. Since you need to understand what type of window you are creating, you should choose Window Style from the Design menu. This will bring up the dialog box shown in Figure 8-2.

In the lower-left corner of this dialog box is a group called Window Type. It is critical that you establish the type of window first, because it can have an impact on what other features are available. For example, response windows cannot include menus. Table 8-2 describes each of the types supported by PowerBuilder. Most of your applications will consist of one MDI frame with microhelp, one or more main windows, and several response windows (or dialog boxes).

For this example, as part of the Time Accounting program, we need a dialog box that gets an employee ID from the user. This ID will be used by several of the other windows to track and report time card information based on that ID. By selecting the ID once in a separate window, the user does not need to keep entering his or her ID more than once.

Since you don't want to relinquish control to other parts of the application until the user enters an ID (or cancels), you should select the Response window type. Notice how several of the other features, such as Resizable, are grayed out, since

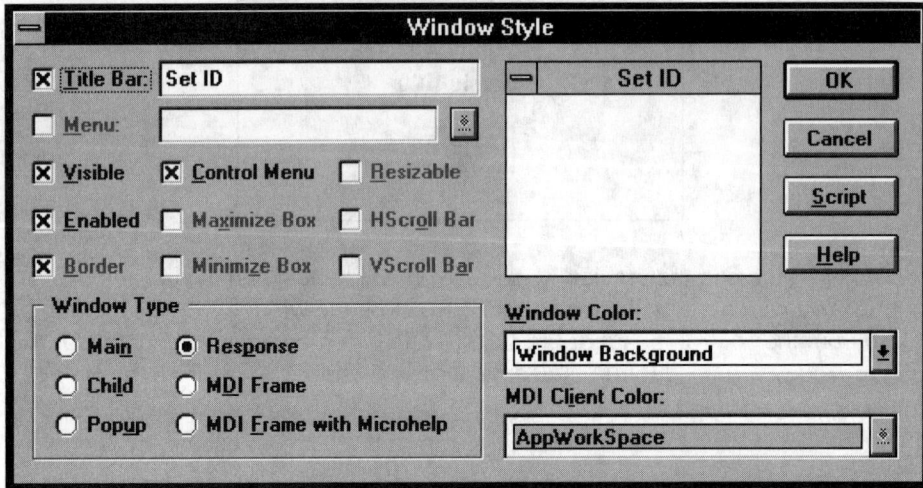

FIGURE 8-2. *The Window Style dialog box*

WINDOW TYPES	DESCRIPTION
Main	A window that can exist on its own, or as a child of another window (especially an MDI frame)
Child	A window bound by its parent. This type has been made obsolete by MDI windows and should no longer be used.
Pop-Up	A window that is activated by another window and remains in front of that window until it is closed or minimized
Response	Also known as a modal window, this type retains control of the application until it is closed. Dialog boxes are of this type.
MDI Frame with Microhelp	A window that acts as the main window of an application and that keeps track of the windows contained in it, known as sheets. See "MDI Windows" later in this chapter.
MDI Frame	Same as above, but with no automatic microhelp support

TABLE 8-2. *Types of Windows Supported by PowerBuilder*

they are no longer applicable to this window type. Change the Title Bar entry to **Set ID**, then choose OK.

Adding Controls to the Window

Once you have established the type of window you are creating, you can begin adding controls to the window. For the Set ID window, follow these steps to create the entire dialog box.

1. Click the SingleLineEdit control icon, then click near the upper-right corner of the white part of the window. Drag it open so that it looks like it will hold up to ten characters.

2. Click the Static Text control icon, then click near the upper-left corner of the window. In the text area, type **Enter Employee ID**. Move and resize the control so that it appears next to the edit control.

3. Create three pushbuttons by clicking the ControlButton icon, holding down the SHIFT key, and clicking three buttons across the lower part of the window.

4. Change the text of the three windows from "none" to **OK**, **Cancel**, and **Help**. Change the font attributes so that the text on each button is bold. Resize the buttons if necessary.

5. For aesthetics you should line up the buttons evenly. The easiest way to accomplish this is to click the Select icon, select all three buttons, then choose Align Controls and Center Horizontal from the Edit menu. While the buttons are still selected, choose Space Controls and the horizontal arrow from the Edit menu.

6. You can make the OK button the default button by right-clicking on the control and choosing Style and Default from the pop-up menu. You can also tell PowerBuilder that the second button is the one that is pressed when the user types **Escape**, by choosing Style and Cancel from the pop-up menu.

When you have finished these steps, your dialog box is finished, and it should look something like this:

```
┌─────────────────────────────────────────┐
│ ▭                  Set ID                 │
├─────────────────────────────────────────┤
│                                           │
│   Enter Employee ID:  ┌───────────────┐   │
│                       └───────────────┘   │
│                                           │
│                                           │
│    ┌──────┐   ┌────────┐   ┌──────┐       │
│    │  OK  │   │ Cancel │   │ Help │       │
│    └──────┘   └────────┘   └──────┘       │
│                                           │
└─────────────────────────────────────────┘
```

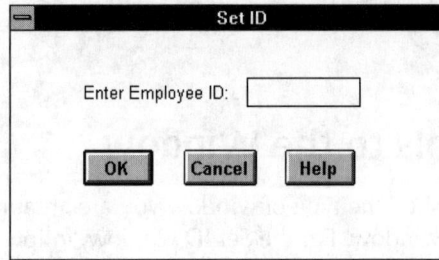

Save this window as w_set_id, and the design is complete. The only task left is the implementation, or what to do when the user chooses the OK button. We will cover implementation scripts in Chapter 9, "Defining How the Program Acts."

Adding the Window to the Application

If you invoke the Application painter, and expand all of the branches, you will not be able to find w_set_id, the window you just created. Why not? Because the window is not referenced by an object in the application. Is the window really saved? Yes, it is part of the library, timeacct.pbl, but it is not part of the application.

To add it to the application, you must modify the object that will open the window. In this particular case, we want to open the window when the user chooses Set ID from the File menu. Therefore, the MDI frame menu will be responsible for displaying this window.

To associate a window with a menu item, you must modify the script associated with that item. Until now we have done the entire design without editing a single script, but we'll have a "sneak preview" of Chapter 9, "Defining How the Program Acts," so you can see your window execute. Here's how:

1. Click the Menu painter icon in the PowerBar, and select the m_genapp_frame menu.

2. Click the File menu in the Painter window, and click the Set ID menu item. A finger should point to that item.

3. Click the Script icon, which should look like a blank sheet of paper.

4. Enter the following text in the script window:

```
Open (w_set_id)
```

This simple one-line script does exactly what you might imagine: It opens the w_set_id window and waits until it gets closed by the user.

5. Choose Return from the File menu. Assuming you've typed everything in correctly, you should return to the Menu painter.

6. Save your work, and run the application. When you choose Set ID from the File menu you will see your newly created dialog box.

Whipping Up Windows Based on DataWindows

In Chapter 7, "Interacting with the Data," you created DataWindows for the Jobs and Employee tables. In order to use a DataWindow in your application you must first associate it with a window. A DataWindow becomes just another control, like a pushbutton or SingleLineEdit box, except that it is created and designed in the DataWindow painter.

In this section we'll use the Jobs DataWindow as the basis for a window that lets the user view and manipulate the job list in the database. Before you can get to the DataWindow, however, you must create a new window. In the Window Style dialog box, set the window type to Main so that it can act as an MDI sheet. Change the title to **Update Jobs** and check Enabled to disable the menu. Return to the Window painter and drag the corners of the white area so that it takes up most of the main window.

Adding a DataWindow Control

It is understandable if you are confused between DataWindow and DataWindow control. The DataWindow is responsible for what information is retrieved from the database and how it is presented. The DataWindow control merely displays the contents of the DataWindow in a particular location in a window. Follow these steps to add the DataWindow control to the Update Jobs window:

1. Click the DataWindow icon in the PainterBar.

2. Click in the upper-left corner of the main window. PowerBuilder creates an empty DataWindow box.

3. Right-click to display the pop-up menu, and choose Change DataWindow.

4. Select the dw_jobs DataWindow from the list. The grid with its headings should appear inside the DataWindow control.

5. Drag the lower-right corner of the DataWindow control so that you can see all of the column headers. Leave a little bit of extra room on the right for a scroll bar.

6. Enable the vertical scroll bar by choosing Style and VScroll Bar from the pop-up menu.

Your screen should now look similar to Figure 8-3. If you would like to change the headings of the grid, you must modify the DataWindow itself, not the control. You can get to the DataWindow painter easily by choosing Modify DataWindow from the pop-up menu.

Adding Data Manipulation Buttons

You may recall that the preview window in the DataWindow painter let you insert, delete, and change the actual data in the database. When you insert the DataWindow into a window object, however, you don't get the manipulation capabilities. If you want users to be able to update the data, you must provide controls to do that yourself.

You can use the commands provided in the DataWindow painter as a model for the controls you add to your window, i.e., commands like **insert**, **delete**, and

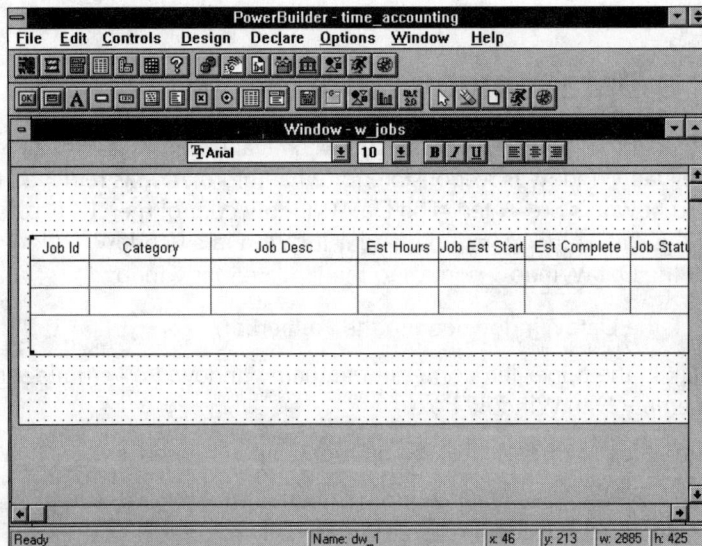

FIGURE 8-3. *Inserting the Jobs DataWindow as a DataWindow control*

update. For variety, you can use picture buttons instead of command buttons. Here's how:

1. Select the DataWindow control in the main window and drag the top of the window down so you have room for buttons.

2. Click the PictureButton icon from the PainterBar.

3. Holding down the SHIFT key, place four buttons across the top of the window. Delete the "none" text from each button.

4. Select the first button, and choose Name from the pop-up menu. PowerBuilder will display the Select Picture dialog box showing available bitmaps.

5. Choose new.bmp from the list. You should now see this display:

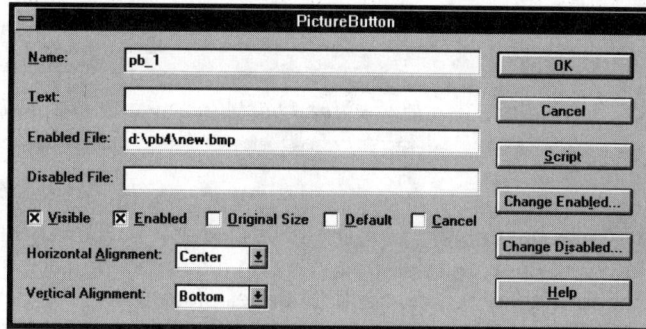

6. Choose Original Size, then OK.

7. Repeat the sequence for the other three buttons. You'll need icons for deleting, updating, and exiting. (We used delete.bmp, update.bmp, and close.bmp.)

8. Adjust the spacing and alignment, and make the Exit button the default button by choosing Style and Default in the pop-up menu.

When you preview your finished product, it should look like Figure 8-4. Again, this is still the design of the window, not the implementation. We will associate commands with each of the buttons when we cover PowerScript in Chapter 9, "Defining How the Program Acts." Save the window as w_jobs.

MDI Windows

A chapter on windows would not be complete without a brief discussion of MDI, or Multiple Document Interface. MDI offers the ability to create an application with

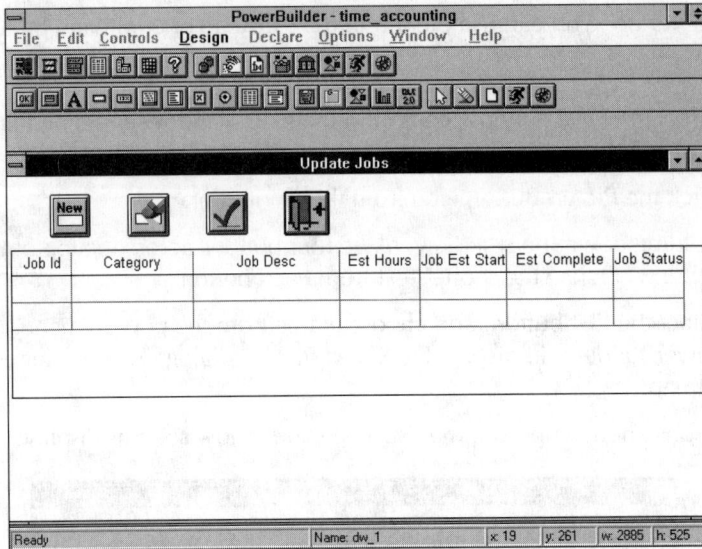

FIGURE 8-4. *A complete window with a DataWindow and picture buttons*

one master, known as the frame, and many slaves, or sheets. Each sheet can be manipulated independently, but the sheets rely on the frame for menu support. Also, a sheet cannot extend beyond the boundaries of its frame. The frame keeps track of all of the sheets so that it can arrange them by tiling or cascading, or take you to a specific sheet that may be hidden.

As you design your application, consider why a user might want to have multiple sheets open at the same time. In the Time Accounting program, users might want to see a time card window and the jobs window at the same time. Or, they might want to see reports on two different departments at the same time. MDI lets them see any combination of sheets at once.

As a rule of thumb, almost all applications should be MDI applications. Even if you can't imagine multiple sheets when you start your development, inevitably you'll find a use for them by the time you finish. Also, an MDI frame gives you microhelp for free, so even if you have a trivial application, you may as well use an MDI frame with microhelp. Trust us—your trivial application will eventually grow into a monstrous application. With PowerBuilder's template application, you can create an MDI application with little effort.

Putting It All Together

At this point you have created the database, the application object, the menu, the DataWindow objects, and the windows. Like a jigsaw puzzle, you now have all the pieces you need in a box (the library), and now you need to connect them together. The next chapter will show you how.

CHAPTER 9

Defining How the Program Acts

If you love to develop applications but hate to program, your introduction to PowerBuilder until now must have been a marriage made in heaven. Well, the honeymoon is over. You can design your application without writing any code, but you must write some code to finish the implementation. This chapter will show you how PowerBuilder has created a language and an environment that make programming as painless as possible.

The first few sections of this chapter introduce you to the terminology and the language of PowerScript. It has been written assuming you have had very little programming experience. If you are an expert programmer in C or another popular language, you should be able to skim this chapter until the section "Implementing Applications;" however, you should not skip the first part entirely.

Understanding the Terminology

Whether you can program in a dozen computer languages or you can't even remember the introductory programming course you had in school, you need to spend a few moments studying the terminology defined by PowerBuilder. Many languages define terms slightly differently, and PowerBuilder is certainly no exception.

Programs in almost all languages consist in some form of actions and data. In PowerBuilder, all actions and data fall into one of two categories: either they are defined by PowerBuilder, or they are defined by you. This is an important distinction, because it helps you understand what things you can control and what things you can't. The following sections describe terms in these two categories.

Actions and Data Defined by PowerBuilder

The following actions and data are predefined; you cannot create them, remove them, or see how they are implemented. You can, however, access them and use them to help you implement your application.

Events

An *event* is a stimulus to an object, usually external. In plain terms, an event is something that can happen. Each object in PowerBuilder has a set of predefined events. Many events are ignored, but a few key events deserve a response. For example, a control button has eleven events, including when the mouse pointer moves into the button's rectangle (getfocus) and when the mouse pointer leaves the button's rectangle (losefocus). Only in rare circumstances would you want to react to either of those events. However when the user presses the button (clicked) you almost always want to respond. Responses for events are written in scripts.

Object Functions

Each object type also defines a set of functions that are available for all instances of that object type. A *function* is a command; it usually performs an action and returns a value. Functions often take one or more *arguments*, or values they need to help with the command. Unlike events, which may be triggered by outside circumstances, functions must be called explicitly by some other script. Here are some of the functions defined for the Control Button object:

```
┌─────────────────────────────────────────────────────────┐
│ ▬                     Browse Object                       │
├─────────────────────────────────────────────────────────┤
│ Paste Values:                                             │
│ ┌───────────────────────────────────────┬─┐  ┌─────────┐ │
│ │ classname ( )  returns string         │▲│  │  Paste  │ │
│ │ drag ( dragmodes m )  returns int     ├─┤  └─────────┘ │
│ │ hide ( )   returns int                │ │  ┌─────────┐ │
│ │ move ( int x, int y )  returns int    │ │  │ Cancel  │ │
│ │ pointerx ( )  returns int             │ │  └─────────┘ │
│ │ pointery ( )  returns int             │ │  ┌─────────┐ │
│ │ postevent ( string e )  returns boolean│ │  │  Help   │ │
│ │ postevent ( string e, long w, long l )  returns boolean│ └─────────┘ │
│ │ postevent ( string e, long w, string l )  returns boolean│ ┌─ Category ─┐│
│ │ postevent ( trigevent e )  returns boolean│ │            ││
│ │ print ( int j, int x, int y )  returns int│ │ ○ Attributes││
│ │ print ( int j, int x, int y, int w, int h )  returns int│▼│ ◉ Functions││
│ └───────────────────────────────────────┴─┘  └───────────┘│
└─────────────────────────────────────────────────────────┘
```

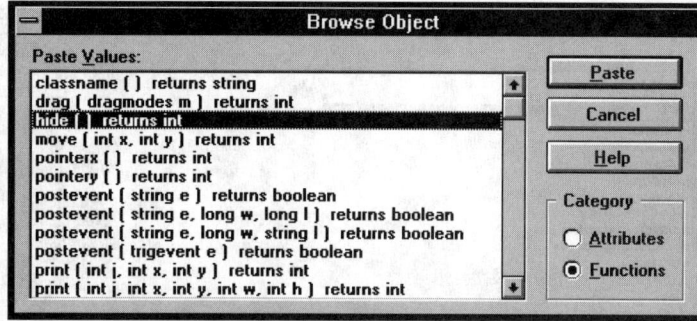

As you can see, you can call a function to remove the button from the window (hide), or even move it to another location in the window (move).

Global Functions

A global function is a command that is not tied to a particular object type. Global functions and object functions together become the set of *built-in* functions. PowerBuilder comes with scores of global functions, such as string manipulation, file I/O, and traditional numeric functions like cosine (Cos) and absolute value (Abs).

If you are modifying a script or function, you can choose Paste Function from the Edit menu to see the complete list of built-in functions:

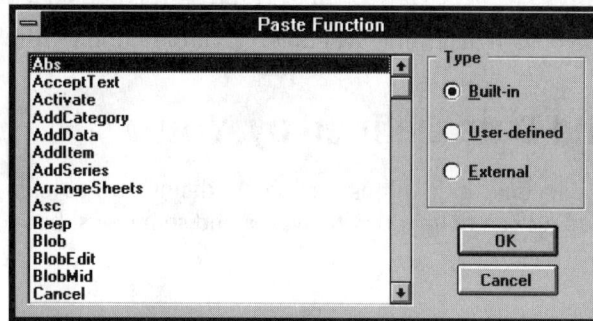

```
┌─────────────────────────────────────────────────────────┐
│ ▬                     Paste Function                      │
├─────────────────────────────────────────────────────────┤
│ ┌───────────────────────────────┬─┐  ┌─ Type ──────────┐ │
│ │ Abs                           │▲│  │                 │ │
│ │ AcceptText                    ├─┤  │ ◉ Built-in      │ │
│ │ Activate                      │ │  │                 │ │
│ │ AddCategory                   │ │  │ ○ User-defined  │ │
│ │ AddData                       │ │  │                 │ │
│ │ AddItem                       │ │  │ ○ External      │ │
│ │ AddSeries                     │ │  │                 │ │
│ │ ArrangeSheets                 │ │  └─────────────────┘ │
│ │ Asc                           │ │                      │
│ │ Beep                          │ │  ┌─────────────────┐ │
│ │ Blob                          │ │  │       OK        │ │
│ │ BlobEdit                      │ │  └─────────────────┘ │
│ │ BlobMid                       │ │  ┌─────────────────┐ │
│ │ Cancel                        │▼│  │     Cancel      │ │
│ └───────────────────────────────┴─┘  └─────────────────┘ │
└─────────────────────────────────────────────────────────┘
```

Obviously just the name isn't much information, but if you know what you are looking for, this window can help. If you're not sure what you need, see Appendix A, "PowerScript Function Quick Reference."

Attributes

An *attribute* is a piece of data that is associated with an instance of an object. Every attribute has a *data type*, which defines the set of possible values for that attribute. Figure 9-1 shows an Object Browser display, where you can see all of the functions

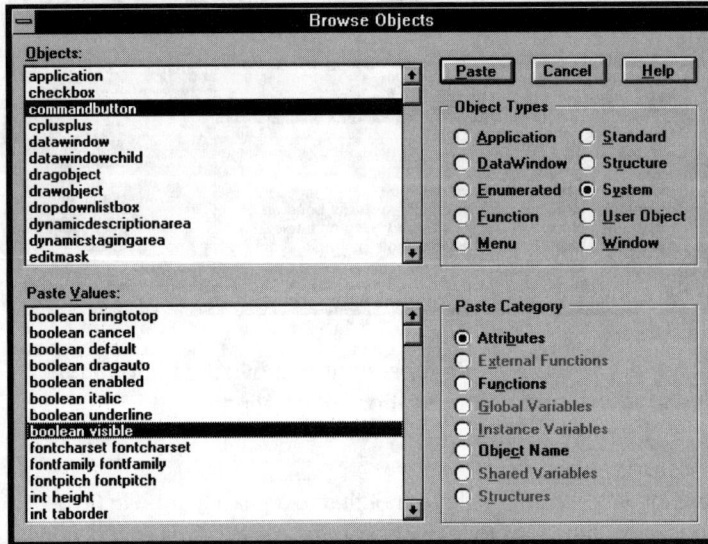

FIGURE 9-1. *The Object Browser lets you view attributes based on object type*

and attributes defined for each of PowerBuilder's object types. With the selected attribute (visible) you can determine whether a control button is visible.

Actions and Data Defined by You

The actions and data described in this section are defined, or at least implemented, by you. PowerBuilder can help you with syntax and semantics, but you control the logic.

Scripts

A *script* defines the actions that take place in response to an event. When an event occurs, such as the user clicking a button, PowerBuilder does all of the generic responses, such as changing the display to make the button look like it has been pushed, then passes control to the script. Other than those filled in by the template application, all scripts are initially empty.

Object Functions

Certain objects, i.e., windows, menus, and applications, let you expand the object definition by creating your own functions. The function will be available to all scripts and functions, but will be attached to a particular object. To declare a new function from within the Menu or Window painter, select Menu Function or Window Function, respectively, from the Declare menu.

Global Functions

If you need to define a function that is general in nature, and might be applicable to other objects, or even other applications, you create a global function. Global functions are defined using the Function painter.

External Functions

An *external* function is one written in the C programming language. If you have a C function that you need for a PowerBuilder application, you do not need to re-create it in PowerBuilder. Instead, compile the function into a DLL (dynamic link library). Then declare it in PowerBuilder as an external function. External functions can be declared either local to a particular object or global to all objects.

User Events

Occasionally you may find it desirable to have objects communicate to each other with user-defined events. In one object, you might declare an event and implement its script. In another object you can trigger that event by calling the TriggerEvent built-in function. User-defined events are most commonly used with UserObjects, which have no predefined events.

NOTE
The term "user" in this context is a bit misleading. User events and user-defined functions are not controlled by the user, but by the programmer. The person running the application cannot create events or functions, nor explicitly trigger or call them.

Local Variables

A *variable* is a location in memory that stores a value. If you have done programming in any of the common languages you are familiar with variables. A *local* variable is one defined inside a script. A local variable can be referenced only by the script where it is declared.

Instance Variables

The same object types that let you declare object functions also support instance variables. An *instance* variable is the same as an attribute, except it is defined and controlled by the programmer.

Shared Variables

A *shared* variable is one that is associated with all objects of a given type. Windows and menus support shared variables. Many PowerBuilder programmers eschew shared variables in favor of the more easily understood global variables.

Global Variables

A *global* variable is one that is changeable by every script and every function within the application. From a programmer's perspective, global variables are dangerous because there is no control over them. Use them with care.

Structures

A *structure* is simply a combination of variables. If you find yourself passing the same four (or more) variables from one function to the next, you can save time and effort by combining them into a structure. It is common practice to create a structure for each table in your database, giving you an easy method of storing a row from the database in memory.

Formatting Your Code

Some languages are very formal in the way that code must be formatted. For instance, many FORTRAN compilers require you to start program statements in column 7 or greater. A comment marker can only be placed in column 6, and line numbers appear in columns 1 through 5. The RPG language uses fixed columns for every line of code to mean different things.

Other languages, like Pascal, C, and PowerScript, are very flexible when it comes to the format of your code—they require almost nothing! Therefore, you need to choose your own guidelines, and train yourself to follow them.

You will begin to develop a personalized style of programming as you become more experienced. This is true for any programming language; without establishing guidelines for yourself, you can write code that even you will not be able to read. Programming style is mostly just a matter of being consistent, especially in the areas of indentation, comments, and variable names.

The following sections offer examples of different programming styles. Use a style that suits you, or modify one of these styles to create your own. But be consistent! Consistency in your programming style will prove invaluable when you return later to re-read your code. It will also enable other programmers to read your code with minimal confusion.

NOTE
Don't feel that you need to make decisions about your style
immediately. Try the different techniques shown here, and then add
changes as you see fit. Your programming style will continually
evolve as you program, but do be careful to ensure that it remains
consistent at any one time, within any one program or project.

Indentation

PowerScript does not require formatting or indentation of any kind; the format that
you use is entirely up to you. The only restriction is that each statement must fit on
a single line, or must be continued with a continuation character (&). For instance,
the following two statements are equivalent:

```
MessageBox("Urgent!", "The database has been corrupted")
MessageBox("Urgent!", &
      "The database has been corrupted")
```

Indentation shows how blocks of code are combined. The number of spaces
that you choose to indent is also a matter of style, although most programmers find
that indenting 2 to 4 spaces per level of indentation is sufficient.
A few examples of indentation are shown below. Don't worry about all the
commands if you don't know them yet; that will come soon.

```
If A = 1 Then
    MessageBox( "Value", "The value of A is 1")
Else
    MessageBox( "Value", "Value has been doubled" )
    B = A * 2
End If

Do While B > A
    B = B - 1
    If B > 1 Then
        MessageBox( "Reducing", "B still needs reducing" )
    Else
        MessageBox( "New Value", "B has been reduced to " + B )
    End If
Loop
```

You may notice that when you have one type of statement within another, you can indent several levels. This helps you later determine what was being done at each decision point.

Comments

While comments are very important in all programming, they are often ignored or played down by programmers. This is because comments are not part of the code necessary for making the program work, and therefore do not appear to be as important.

> **NOTE**
> Comments are not required in programs. You should, however, try to get into the habit of commenting your code. Although comments may not seem important when you are writing a program, they will be very important when you come back later and try to decipher what you have written.

Comments do not need to be lengthy, but they do need to explain what is happening in the program. This should be plain enough so that you, the programmer, or other users will be able to understand the code in the future. It is not necessary, or even desirable, to comment each line of code. However, you should put comments in the following places:

- *At the beginning of the script file*   These comments describe what is in the file, possibly who wrote it and when, and any other files that it may be linked to or dependent upon. In addition, it is often helpful to add the version of PowerBuilder used, and the steps required for building the program (the libraries used, etc.).

- *At the beginning of each function*   Function comments describe how the function is called, what it does, and what parameters are used with it. *Parameters* are the values or variables sent into and returned from functions.

- *In any area of code where the algorithms are not straightforward*   These comments will later help you remember why things were done in a particular way.

NOTE

Algorithms are the steps and decisions required to perform a given task. For instance, there are two common algorithms used to search for a given item in a list. If the list is in order (numerically or alphabetically), you can use a binary search, but if they are not in order, you will need to use a sequential search.

A sequential search does not require a complex algorithm; you simply look at each item until you find the one you wanted. A binary search, on the other hand, involves repeatedly splitting the list in half until the desired answer is in the portion that is left. This type of algorithm is more complex, and should be commented (so you don't forget how it is supposed to work).

In PowerScript, there are two ways to add comments to your scripts. In the first format, comments start with two characters: a slash and an asterisk (/*), with no spaces between them. These comments end with the same two characters in reversed order (*/). They can be written on a single line, or can cross multiple lines. The following example shows comments on a line, and comments crossing several lines.

```
/*
   Function to determine a big number

   This function returns a number that is all the
   numbers equal to or less than i, multiplied
   together. For instance, if i=3, then this
   function will return 1*2*3, or 6.

   Input:      The base number, i
   Output:     The big number
*/


Function : BigNumber
( i : Integer ) : Integer;
Private:
   int big, count

   big = 1  /* start out with 1 */
```

```
/* Multiply for each number. Skip 1 since
   multiplying by 1 doesn't change the
   result. */
For count = 2 To i
   big = big * count
Next
Return big  /* send the number back */

END /* function */
```

While you may not yet understand how this example works, notice how the comments help you to better understand what is happening. Also notice that the format of a comment can change from line to line; some comments are on a single line, while others span several lines. How you format your comments will be a matter of choice, based on how you want your final program to look.

If you use lots of single line comments, you will like to know about the second type of comment. These comments begin with the // character pair, and end at the end of the current line. The above example, using these new comments, might be typed like this:

```
// Function to determine a big number

// This function returns a number that is all the
// numbers equal to or less than i, multiplied
// together. For instance, if i=3, then this
// function will return 1*2*3, or 6.

// Input:      The base number, i
// Output:     The big number


Function : BigNumber
( i : Integer ) : Integer;
Private:
   int big, count

   big = 1  // start out with 1

   // Multiply for each number. Skip 1 since
   // multiplying by 1 doesn't change the
   // result.
   For count = 2 To i
      big = big * count
```

```
    Next
    Return big  //send the number back

END // function
```

While many programmers just display their comments, others go further,
adding lines and positioning their comments in an attempt to make their code look
nice, as shown here:

```
/* -----------------------------------------------------
    Function to determine a big number

    This function returns a number that is all the
    numbers equal to or less than i, multiplied
    together. For instance, if i=3, then this
    function will return 1*2*3, or 6.

    Input:      The base number, i
    Output:     The big number
    --------------------------------------------------- */

Function : BigNumber
( i : Integer ) : Integer;
Private:
    int big, count

    big = 1                             /* start out with 1 */

                    /* ------------------------------------
                        Multiply for each number. Skip 1 since
                        multiplying by 1 doesn't change the
                        result.
                        ------------------------------------ */
    For count = 2 To i
        big = big * count
    Next
    Return big                  /* send the number back */

END /* --------------- function Big ------------------*/
```

While this may appeal to you from a pictorial viewpoint, remember that
consistency is the rule, and drawing pretty boxes often takes a good deal of time,
especially if you have several dozen, or several hundred, functions to comment! In

addition, the more characters that are in your source files create more work for the compiler, which may increase the time required to build your programs.

NOTE
Comments that are aligned are very easy to read—an important consideration for maintaining (making changes to) your code in the future. Just remember that art work takes a lot of time, and is best saved for the final version of your program, when there are no other changes that need to be made.

Selecting Variable Names

Variables are data storage locations within your programs. You should name them in a way that will be simple to recall as you continue programming. Several ideas for naming variables are described in this section. The choice of styles for naming your variables is up to you, but do remember to be consistent.

Assign your variables long enough names that you'll be able to remember easily what each one is used for, but not so long that you dread typing them in for each statement. For instance, there is no need to call variables i, p, and t when you could call them interest, payment, and total. On the other hand, longer names such as interest_rate_for_the_loan, payment_for_the_loan, and total_amount_paid_on_the_loan would be tedious to type over and over, and unnecessary for most programs.

Capitalization is not significant in PowerScript. This means that variables named aVariable, avariable, and AVARIABLE would all represent the same variable to the compiler.

Listed here are some common options for capitalization:

CONVENTION	EXAMPLES
All Lowercase	interestrate
	paymentamt
	lastamtdue
All Uppercase	INTERESTRATE
	PAYMENTAMT
	LASTAMTDUE
First Letter Capitalized	Interestrate
	Paymentamt
	Lastamtdue

First Letter of Each Word Capitalized	InterestRate
	PaymentAmt
	LastAmtDue
Words Separated with Underscores	interest_rate
	payment_amt
	last_amt_due

These conventions are all acceptable, but the last two are more readable than the others, and are the ones seen most often in the code of professional programmers.

NOTE
Even if the language you use is not case-sensitive, variable names that include mixed uppercase and lowercase letters will help make your program much easier to read. Look at the examples above, and pick one that suits you. Remember to be consistent!

Declaring Variables and Constants

Throughout the early chapters of this book, you learned about different types of data that can be stored in a PowerBuilder database, such as integers, real numbers, and character strings. In this section, you will see how a programmer would define these pieces of data in a script. In order to store data, there must be some mechanism to hold onto the data, so that its value is retained as your program runs. One of these mechanisms is the variable, which is used to store data that can be changed (or varied) during the program.

Before a variable can be used to hold data, it must be declared. A declaration includes both the variable name and its data type. When the variable is declared, the computer puts some memory aside specifically for the use of that variable. The specific location in memory is usually not important; your program uses the variable's name to tell the computer where to look. In the next sections, you will see examples of how this works.

Standard Data Types

Standard data types are the types of variables that are available in your scripts. They include integers, floating point numbers, characters, and strings. Another type of variable supported in your scripts, is the Boolean, or logical, type. These are variables with TRUE and FALSE values.

Integers

Integers are the counting numbers that you deal with in normal conversation ("I am thirty years old," "It is 25 degrees outside," "You were traveling 75 in a 55-mile-per-hour zone," etc.). These numbers are used very often in programming; for instance, integers are used for counting how many times something happens.

The following example shows variables being declared in PowerScript. Notice that the variable name always follows the data type (int, in this case).

```
int myAge
int carSpeed, loopCount
```

You may place each variable on a separate line, or may combine the variables on a single line, separating them with commas.

Characters and Strings

Character variables each use one byte (8 bits) of computer memory, holding only one printed character. A *string*, on the other hand, is a sequence of characters, used to hold names, addresses, etc. A string takes up one byte of computer memory for each character it holds. Typical strings might include:

```
George Jetson
Leaning Tower of Pisa
ABC
```

In PowerScript, the variable type for holding a single character is called **char**, while the variable type for holding a string is called **string** (pretty straightforward!). Here are some example definitions for these variable types:

```
string myName = "John Ribar"
char firstInitial
```

You may notice that you can define a value for a variable at the same time you declare the variable. In the above example, the variable *myName* is declared as a string variable, and given a value of "John Ribar", all in the same command.

Flow Control

To streamline your work as a programmer, you need to learn how to use flow control statements. Flow control statements allow programmers to control the order in which the program statements will be executed, and often even how many times they will be repeated (if at all).

Looping

Looping is the process of repeating a piece of code, whether one statement or a large group of statements, multiple times. Some loops repeat a specific number of times, while others repeat until a specific condition is met. Be careful when you specify the exit conditions (the condition that makes the loop end), or you may create an infinite loop; these loops continue forever, locking up your computer and generally requiring you to reboot!

The sections which follow describe two main types of flow control statements. The first type is used to make a decision and then run selected code, according to the results. The second type is used to repeat sections of code multiple times, in a controlled manner.

Making Decisions

The first type of control statements are those used when a decision is necessary. An IF statement checks the value of a Boolean variable, or an equation with a Boolean answer. If the value is TRUE, specific code is executed. If the value is FALSE, then no code is executed, unless there is an ELSE clause. An ELSE clause is used to specify an alternate course of events—something that the program should do if the condition in the IF statement is FALSE.

A CHOOSE CASE statement will first check the value of a specified variable and then, depending on that value, jump to a specific section of code.

IF...THEN...ELSIF...ELSE Statements

An IF statement is used when there is a decision to be made that will effect whether certain lines of code should be executed. It has several forms, which are discussed here.

```
If <condition> Then
    <actions>
End If
```

In this format, a single condition is checked. If the condition is found to be TRUE (e.g., A = B, C > 0, etc.) then the actions will be taken.

```
If <condition> Then
    <first_action>
```

```
Else
    <second_action>
End If
```

Here, a condition is checked. If it is found to be TRUE, the first action is taken; otherwise, the second action is taken.

```
If <condition1> Then
    <first_action>
ElseIf <condition2> Then
    <second_action>
Else
    <third_action>
End If
```

In this final example, there are several possibilities. If the first condition is TRUE, the first action will occur. If the second condition is TRUE, the second action will take place; otherwise, the third action will be performed.

CHOOSE CASE Statements

CHOOSE CASE statements are similar to IF statements that have lots of ELSE and ELSE IF clauses. However, when a CHOOSE CASE statement is used, the result is a more readable piece of code. You will see this in the next example, which replaces a possible string of IF...ELSE statements with a single CHOOSE CASE statement.

```
int month
Choose Case month
    Case 1
        MessageBox( "Cold Weather", "It sure is cold outside" )
    Case 2 to 5
        MessageBox( "Warming Trend", "Get warmer little by little")
    Case 7, 9, 11, 12
        MessageBox( "Holidays", "Days off coming up soon")
    Case Else
        MessageBox( "Others", "Must be another normal month")
End Choose
```

You will probably notice that there are several ways to specify the valid responses. In the first case, only a single value was allowed (1). In the second case, a range of numbers (2 to 5) was allowed. The third example (7, 9, 11, 12) shows a selection of specific items, separated by commas. And the final case is the ELSE case, into which all other values will fall.

NOTE

When deciding whether to use a group of IF statements or a CHOOSE CASE statement, consider the nature of the arguments. An IF statement can take any equation or condition that returns a value of TRUE or FALSE. A CHOOSE CASE statement, on the other hand, is limited to specific (non-fractional) values.

Repetitive Processing

Very often, you will want a section of code to be performed several times. Sometimes, you will know how many times the code should execute when the program is run (printing reports for 12 months, calculating payroll for 20 employees, etc.). In other cases, you will want the program to keep going until the user decides to quit.

In computer programming, repetitive processing tasks can be simplified with the use of loops. In PowerScript, FOR, WHILE, and UNTIL loops are all available.

FOR Loops

A FOR loop is used to execute a target statement or group of statements multiple times. To use a FOR loop, you use an index variable. This variable keeps track of how many times the loop has been run. In constructing a FOR loop, you first initialize the variable, and then set a limit that will cause the program to exit the loop when appropriate.

The general format of the FOR loop is shown below.

```
For <variable> = <start> To <end>
   <actions>
End For
```

The variable, as with all other variables, must be declared before it is used in the FOR loop. The start and end values give the number of times the actions will be repeated. For instance, to perform specific actions for each month of the year, you might use

```
For month = 1 To 12
   // some action goes here
End For
```

DO WHILE and DO UNTIL Loops

DO WHILE and DO UNTIL loops are very much like IF statements that can be executed more than once. Each of these loops has a control statement that, each time the loop is finished running, checks to determine whether the loop should continue to run. (Recall that in the IF statement, the control statement only applied the first time through.) There are four basic forms of these statements, all of which include the Loop keyword.

This format is used when you want to check the condition before the loop, and may not even get to perform the actions once (if the condition is FALSE, that is).

```
Do While <condition>
    <actions>
Loop
```

The next format is used when the actions should be executed at least one time, but may not need to be run any more than that. This format is as follows:

```
Do
    <actions>
Loop While <condition>
```

The WHILE statements continue to execute as long as the condition is TRUE. The UNTIL statements, on the other hand, continue to execute while the condition is FALSE, and stop when it becomes TRUE. The format of the UNTIL statement which checks before the actions is

```
Do Until <condition>
    <actions>
Loop
```

while the format for having the check after the actions is like this:

```
Do
    <actions>
Loop Until <condition>
```

More About WHILE and UNTIL Loops

The different WHILE and UNTIL loops are nearly identical in purpose. The difference is the timing of execution of the condition statement. With an IF statement, the control statement determines whether the line or block of target code would be executed at all. With WHILE and UNTIL loops, the control statement determines whether the target code will be executed again.

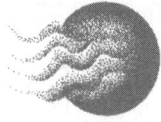

NOTE

In a WHILE or UNTIL statement that has the control statement *after* the target statements, the body of the loop (the target statement or block) will always be executed at least one time. The condition is checked after each execution of the loop. When the control statement is located *before* the body of the loop, the body of the loop may not be executed at all.

The Infamous GOTO Statement

There is one last control statement that you should know about, a statement called GOTO. This is a very powerful—and extremely dangerous—statement. The GOTO statement was always popular in early BASIC programming, because one of the only ways to get from one point to another in your program was to GOTO a specific line number, as shown in this example:

```
10 PRINT "How old are you?"
20 INPUT Age%
30 IF Age% > 18 GOTO 60
40 PRINT "You are an adult"
50 GOTO 70
60 PRINT "You are not yet an adult"
70 PRINT "See you next time"
```

As you can probably see just from this small example, it can become very difficult to read and trace the execution of this type of program. For this reason, programmers who use the more structured languages (Pascal, Modula-2, C, C++, PL/I, and even the newer versions of BASIC and FORTRAN) have frowned upon the use of the GOTO statement. This holds very true with PowerScript programming as well.

With the variety of looping and control statements now available, GOTO can be nearly eliminated. Here is a similar program written in PowerScript, without the use of a GOTO statement:

```
int Age = 17
If Age > 18 Then
    MessageBox( "Legal Age", "You are an adult")
Else
    MessageBox( "Under-Age", "You are not yet an adult")
End If
```

If you can avoid using GOTO statements, it will save you immense time and effort in the debugging and maintenance of your programs.

Accessing Functions and Data
When you need to call a function, you use the function name followed by the arguments enclosed in parentheses. For example, the statement

```
close(Parent)
```

calls a function named **close**, with the variable *Parent* passed to the function as an argument. The syntax for calling a function or referencing data depends on how that function or data was defined, as you can see by this table:

IF DEFINED AS A(N)...	ACCESS USING...
global function	function_name
object function	object_name.function_name
attribute	object_name.attribute
local variable, global variable	variable_name
instance variable	object_name.variable_name

Function Call   A function call returns a value, so it is normally part of an assignment statement, such as this:

```
status = close(Parent)
```

If you don't care about the value returned by the function, you can call the function on a line by itself:

```
close(Parent)
```

Using the PowerScript Painter

PowerBuilder officially supports two painters for writing code: the PowerScript painter and the Function painter. Actually, there is almost no difference between the two. The Function painter lets you modify the arguments of the function, and since events don't have arguments, the PowerScript painter has no support for arguments.

One of the key features of both painters is that you cannot exit out of the painter until all the code in it compiles. This feature is wonderful in making sure

you don't accidentally execute uncompilable code, but it has several other implications:

- If you are turning off your computer for the day, and you have errors in your code, you must comment out the lines with the errors before you can exit PowerBuilder.

- You must implement features in the proper order. For example, if you realize you need a function in another object, you must declare that function first before you try to call it from a script or other function.

- If you delete an object from a library, and an existing object references that object in a script, you will not be able to open that object in a painter, and must redo the object from scratch. Therefore it is a good idea to never delete objects, unless you are absolutely certain they are unused.

Implementing Applications

The remainder of this chapter lets you see how scripts, functions, variables, and attributes work together to complete the implementation of an application. It takes the objects designed in the previous chapters and glues them together using PowerScript.

Let's start with the time_accounting application object. When you run an application PowerBuilder triggers the Open event of the application object. If the script for the Open event is empty, the application won't do anything. The template application loads a script for this event, most of which you can see in Figure 9-2. After some initializations, the script calls a global function called Open, and passes it the name of the MDI frame window. You don't need to make any changes to the script at this time, so close it.

By the way, did you ever wonder how PowerBuilder creates the tree structure in the application window? It searches the scripts and object functions for other objects, and those become the next level of objects in the display. If you change the window referred to in the Open script from w_genapp_frame to some other window object, the display in the application window would change as well.

Implementing MDI Frames

One of first things that the Open built-in function does is trigger the Open event for that window. If you bring up the Window painter with the w_genapp_frame

PowerScript/Function Painter—What You See
The painters for editing scripts and editing functions are virtually identical.

PainterBar Icons

Undo	Cancels the last textual change you made.
Cut, Copy, Paste	Standard clipboard commands.
Clear	Deletes the selected text.
Select All	Selects the entire script or function.
Comment	Prepends each of the selected lines with comment indicators (//).
Uncomment	Removes comment indicators from each of the selected lines.
Paste SQL	Click this icon to display the SQL paster, which helps you build an SQL statement interactively.
Paste Statement	If you are unsure of the syntax of a statement, click here to choose the statement kind.
Browse Object	Displays a dialog box showing the functions and attributes defined for this object type.
Browse Objects	Displays a more complex dialog box showing attributes, variables, and functions defined for any object defined by you or PowerBuilder.
Edit (function only)	Click this icon when you need to modify the arguments of a function.
Return	Although the icon will change depending on the context, the last icon always returns you to your previous painter.

Main Window
The main window contains the PowerScript statements that will be executed when the script or function is run. If you compile and have errors, the window will display the error messages at the bottom of the window.

Drop-Down List Boxes

Select Event (script only)	Lets you change scripts to one associated with a different event.
Paste Object	Displays a list of the subobjects visible to the script or object function. If you click one, the name will be pasted at the current cursor location.
Paste Global	Displays a list of the global variables and their data types. Click one to paste the variable name in the script.
Paste Instance	Displays a list of all instance variables for pasting.
Paste Argument (function only)	Displays the names of the arguments defined for the function for pasting.

```
┌─────────────────────────────────────────────────────────────┐
│ ─              PowerBuilder - time_accounting          ▼ │ ≑ │
│ File  Edit  Search  Declare  Compile  Window  Help           │
├─────────────────────────────────────────────────────────────┤
│ [toolbar icons]                                               │
├─────────────────────────────────────────────────────────────┤
│ [toolbar icons]                                               │
├─────────────────────────────────────────────────────────────┤
│ ─             Script - open for time_accounting        ▼ │ ▲ │
├─────────────────────────────────────────────────────────────┤
│ Select Event  ↕│Paste Object ↕│Paste Global ↕│Paste Instance↕│
├─────────────────────────────────────────────────────────────┤
│ sqlca.userid     = ProfileString ("pb.ini", "database", "userid",    "") │
│ sqlca.dbpass     = ProfileString ("pb.ini", "database", "dbpass",    "") │
│ sqlca.logid      = ProfileString ("pb.ini", "database", "logid",     "") │
│ sqlca.logpass    = ProfileString ("pb.ini", "database", "LogPassWord", "") │
│ sqlca.servername = ProfileString ("pb.ini", "database", "servername", "") │
│ sqlca.dbparm     = ProfileString ("pb.ini", "database", "dbparm",    "") │
│                                                               │
│ /* Uncomment the following for actual DB connection */        │
│ /*connect;*/                                                  │
│ /* */                                                         │
│ /*if sqlca.sqlcode <> 0 then*/                                │
│ /* MessageBox ("Cannot Connect to Database", sqlca.sqlerrtext)*/ │
│ /* return*/                                                   │
│ /*end if*/                                                    │
│                                                               │
│ /* Open MDI Frame window */                                   │
│ Open (w_genapp_frame)                                         │
│                                               0020:0001       │
├─────────────────────────────────────────────────────────────┤
│ Ready                                                         │
└─────────────────────────────────────────────────────────────┘
```

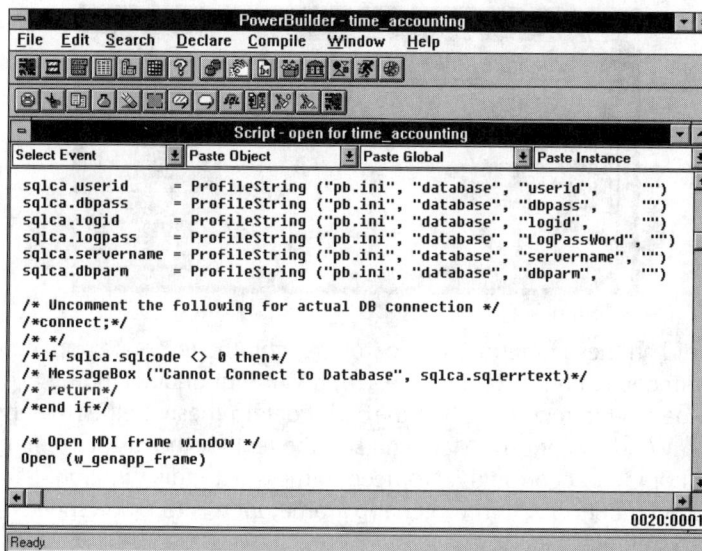

FIGURE 9-2. *The template application supplies an implementation for the Open event of an application*

window and click the Script icon (it resembles a piece of paper), you should see the script for the Open event. It should look like this:

```
/* Modify menu text for platform */
f_setmenutext (menuid)

/* Create the initial sheet */
f_newsheet
```

(If you see a different script, click the Select Event list box and click the Open event.) Since you can read PowerScript, you can see that the listing contains two comment lines and two function calls. By convention, we know that the functions are user-defined since they start with f_.

What do these functions do? If we trusted the comments, we could assume that the first one modifies the menu text for the platform. OK, what does that mean? To get more information we must look at the function itself. Choose Window Functions from the Declare menu, and you will see this dialog box:

```
┌─────────────────────────────────────────────────────┐
│ ─        Select Function in Window                    │
├─────────────────────────────────────────────────────┤
│ Functions:                          ┌──────────────┐  │
│ ┌─────────────────────────────────┐ │     OK       │  │
│ │ f_closesheet                    │ └──────────────┘  │
│ └─────────────────────────────────┘ ┌──────────────┐  │
│ ┌─────────────────────────────────┐ │   Cancel     │  │
│ │ f_closesheet                    │ └──────────────┘  │
│ │ f_enableprint                   │ ┌──────────────┐  │
│ │ f_getsheetcount                 │ │     New      │  │
│ │ f_newsheet                      │ └──────────────┘  │
│ │ f_setmenutext                   │ ┌──────────────┐  │
│ │                                 │ │   Delete     │  │
│ │                                 │ └──────────────┘  │
│ │                                 │ ┌──────────────┐  │
│ │                                 │ │    Help      │  │
│ └─────────────────────────────────┘ └──────────────┘  │
└─────────────────────────────────────────────────────┘
```

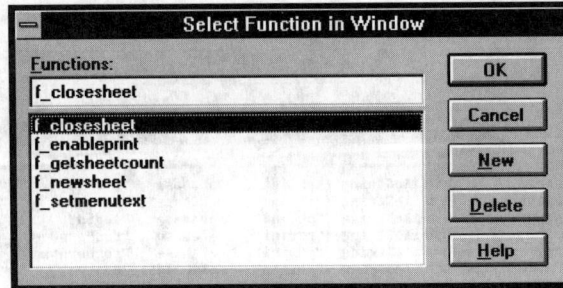

Where did all these functions come from? Right, the template application. Choose f_setmenutext and examine the script. Without understanding every detail you should be able to recognize that the script determines whether the application is running in Windows or on a Mac, and sets the text for the last item in the File menu to Exit or Quit accordingly. No need to mess with this function.

The second function call in w_genapp_frame.open is to f_newsheet. The code for this function looks like this:

```
w_genapp_sheet l_wSheet

    /* Enable printing */
    f_enableprint (true)

    /* Open a new instance of a sheet */
    return OpenSheet (l_wSheet, this, 3, layered!)
```

Now that you can read PowerScript, you can see that the function defines a local variable l_wSheet, calls a function to enable printing, and finally calls OpenSheet to open an MDI sheet using the window object w_genapp_sheet. We can use this function as a guide for opening MDI sheets for other window objects as well.

In Chapter 8, "Designing Windows and Dialog Boxes," you created a window called w_jobs, so you need a function that opens a w_jobs window when called. Follow these steps:

1. Select the text and copy it into the clipboard.

2. Choose New from the File menu.

3. Enter the name of the new function, f_newjobs, and choose OK.

4. Paste the contents of the clipboard into the main window.

5. Replace w_genapp_sheet with w_jobs.

6. Replace l_wSheet with l_wJobs in both places you see it.

7. Save your changes and close the window.

Now go back to the Open script for the w_genapp_frame window. When do we want to create a Jobs window? Every time we start the application? No, only when the user chooses Jobs from the Update menu. In fact, we don't want to automatically open any sheet. For this reason you need to comment out the call to f_newsheet in the script. Save it, and return to the Window painter.

Implementing Menus

You have just declared a function in w_genapp that opens the w_jobs window, and now you want to call that function when the user chooses the proper menu item. Therefore, you need to modify the script associated with that menu item. Here's how:

1. Click the Menu painter icon, and choose the m_genapp_frame menu. You should see the menu you created in Chapter 6, "Organizing with Menus and Toolbars."

2. Select the Update menu, then the Jobs... menu item. There should be a finger pointing to the selection.

3. Notice that the Script icon in the PainterBar looks like a blank page. Click that icon.

4. In the PowerScript painter, enter this line:

```
w_genapp_frame.f_newjobs ()
```

5. Save the script and close the painter. The Script icon should now look like a filled-in page, indicating that the script has code in it.

You should now have the menu script calling a function, which in turn opens the Jobs window. Run the application, choose Jobs from the Update menu, and your screen should look like Figure 9-3. It looks like there's good news and bad news. The good news is you have successfully opened a new window in your application. The bad news is that there's no data in the window.

In some cases, such as dialog boxes, a menu script can open the window directly, rather than through another function. Remember the w_set_id window

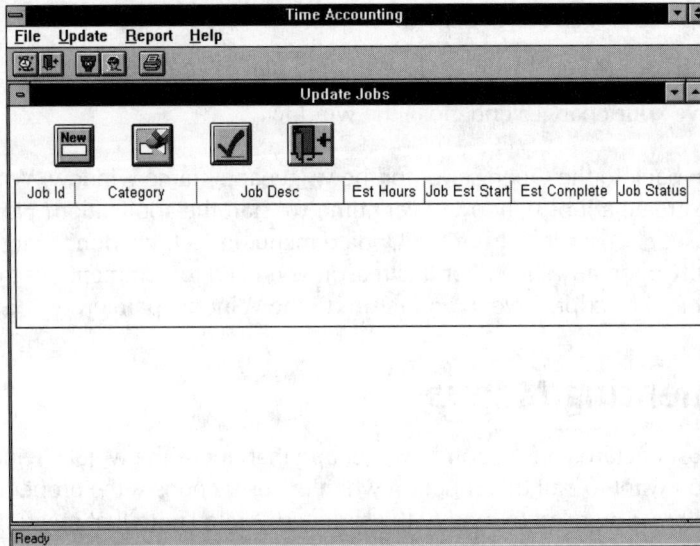

FIGURE 9-3. *Displaying your created window from a menu command, but without any data*

you created in Chapter 8, "Designing Windows and Dialog Boxes"? Let's associate that window with the Set ID command in the File menu:

1. Bring up the Menu painter with the m_genapp_frame menu.

2. Locate and select the Set ID item in the File menu.

3. Click the Script icon, and enter this line:

```
Open (w_set_id)
```

Since the MDI frame window does not need to track this window, you can Open directly in this script. Test your change by saving your work and running the application.

Implementing Windows

PowerBuilder is intelligent enough that when it opens a window, it displays each of the controls in the window. It cannot, however, place data in DataWindows automatically. This means you must modify the Open script of the w_jobs window to tell the DataWindow to retrieve the data.

Bring the w_jobs window into the Window painter. Notice that the Script icon is blank. Click that icon, and enter this text:

```
CONNECT;
dw_1.settransobject (sqlca)
dw_1.retrieve
```

These three statements must all be done in sequence in order to load a DataWindow with records in the database. The CONNECT; statement is an SQL command that establishes a connection to the database. The second statement is a call to a DataWindow function SetTransObject that determines the transaction object. A *transaction object* is a location in memory that serves as a communication area between the script and the database. PowerBuilder includes a transaction object as part of the default global variables, called SQLCA. Since you are only working with one database, you don't need to define any additional transaction objects. Finally, the Retrieve function uses the transaction object to retrieve records from the database according to the selection criteria defined by the DataWindow.

After entering this script and saving your work, rerun the application. This time your Jobs window should display the records in the Jobs table, similar to Figure 9-4.

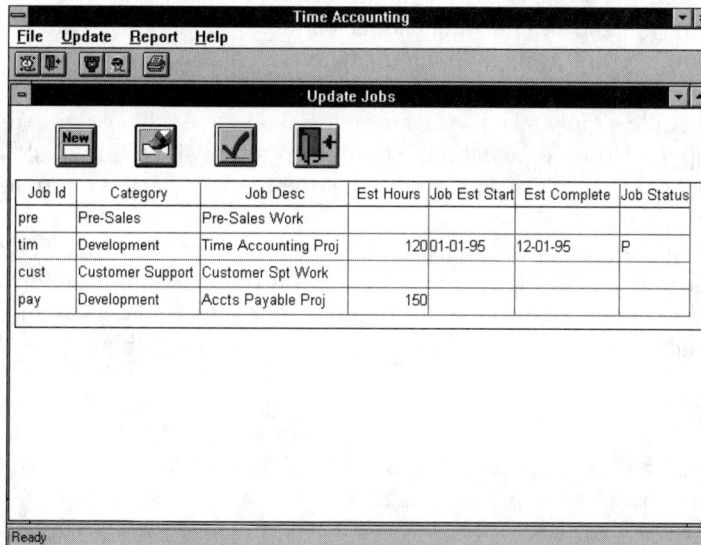

FIGURE 9-4. *The Update Jobs window now displays the records from the database*

Implementing Window Controls

By following the steps outlined in this chapter, you have been able to add two windows to your application. In both cases, however, none of the controls are implemented. If you tried to press any of the buttons while testing the windows, you noticed that there were no responses. To make a control react properly, you must implement its script(s).

Let's start simple, with the Cancel button in the w_set_id window. Load this window in the Window painter, select the Cancel button, then click the Script icon. In the PowerScript painter, type this simple statement:

```
close (Parent)
```

This statement tells PowerBuilder to close the button's parent window, which is the w_set_id dialog box. If you recall from Chapter 8, "Designing Windows and Dialog Boxes," you changed the style of the button to enable the Cancel feature. This means that pressing the ESC key will execute this script and therefore close the window.

The OK button is a bit more complicated. The purpose of this dialog box is to establish an employee ID so that the user can enter it once, and the application will use that value for time card entry, validation, and reports. This implies that we need a variable that all windows can access. Define a global variable of type string called current_emp_id by choosing Global Variables from the Declare menu, and entering **string current_emp_id** in the dialog box.

Now let's think about what we want to do when the user chooses the OK button. We could simply take the text from the single-line edit box and assign it to current_emp_id. However, what if the user enters an invalid ID? It would make sense to check that in this dialog box, so the user doesn't have to return to it later to make any corrections.

Validating the user input means we will need to access the Employee table in the database with a SELECT statement. We'll retrieve the record from the table whose ID matches the one entered by the user. Since the SELECT statement must place its result somewhere, we'll need to declare a local variable:

```
string temp
```

Now you can use the SQL paster to help with the syntax of the SELECT statement. Follow these steps:

1. Click the Paste SQL icon. You will see this display:

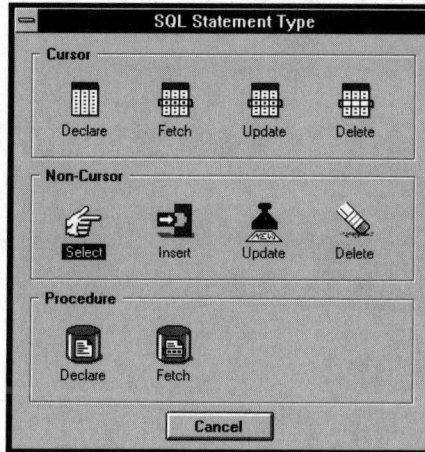

2. Choose Select. PowerBuilder will display the Select Tables dialog box. Choose the Employee table, then choose Open. You will see the SQL Paster window, shown in Figure 9-5.

3. Click the emp_id column in the table, since that is what you want to retrieve.

4. In the Where section, select the "employee"."emp_id" column, and set the Value to :sle_1.text, which is the text attribute from the SingleLineEdit control called sle_1.

5. Click the Into icon, and enter **temp** as the Program Variable.

6. Return to the script, and the SELECT statement will appear with the proper syntax.

The entire text of the script is given here. After the SELECT statement, the script checks the SQL error to see if the selection was successful. If so, the global variable is updated; if not, the user sees an error message and must try again.

```
string temp

CONNECT;
SELECT "employee"."emp_id"
  INTO :temp
  FROM "employee"
  WHERE "employee"."emp_id" = :sle_1.text  ;
```

```
if SQLCA.SQLCode = 0 then
  current_emp_id = sle_1.text
  close (Parent)
else
  MessageBox ("Employee ID Not Found", "Please Try Again", exclamation!)
end if;
```

Save your work, run the application, and verify that these scripts operate the way you expected them to.

Congratulations!

You are now well on your way to having a complete application. The design work done in Chapters 5 through 8 and the implementation work done in Chapter 9 should give you enough information to complete either the Time Accounting program or an application of your choosing.

So what good is the rest of the book? Well, Chapters 10 and 11 will help make your application more professional, with more sophisticated objects and online

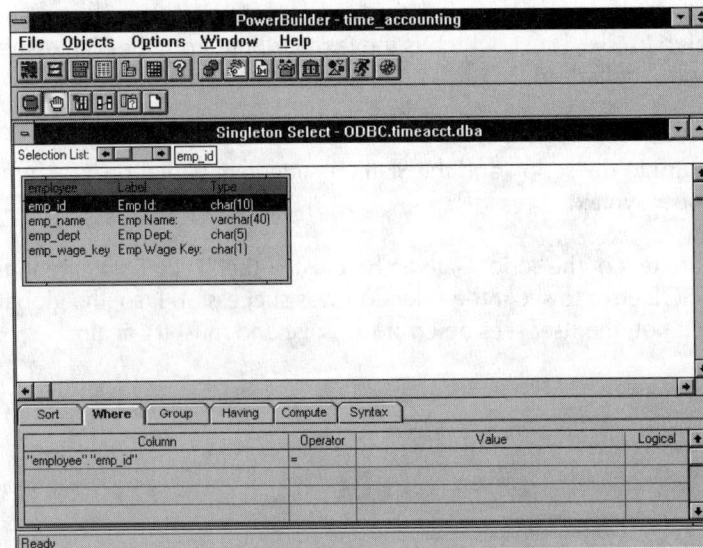

FIGURE 9-5. *The SQL Paster helps you define SQL statements that are syntactically correct*

help. Chapters 12 and 13 will provide explanation on using libraries and projects. Chapter 14 will introduce you to some other features of the Enterprise series in addition to PowerBuilder. Finally, Chapter 15 will show you how to test and debug your program to give you that perfect finish.

CHAPTER 10

Adding Some Sophistication

You have now been introduced to each of the major painters used to develop applications. This chapter has two purposes:

■ It lets you experiment with more advanced data windows, window objects, and window controls.

■ It leads you through the development of the main window of the Time Accounting application, to give you the opportunity and satisfaction of seeing the program work. (If you want to get an idea of what you'll be creating, sneak ahead and look at Figure 10-6.)

If you've reached this chapter, it can be assumed that you are comfortable using PowerBuilder, and you are ready for more advanced features. If you've been struggling through the examples, or you are merely following the steps one by one without grasping the concepts, you are encouraged to go back to Chapter 4 and reread to here. The pace of this chapter is much faster— we provide the major steps and assume you can fill in the rest.

A Regal Report

A data window can be used for more than simply viewing and updating tables in a database. Data windows can also process the information and display it in a way that is more useful to the users. This data can be in the form of summary reports, composite reports, histograms, bar charts, and others.

If you experiment with the presentation styles for data windows, you will discover that some of them are more suited for report-like displays than for interactive updates. This section covers one such style—the Group.

Creating a Group Data Window

To create a group data window, obviously you must start in the Data Window painter. From there you must do the following:

1. Create the window using Quick Select and the Group presentation style.

2. Once in the Quick Select dialog box, choose the time_card_entry table, then columns tc_date, tc_job_id, and tc_num_hours, in that order.

3. Set the sort criteria so that the table is ordered by date in ascending order.

4. When you choose OK, PowerBuilder will display a small dialog box that sets the report title. Clear out the title; you won't need it for this report.

You should now be at the Specify Group Columns dialog box, shown here:

```
┌─────────────────────────────────────────────────────────┐
│ ─             Specify Group Columns                        │
├─────────────────────────────────────────────────────────┤
│ 1) Drag and Drop items.                        ┌─────────┐ │
│                                                │   OK    │ │
│                                                └─────────┘ │
│ Source Data                  Columns           ┌─────────┐ │
│ ┌──────────────┐             ┌──────────────┐  │ Cancel  │ │
│ │tc_date       │             │tc_date       │  └─────────┘ │
│ ├──────────────┤             │              │  ┌─────────┐ │
│ │job_id        │             │              │  │  Help   │ │
│ ├──────────────┤             │              │  └─────────┘ │
│ │tc_num_hours  │             │              │             │
│ └──────────────┘             │              │             │
│                              │              │             │
│                              │              │             │
│                              └──────────────┘             │
│  ☐  New Page on Group Break                                │
│  ☐  Reset Page Number on Group Break                       │
└─────────────────────────────────────────────────────────┘
```

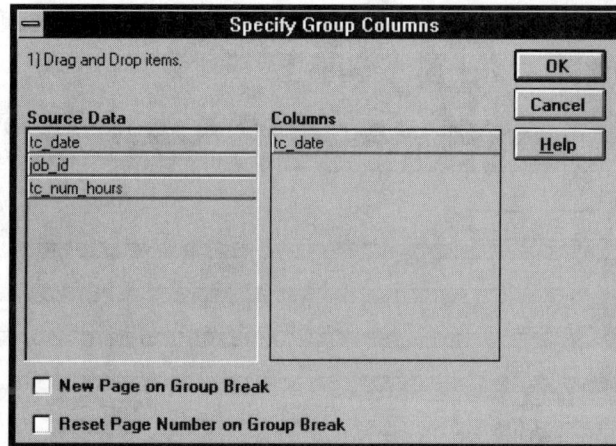

The purpose of the Group presentation style is to allow you to organize your report to show the records with some commonality together, and to do calculations based on that commonality. In this report we want to display the time card entries grouped by date so the user can quickly glance at the total hours for each day and determine whether the time card is complete.

To finish the initial specification of the data window, drag the tc_date column to the right side of the dialog box and choose OK. Your screen should now look like Figure 10-1. If you are unfamiliar with the gray bands of the data window, study the descriptions in Table 10-1.

Creating Retrieval Arguments

For this particular report we are only interested in the data for one individual, which explains why the employee ID column was not included in the data window. Also we don't want every record, but only those after a particular date. Of course we don't want to "hard-code" an ID and a date, but rather we want to determine that information somehow during program execution.

To narrow down the number of records retrieved, we start by creating retrieval arguments. A *retrieval argument* is a value the data window uses to help retrieve data from the database. Note that there are no scripts or functions associated with a data window, so this is one of the only ways to pass information to it.

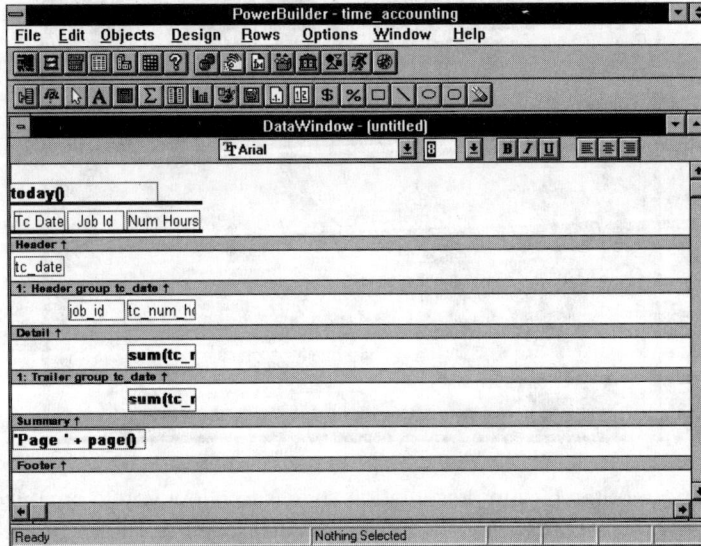

FIGURE 10-1. *A group data window*

DATA WINDOW BAND	DESCRIPTION
Header	Text that will appear at the top of every page, regardless of grouping
Header for group	Text that will appear at the beginning of every group
Detail	Text that will appear for every record retrieved from the database
Trailer for group	Text that will appear at the end of every group, including calculated fields
Summary	Text that will appear after the last group, including any fields calculated against all retrieved records
Footer	Text that will appear at the bottom of every page, regardless of grouping

TABLE 10-1. *The bands that are used for report-style data windows*

To create the retrieval arguments for this data window, choose Data Source from the Edit menu, then Retrieval Arguments from the Objects menu. You should see this dialog box:

As the illustration indicates, enter retrieval arguments for both employee ID and start date.

Setting the Select Criteria

Now that you have variables representing the selection constraints, you can modify the SQL query. At the bottom of the data source window you will see tabs for sorting, selecting (WHERE and HAVING), and grouping, as well as a tab to see the actual syntax of the generated SQL SELECT command.

For this example we need two WHERE criteria: The emp_id field must match the employee ID retrieval argument, and the tc_date field must be after the start date retrieval argument. When referring to variables and controls in the SQL statement, you must precede them by a colon. Thus when you enter the WHERE criteria you should end up with the display shown in Figure 10-2.

If you like, you can test the syntax you created by displaying the Preview window. When you do, PowerBuilder will display the Retrieval Arguments dialog box, where you enter the values to be used in the test. When you choose OK the report will be displayed.

NOTE
If you haven't entered any data into this table, you must do so from the Database painter. You should enter several records with different dates and employee IDs to verify that your data window is acting as you expect.

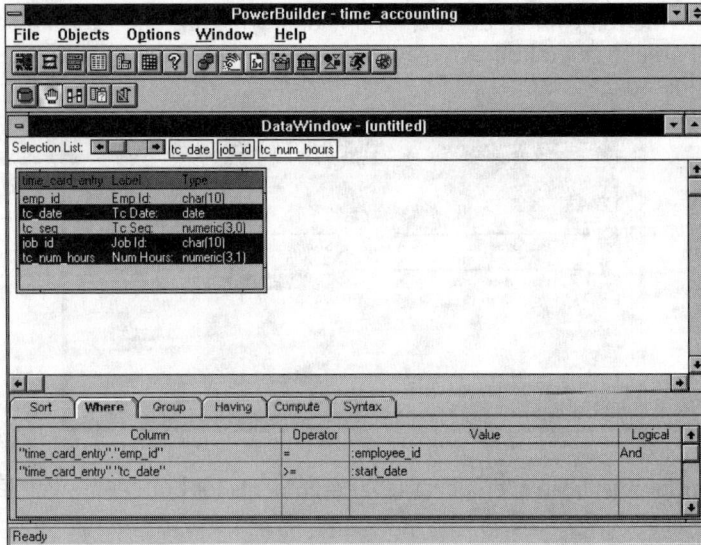

FIGURE 10-2. *The Data Source display showing the WHERE criteria*

Finalizing the Layout

Before you are finished with the data window you should finalize the report layout. This window displays the data vertically, and we want to show as much data as possible. Therefore it makes sense to eliminate as much extraneous information as possible. You can remove the page number references, since this window will be part of an interactive window rather than a report. You might also get rid of the date at the top of the window, since more relevant dates are included as part of the data.

You should also take this opportunity to alter column headings, fonts, and formats. For instance, the day of the week is important information when trying to enter time card information. If you set the format of the tc_date field to "mm/dd/yy (dddd)" you will display the date as well as the day in parentheses. The final report layout as we have chosen it appears in Figure 10-3.

A Wondrous Window

As you recall from reading Chapter 7, "Interacting with the Data," a data window can appear in an application only when it is included as part of a data window control in a window object. This section will guide you through the creation of the

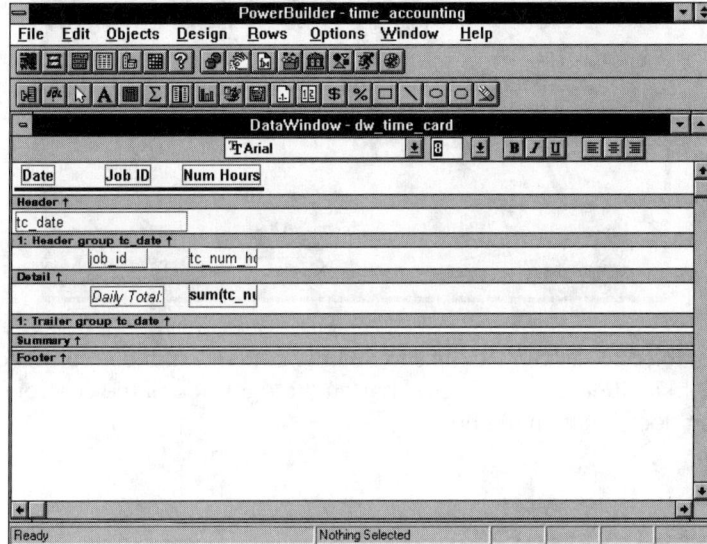

FIGURE 10-3.   *The final layout of the report*

window that includes the group data window created in the previous section. The data window is report-like, and therefore not designed to be updated interactively. This means the window object that controls it must include all of the controls necessary to update the table in the database. The window object will include several new enhancements to controls that you've probably never seen before, whose purpose is to make using the window a little more pleasurable.

The Data Window Control

The entire left side of the window will be a data window control. Using the method you learned in Chapter 8, "Designing Windows and Dialog Boxes," create a data window control, change the data window associated with the control to be the group data window (we called it dw_time_card), and expand the boxes so they take up the left half of the main window.

When PowerBuilder creates a data window control, it assumes that it will be editable by the user, and that the entire data window will fit in the control. Neither of these assumptions are valid for this particular control. To correct them, choose Name from the pop-up menu to display this dialog box:

```
┌──────────────────────────────────────────────────────────────┐
│ ─          DataWindow - dw_time_card                          │
├──────────────────────────────────────────────────────────────┤
│ Name:  dw_1                                    ┌──────────┐    │
│                                                │    OK    │    │
│ Title:                                         └──────────┘    │
│                                                ┌──────────┐    │
│ ☒ Visible     ☐ Enabled      ☐ Title Bar      │  Cancel  │    │
│                                                └──────────┘    │
│                                                ┌──────────┐    │
│ ☐ Control Menu  ☐ Maximize Box  ☐ Minimize Box│  Script  │    │
│                                                └──────────┘    │
│                                                ┌──────────┐    │
│ ☐ Resizable   ☐ HScroll Bar   ☒ VScroll Bar   │ Change.. │    │
│                                                └──────────┘    │
│                                                ┌──────────┐    │
│ ☒ Live Scrolling ☐ H Split Scrolling Border: Box ▼│  Help  │  │
│                                                └──────────┘    │
└──────────────────────────────────────────────────────────────┘
```

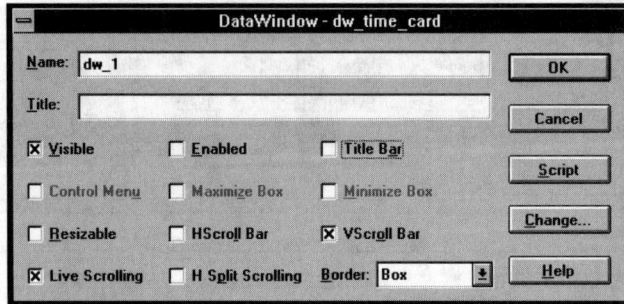

Click Enabled to disable attempts to edit the contents of the report, and click VScroll Bar to include a vertical scroll bar on the right side of the control if the entire report does not fit in the box.

The Date Control

Stop and think for a minute about how the typical user would use the Time Card window. Most people put off doing their time cards until the last possible moment, then enter all their data at once. In many cases their doing the same job for the same number of hours each day, so the only thing that changes is the date. Therefore, it is important that entering and changing the date are as convenient as possible.

The obvious choice for date entry is an edit mask control. With the edit mask you can display the separators (dashes or slashes) and allow the user to enter a date while automatically skipping over the separator. You can make things even easier with a *spin control*, which is the name given to the set of up and down arrows that increment or decrement the value in the edit box.

To create the spin control, use these steps:

1. Create an edit mask control, and place it in the desired location in the window.

2. Choose Name from the pop-up menu.

3. Set the Type to Date, then click Spin Control. You should see the dialog box change so that it looks like Figure 10-4.

Don't worry about the spin range; when PowerBuilder creates a spin control for a date field, the max value is determined by the valid values for a month, or a date for the month entered.

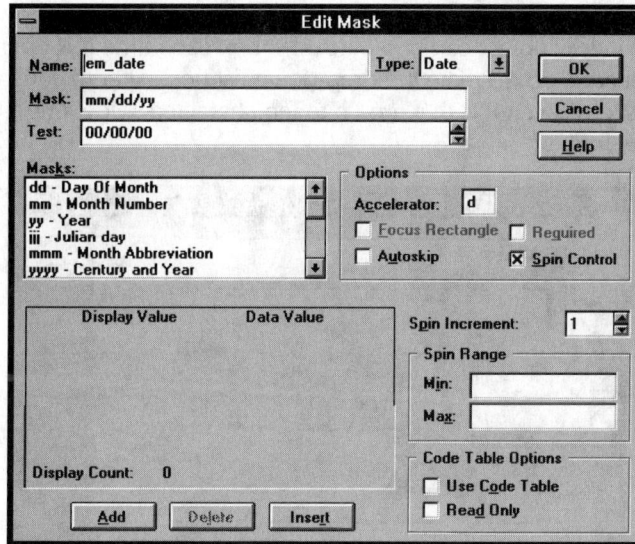

FIGURE 10-4. *Making date entry easier using an edit mask with a spin control*

Although the spin control is nice, the real time-savers are assigning a default date and selecting the day part of the date. We'll implement both of these features as part of the Open script for the window control later in this chapter.

The Job ID Control

What is the best way to make choosing a job ID easy?

- Create radio buttons for the job IDs. (Not practical, since there are too many.)

- Create a list box containing all job IDs. (Better, but each user may only use a subset of the available jobs.)

- Use a single-line edit control, but provide a way for the user to browse through the job database. (This is a common solution, but still not very easy.)

- Create a list box containing the job IDs that the current employee has used in the past, and allow them to add new ones. (Wow, sounds easy for the user, but hard for the programmer.)

Actually the last option is not as hard as it sounds. You will see how the Open script for the window object can populate a list box each time it is opened. Right now, all you need to do is create the drop-down list box. After making it large enough to fill six or seven IDs that are up to ten characters wide, choose Name from the pop-up menu:

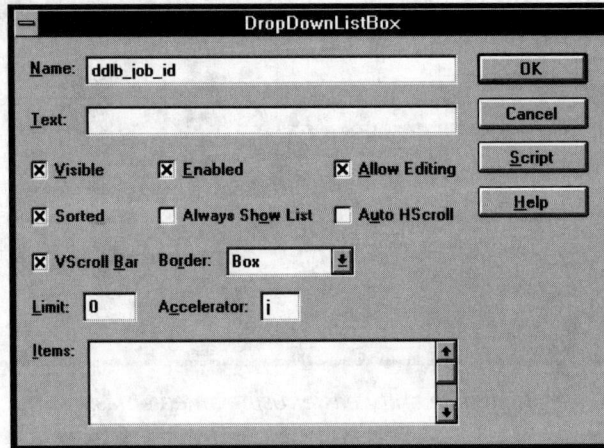

The only change you need to make here is to check Allow Editing. This enables the user to enter a job ID that is not in the list.

The remaining controls in the Time Card window are pretty standard: an edit mask for number of hours, to restrict users to one decimal place; three pushbuttons, "Insert Entry," "Erase Date," and "Close"; and static text to identify the input controls. When you are done with the design, your preview window might look something like Figure 10-5. The design of the window is complete—the implementation will take a little more effort.

Retrieving Job IDs for an Employee

To retrieve the job IDs and place them in the list box, we will create a window function called f_get_job_ids. The key to implementing this function is a *cursor*. A cursor in the database world, not to be confused with the flashing box on your screen that shows where text will be input, is a location in memory that can store multiple records.

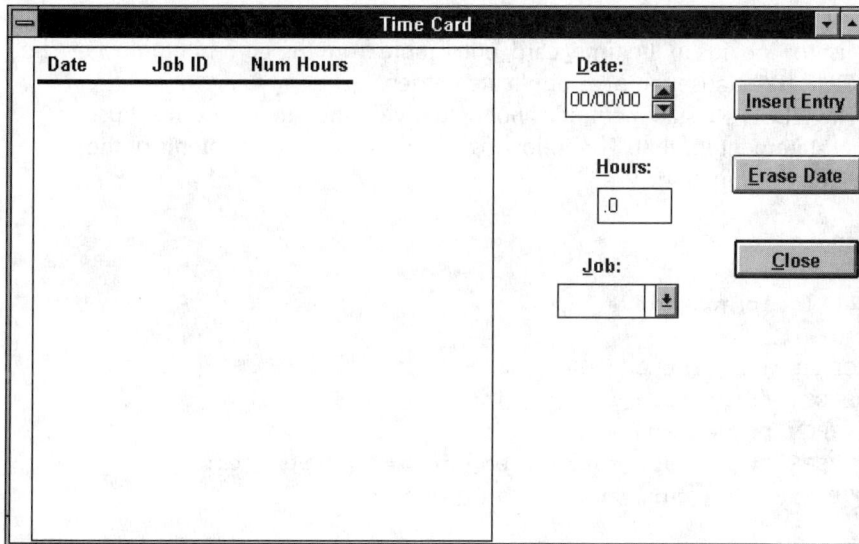

FIGURE 10-5.   *The Time Card window as it appears in the preview window*

To define a cursor you must create a DECLARE statement. Here's how:

1. Click the Paste SQL icon, then click the Declare icon in the Cursor group.

2. Select the time_card_entry table.

3. Click job_id in the selection list.

4. In the Where section, select where the emp_id equals the global variable :current_emp_id.

5. In the Group section, drag the job_id column to the right side of the window.

When you return to the Function painter, you will be prompted for a Name, such as job_list. PowerBuilder should then create this statement:

```
DECLARE job_list CURSOR FOR
  SELECT "time_card_entry"."job_id"
    FROM "time_card_entry"
   WHERE "time_card_entry"."emp_id" = :current_emp_id
GROUP BY "time_card_entry"."job_id"  ;
```

In English, this statement tells the database manager to set aside memory called job_list for job_ids in the time_card_entry table from the current employee. The "GROUP BY" clause removes duplicate entries.

The DECLARE statement does not actually do the query; you must use an OPEN statement for that. The following listing is the entire contents of the f_get_job_ids function:

```
string a_job

Reset (ddlb_job_id)

 DECLARE job_list CURSOR FOR
   SELECT "time_card_entry"."job_id"
     FROM "time_card_entry"
    WHERE "time_card_entry"."emp_id" = :current_emp_id
GROUP BY "time_card_entry"."job_id"   ;

OPEN job_list;
a_job = ""
do
    if a_job <> "" then
        ddlb_job_id.AddItem(a_job)
    end if;
    FETCH job_list INTO :a_job;
loop until sqlca.SQLCode <> 0

CLOSE job_list;
return 0
```

After the OPEN statement, the main part of this function is a loop that calls FETCH to look at the records in the cursor one at a time and adds each job ID to the list (by calling AddItem).

Initializing the Window

Once you have implemented the f_get_job_ids function, you can create the rest of the Open script for the Time Card window:

```
if current_emp_id = "" then
  Open(w_set_id)
end if;
```

```
dw_1.settransobject (sqlca)
dw_1.retrieve (current_emp_id, RelativeDate(today(),-30))

em_date.text = String(today())
em_date.selecttext (4, 2)
f_get_job_ids ()
```

The first action this script does is check to see if the user has set an employee ID. If not, it brings up the Set ID dialog box (from Chapter 8). Then it tells the data window control to retrieve the data. The retrieval arguments (the current employee ID and the start date of 30 days ago) are passed as parameters so that no user interaction is required. Finally, the date mask is initialized to the current date, and the two characters that represent the day are selected.

Adding a New Time Card Entry

To update a database table with a new entry, follow these steps:

1. Allow the user to enter any non-computable fields in window controls.

2. Convert any string controls to the data types expected by the database.

3. Paste an SQL INSERT statement containing the new values.

This listing shows how we did these steps for the Time Card window:

```
Date insert_date
Decimal num_hours
insert_date = Date(em_date.text)
num_hours = Dec(em_num_hours.text)

    INSERT INTO "time_card_entry"
            ( "emp_id",
              "tc_date",
              "tc_seq",
              "job_id",
              "tc_num_hours" )
    VALUES ( :current_emp_id,
             :insert_date,
             1,
             :ddlb_job_id.text,
             :num_hours )   ;

dw_1.retrieve (current_emp_id, RelativeDate(insert_date, -5))
```

The final statement tells the data window control to regenerate the report, now that there is new data in the database.

Deleting Entries

Deleting a record from a database table without an interactive data window is a little more tricky. You don't want to require the user to enter each piece of data for that record, then attempt to find that record before deleting it—that's too much work for the user. We have solved that problem for the Time Card window by having the user enter a date in the date field, then deleting *all* records from that date. We feel that most dates will only contain one or two entries per employee, so this alternative is actually more convenient for the user.

Here is the script for the Clicked event for the "Erase Date" pushbutton:

```
Date delete_date

delete_date = Date(em_date.text)

  DELETE FROM "time_card_entry"
   WHERE ( "time_card_entry"."emp_id" = :current_emp_id ) AND
         ( "time_card_entry"."tc_date" = :delete_date )   ;

  dw_1.retrieve(current_emp_id, RelativeDate(delete_date, -5))
```

If you managed to fill in the pieces not completely described in this chapter, you should end up with a working window that looks something like Figure 10-6.

Yearning for More?

It would be nice to provide examples for each of the many other types of data windows and each built-in function. The real secret, however, is to master enough of the techniques to be able to go exploring through PowerBuilder to accomplish your tasks. Take full advantage of the online help in PowerBuilder; it contains

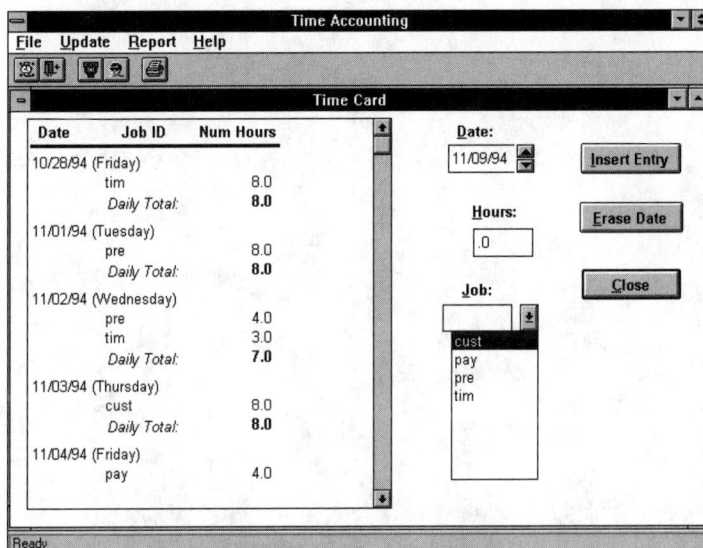

FIGURE 10-6.   *The Time Card window as it appears in the working application*

complete descriptions of every option in every database, and every parameter of every function. And speaking of online help, read on to see how to enhance your own applications with online help.

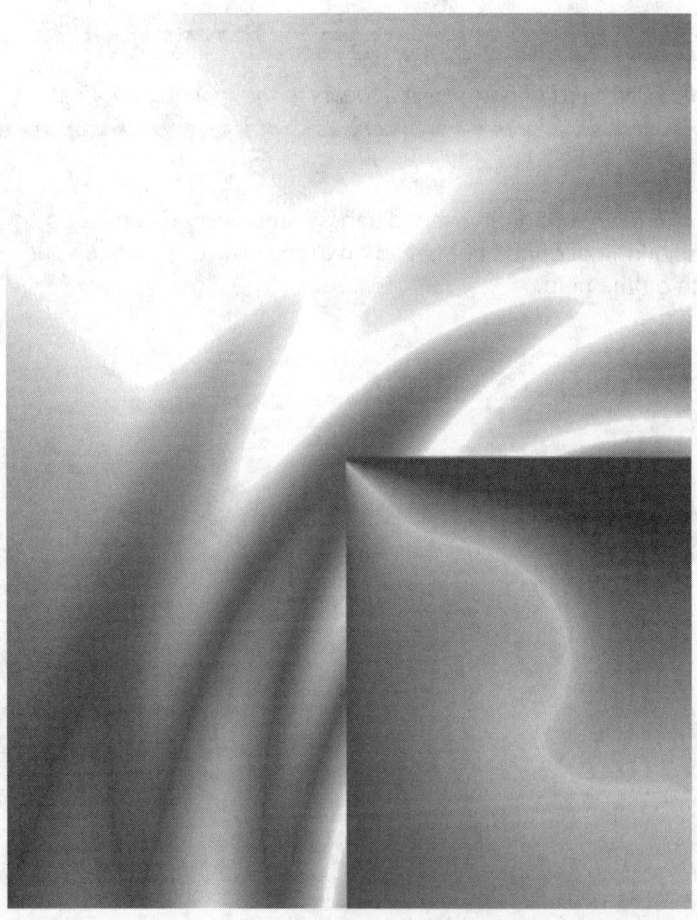

CHAPTER 11

Adding Help for Your Users

If you've gotten this far, and you've followed along with the book by creating an application, you might think that you're almost done. After all, you've designed a database, added a beautiful user interface, and connected all the pieces together. What else could you possibly need to do?

In this chapter and in the next few chapters, you'll learn about some of the finishing touches that you need to add. These will help make your application more polished, appearing more like a professional, commercial application.

In this chapter, we'll start by adding a help facility to your application. And while we won't cover all the possibilities here, the Windows Help facility is very robust; if you continue your research, you'll find that you can add text of different fonts, sizes, and colors, bitmaps and other graphic files, special bitmaps with embedded hotspots, cross-reference links to topics throughout your help file, buttons, and keywords, all to make traveling through the help file easier for the user.

First, though, let's start with the basics.

Piecing Together a Help Facility

One of the nice features in Windows, specially designed for users and programmers alike, is the Help facility. This program allows all Windows programs to have similar help capabilities, without needing to write the routines over and over and over. In fact, to use the Help facility, you probably have all of the tools you need.

The PowerBuilder manuals say little about using the Windows Help facility, referring you instead to the Microsoft Windows Software Developer's Kit (SDK). Here's a pop quiz: How many of you have a copy of the Windows SDK handy? Raise your hands if you do.

Back to reality—the reason you are using PowerBuilder to generate applications in the first place is so you won't need to be a programmer, or hire one. So let's try to create some help right here, without the SDK.

There are three steps in the creation of help files:

1. Create the text for the help in a suitable word processor.

2. Create a project file for your help.

3. Use the Help Compiler to create the actual help file (with an HLP extension) from your text and project files.

So the first step is the creation of the text you want to use as help for your users.

Find a Good Word Processor

The first step in creating your help files is to use a word processor that supports the RTF (Rich Text Format) file format. Microsoft Word for Windows works fine, as do most other full-featured Windows word processors.

Open a new document, and we'll start adding text, with little of the trouble you might expect from something that sounds as daunting as a "Software Developer's Kit." By the way, the SDK comes in a box bigger than PowerBuilder Enterprise. If you really like a lot of heavy books, you might look into it. The book in the SDK that deals with help files (called "Programming Tools"), luckily, is only about 250 pages, and it is much less than a half-inch thick. The chapter on help files is less than 50 pages long. What I'm trying to say is, don't buy the SDK just to learn about creating help files!

Back to creating the help file. Your word processor needs to support footnotes, underlined text, double-underlined or strikethrough text, and hidden text. These are the formats that are used in generating the help file commands.

You will be creating a text file that is broken into *topics*. Each topic tells about one part of your application. For instance, you might create one topic for each of your screens, one for each field in each screen, one for every menu selection, and even one for a general introduction.

So to get started, enter the information into the word processor, breaking the text down into topics. Each topic should have a unique title and should appear on its own page in the word processing file. This is done by adding a hard page break before each topic begins. In Word for Windows, this is done with the Insert | Break | Page menu sequence, and it looks like Figure 11-1.

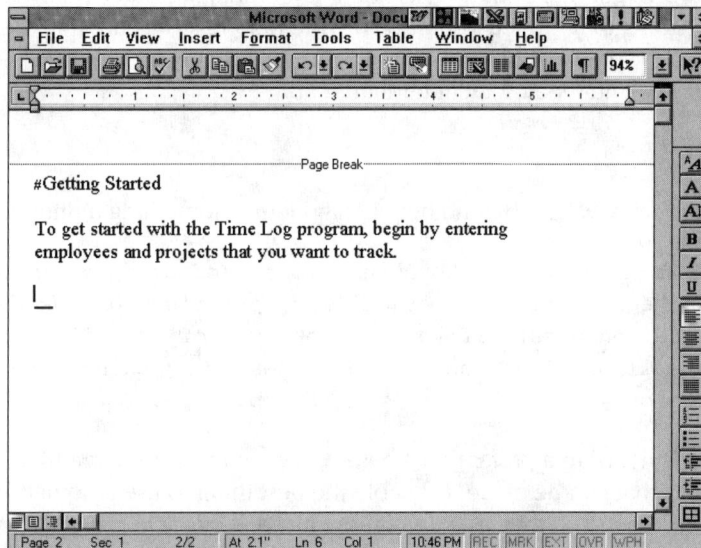

FIGURE 11-1. *The page break is used to separate help topics*

Tags

In order to start your new topic, place one or more of the following tags at the top of the page, before the topic title. A *tag* is a footnote indicator, using a special character. Here are the most common tags:

#footnote   This is a context string, used to help your user find a specific help topic. The *footnote* is the name that will be searched for by the user or by your application. This is also the address used by any hypertext links in your help document (see "Adding Hypertext Links" later in this chapter); anytime you try to jump around in a help file, the context tags are used as the destinations. Therefore, these are the most important tags to have in your document.

$footnote   This is the title that will be placed in the help window when the specific topic is displayed. This title is optional.

Kfootnote   The K tag is used to associate keywords with the topic. This is used by the Windows Help facility to allow the user to search for keywords when they are not aware of the exact context name.

Okay, you've got one or more tags at the top of the page, so type in some help text. I'm not going to try to tell you how to write help text. Be sure that the help is useful, though. There is nothing so annoying as help that is useless. For instance, your help for the File Open selection might read:

```
Open a file
```

This is probably worse than no help at all. Here is something a little better:

```
This menu item allows you to open a file, and bring it into the
application for processing (or editing, printing, or whatever
your application does). If you are not sure of the file name you
need, you will be given the option of searching through the
directories on your hard disks to find the file.
```

This text is not from a professional help writer, so there are certainly improvements that can be made. Probably the best thing to use is something you would say to someone if they asked you how a specific function worked. You designed the application, so nobody knows better than you how it should work. Put some of that knowledge into the help file.

Spend a little time with this task. It may seem like a waste. But the first phone call that you *don't* get asking for help will be well worth the trouble.

Once you have created your help topics, you can add some links or pop-ups, which are explained in the following sections.

Adding Hypertext Links

A *hypertext link* is a special word or picture in your help text which can be selected with a mouse. When this is done, the user is immediately taken to the matching help topic. In this way, users can search for related topics, without knowing exactly where they are. When they are done reading, they can use the Back button in Windows Help to return to where they started.

This type of moving around is often referred to as *hypertext*. Have you ever looked up a subject in an encyclopedia, noticed it said "see also" a related topic? You might have started flipping pages looking for the other topic, and even forgotten what you were looking for. If your encyclopedia had hypertext, you would have been able to go to that related topic immediately.

To add a hypertext link, format the word that will act as a link with a double-underline. The word will become a *hotspot* (where the mouse pointer may change to a finger). In Word for Windows, this is done with the Format | Font | Underline | Double menu sequence. Then, follow the word with **/v** and the name of the context tag where the link will take the user.

Hypertext links show up in a different color in your help screens, so that they are easily seen, and they can be selected by the user without any other work. Links are often at the end of each topic, but they can also be part of the topic's text. By the way, when you select the hotspot, you are transported to the new help topic, and the old one goes away. Use the Back button to return to your starting place.

Adding Pop-ups

A *pop-up* is similar to a link, but you are left in your original help topic, and a small window (a pop-up) shows the requested information (see Figure 11-2). This is useful for definitions, or other small pieces of information that a user might need.

A pop-up is created by highlighting your keyword (or hotspot), and formatting it with an underline (single this time). Then, follow it with **/v** and the name of the context tag, as was done for the links. When the user presses the hotspot, the context you selected will be shown in a small window.

Figure 11-3 shows a typical page from a help document in Microsoft Word.

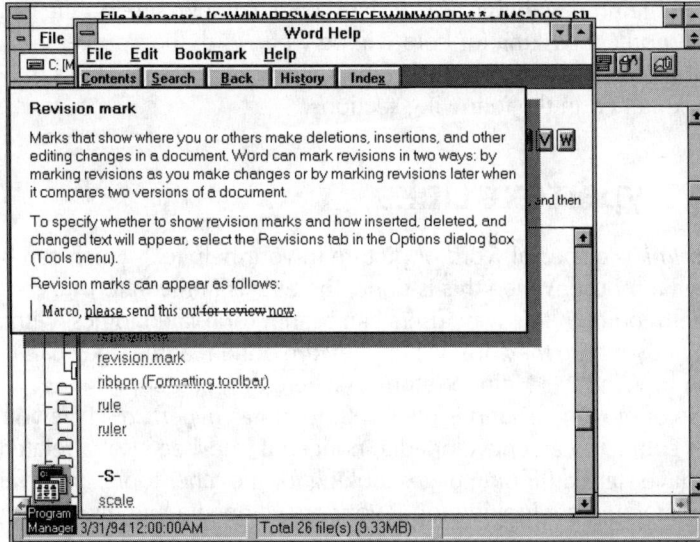

FIGURE 11-2. *A pop-up shows a small piece of information on the current help topic topic*

Tags

 # $ K Opening a Time Card Entry

Pop-up

The Open command in the File menu lets you update your time card/vTime_Card. If you have not set your employee ID, you will be prompted to do so.

For more help, see:

Updating a Time Card/vTime_Card_Window
Setting the Employee ID/vSet_ID_Window

HyperText links

#File_Open
$File|Open
KTime Card, opening; Opening a Time Card, File Open

FIGURE 11-3. *A sample help topic with tags, links, and a pop-up*

Project Planning

Once you have an RTF file created, you need to create a project file. Unlike the RTF file, a project file is a straight ASCII file, the kind that programs like Notepad generate (in other words, you don't want any word processing stuff in it). The project file, which has an extension of PRJ, is used to tell the Help Compiler how to build your help file. It lists the names of the RTF files to be used to create your help file, plus any special options.

To get started, a simple project file might look like this:

```
[OPTIONS]
COMPRESS=TRUE

[FILES]
TIMEACCT.RTF
```

This mundane-looking file specifies that the help will be stored in compressed format, and that all of the help is located in a single RTF file, TIMEACCT.RTF. If you want to get into hypermedia, graphics, and all the really fun and exotic things that can be done in a help file, your project file will become more complex. In this case you'll need additional reading material. There are some good books listed at the end of this section for your consideration.

Once you have a project file defined, use the Microsoft Help Compiler (commonly named HC.EXE or HC31.EXE) to create your final help file. Just use the command HC (or HC31) with the name of your project file, like this:

```
HC TIMEACCT.PRJ
```

The file TIMEACCT.HLP will then be created for you. Of course, you still need to attach this help file to your PowerBuilder application, but you've completed the hard part.

The following books might be of assistance in developing advanced help files:

- *Developing Online Help for Windows*, by Scott Boggan, David Farkas, and Joe Welinske (Sams Publishing).

- *Designing and Writing Online Documentation*, by William K. Horton (John Wiley and Sons, Inc.).

- *Microsoft Word Technical Reference* (Microsoft Press).

You can find some immediate help later in this chapter in the "RoboHelp to the Rescue" section. There we'll see how to get around this very intense process with additional tools, but first, how do you use the help file within your PowerBuilder application?

Using Help Files Within PowerBuilder

In order to show the topics from your help file within a PowerBuilder application, you will be using the ShowHelp() function in your scripts. The format of this function is

```
ShowHelp( helpfile, helpcommand [,typeid] )
```

Helpfile is the name of the HLP file you will use (the one you created earlier in this chapter). *Helpcommand* is one of the following commands:

COMMAND	DESCRIPTION
Index!	With this command, the Typeid parameter is not required. The Index! command causes the index of the help file to be displayed. This shows all the context items that are available in the file, allowing the user to choose where to start in their viewing of the help file.
Topic!	With this command, the Typeid parameter is the number of a topic that should be displayed. This is very common for programmers in other Windows languages. An example of this usage is as follows:

```
ShowHelp( "TimeAcct.HLP", Topic!, 23 )
```

Of course, to use this you need to know the numbers of all the topics in the help file. An easier method is to use the Keyword! command.

Keyword! — With this command, the Typeid parameter is the name of a keyword that should be displayed. This is very simple to use. An example of this usage is as follows:

```
ShowHelp( "TimeAcct.HLP", Keyword!, "TimeCard" )
```

Notice that you are asking for help for a specific topic, namely TimeCard. There must be an associated keyword in your help file.

Using the Topic! and Keyword! commands, you are able to give what is called *context-sensitive* help. This means that the help is different for each place where the user might be in the application. This is very helpful to the user; they don't need to go through the whole help system to find the information they need!

What next? How about an easier way to create your help files? You still need to use ShowHelp() in your applications, but there are easier ways to create the actual help files.

RoboHelp to the Rescue

There are some special programs that are designed to help you create help files with ease. One of these is called RoboHelp, supplied by Blue Sky Software (their address is noted at the end of this section). There are other tools available, of course, but RoboHelp is suggested as an add-on to PowerBuilder, and therefore it might be easier to use with the Enterprise.

RoboHelp works with Word for Windows but adds several specialized buttons for automating the creation of your help file, topics, cross-references, etc. (See Figure 11-4.) There are buttons for adding topics, jumps, pop-ups, graphics, and more.

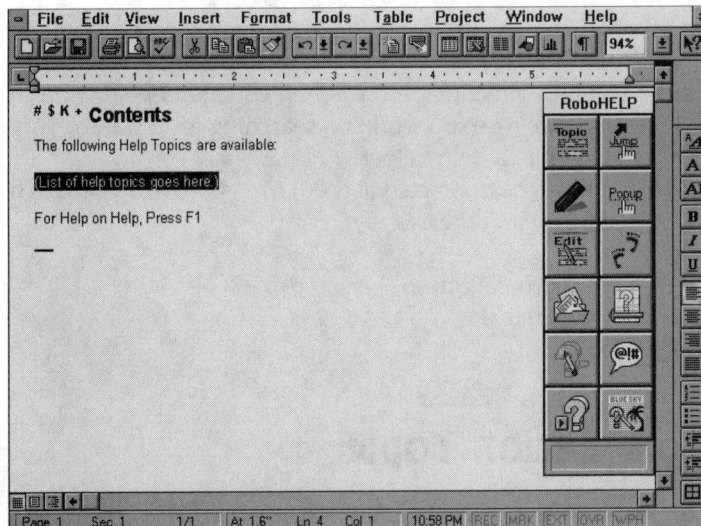

FIGURE 11-4. *RoboHelp adds help automation buttons to Word for Windows*

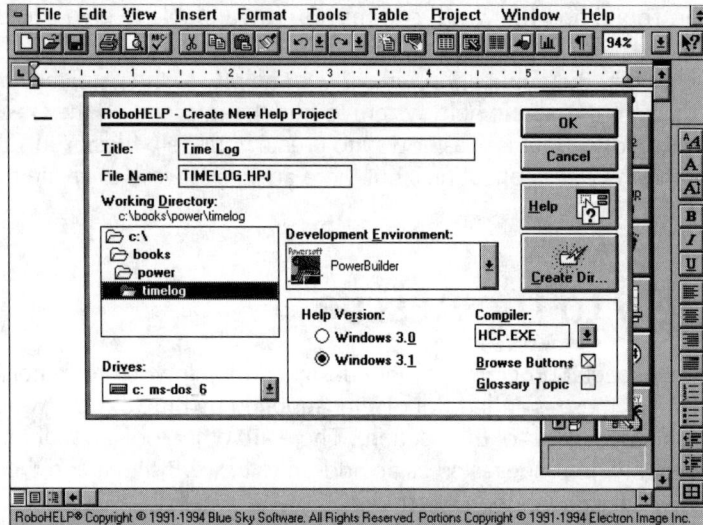

FIGURE 11-5. *Creating a new help project with RoboHelp*

You start by creating a project, using the dialog box shown in Figure 11-5. This dialog box starts your PRJ (project) file and begins to place the items there that you create (RTF files, graphics selections, etc.). When you are done, the help file is complete; no funny codes, no extra work, no searching for lost files. This is why you might want to look into a help helper.

Blue Sky Software can be contacted at (800) 677-4946, (619) 459-6365, or via fax at (619) 459-6366. Their address is

Blue Sky Software Corporation
7486 La Jolla Blvd., Suite 3
La Jolla, CA 92037

Next Completion Topic

In this chapter, you learned how to add help to your application. You even learned about a product that helps automate the help process. In the next chapter, you'll learn about using and sharing libraries, which allows you to better share your discoveries with others and to build from the work others have done before you.

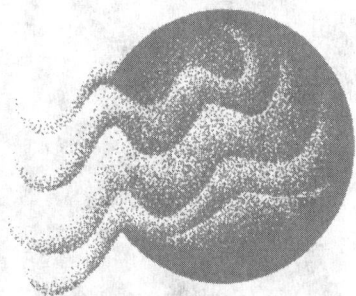

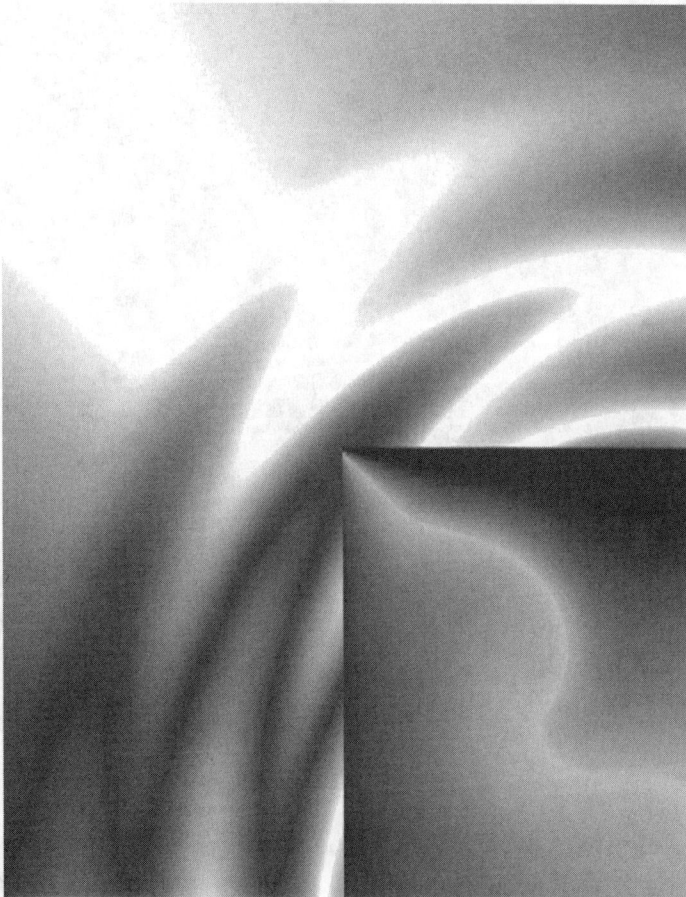

CHAPTER 12

Using and Sharing Libraries

As you have been using PowerBuilder, you have probably noticed that all the items you have created, including menus, windows, buttons—in fact, everything—has been stored in a file with the PBL extension. PBL stands for PowerBuilder Library. In this chapter, you'll learn more about libraries, and how to manage them for the best results in your PowerBuilder programming efforts.

What is a Library?

In PowerBuilder, a library is simply a collection of objects. This includes all of the objects that you have created in PowerBuilder thus far.

Some libraries are small, containing only a few objects. This might be the case if you are putting together a personal database, with little regard for how the uninitiated user will handle the application. It can also be the case when you are combining objects from other projects into small, easily manageable groups.

Other libraries can be extremely large. If you have created a major application, there might be dozens or even hundreds of objects that are being maintained. So before we go on, lets talk about how these libraries should be organized.

Why do you need to worry about libraries? If you only produce tiny applications, with a few menu items, a data table or two, and a data window, you probably don't. But when you get beyond this size, or start working with other people, the library concept becomes very worthwhile. Libraries become places where you can store your objects for later retrieval, for quick organization, and for sharing with others in your organization.

Organization of Your Libraries

Powersoft recommends that you try not to put more than about 50 or 60 objects into any single library. This is because as the libraries get larger, they get slower. Building your applications will slow greatly if PowerBuilder needs to look through a great big file of hundreds of objects trying to find the ones it needs.

For smaller applications, this limit should not be a problem. In fact, even a few more objects won't hurt if that is all your application requires. But when you start building those monster applications, you will want to start breaking them into separate libraries. Have no fear, PowerBuilder doesn't care if you use one library or a thousand.

There are several ways you might consider breaking your project into separate files. Once you have done this, you can use the Library painter (covered in the next section, and shown in Figure 12-1) to actually move the objects around.

First, you might consider breaking the libraries up by the objects that you will be putting in them. For instance, you might have a library with all your menus, another with the global functions you developed, and others for your windows, DataWindows, and other objects. This is a good method when you are working alone, or when your project is broken down for each person to work with a different part of the user interface (Bill does menus, Sandy does reports, you do the

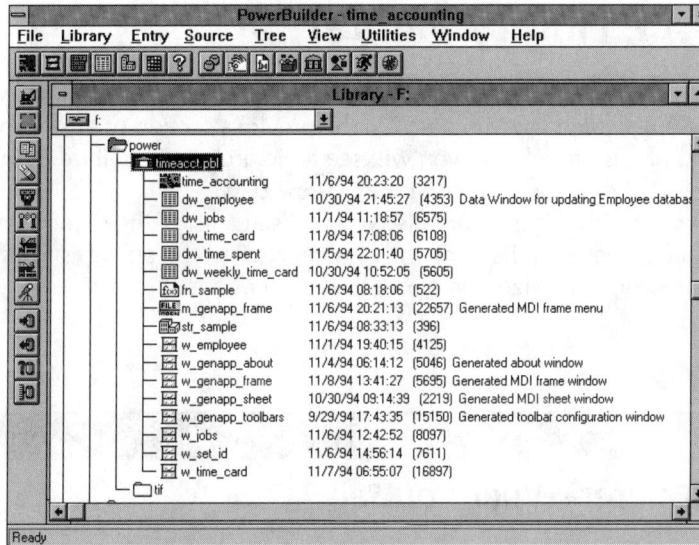

FIGURE 12-1.   *The Library painter helps organize all your objects*

DataWindows, etc.). In this way, consistency can be maintained simply; only one person works on each type of object.

A second way to break up your libraries might be by function. For instance, you might be working on a large accounting package. Jim is doing all the windows and menus that are related to the accounts payable module, Deb is doing the same for the General Ledger module, and Greg has the responsibility for the Accounts Receivable module. As these are all completed, you have the task of tying them all together. This type of breakdown makes it simpler for each person to keep their files available for working, but it becomes more difficult to present a consistent approach to the user interface. If you are managing this process, this is your task (in the above scenario); you need to define the standards that everyone will follow to create a user-friendly, consistent environment.

Of course, your project might be so large that Deb will have a library for the general ledger algorithms, another for her menus, and a third for the windows and data presentation objects. Jim and Greg will do something similar with their modules. This is okay, as long as your team knows the standards, and can keep things organized.

Now, let's see how the Library painter actually works.

Using the Library Painter

The Library painter allows you to quickly move objects into the libraries where they best belong (which was discussed in the previous section of this chapter). When the painter is brought up, you will see a hierarchy of the libraries in the currently selected directory, as shown in Figure 12-1.

If you double-click on a library file, you will see a list of the objects within that library, displayed beneath the library file name. Each of the objects shows the date and time of creation, the size of the object, and a comment.

Library Painter—What You See

PainterBar Icons

Create	Creates a new library file.
Select All	Selects all the objects in the current library file.
Copy	Copies the highlighted object to another library.
Erase	Deletes the highlighted object from the library.
Move	Copies the highlighted object to another library, and then deletes it from the original library.
Regen	Regenerates the object code version of the object from the source code in the library.
Export	Exports the highlighted object to an ASCII file.
Import	Imports an ASCII file, and creates a new object.
Browse	Allows you to look through the library, one object at a time.
Check In	Places an object into the highlighted library from your working directory, replacing the same object that existed in the library previously.
Check Out	Removes a copy of an object into your working directory.
Check Status	Determines whether the highlighted object is checked out by anyone else.
Directory	Returns you to the full directory display of library files.

The comment now becomes very important. If you look closely at Figure 12-1 again, you'll see that there are quite a few entries in the library that is being viewed. Your libraries will also begin to get large as you continue to create objects for each application. The comment is the only thing you have to really remember what an object was used for, besides the name of the object, of course.

Because the comment is so important, if you right-click on an object, there is a menu selection specifically for modifying the comment. With this menu chosen, you will be greeted with the dialog box shown here:

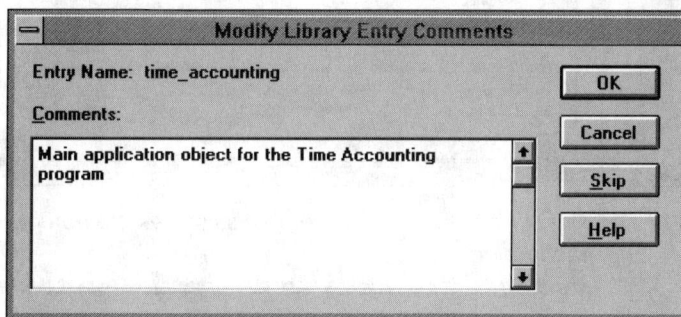

```
┌─────────────────────────────────────────────────────────┐
│ ▬   │          Modify Library Entry Comments              │
├─────────────────────────────────────────────────────────┤
│   Entry Name:  time_accounting              ┌──────────┐  │
│                                             │    OK    │  │
│   Comments:                                 └──────────┘  │
│   ┌───────────────────────────────────┬──┐ ┌──────────┐  │
│   │ Main application object for the   │▲ │ │  Cancel  │  │
│   │ Time Accounting program           │  │ └──────────┘  │
│   │                                   │  │ ┌──────────┐  │
│   │                                   │  │ │   Skip   │  │
│   │                                   │  │ └──────────┘  │
│   │                                   │  │ ┌──────────┐  │
│   │                                   │▼ │ │   Help   │  │
│   └───────────────────────────────────┴──┘ └──────────┘  │
└─────────────────────────────────────────────────────────┘
```

Simply add, delete, or change the comment, and when you are done, you'll see it immediately updated in the library hierarchy.

Browsing the Class Hierarchy

When you have a library selected, you can view the class hierarchy with the Browse Class Hierarchy selection from the pop-up menu. The hierarchy will look something like that shown in Figure 12-2.

The browse view of the hierarchy shows all the objects, and which objects they are derived from. In other words, this is the inheritance tree of the objects. By the way, this is another way that you might consider organizing your libraries—putting all descendants of a common object into the same library.

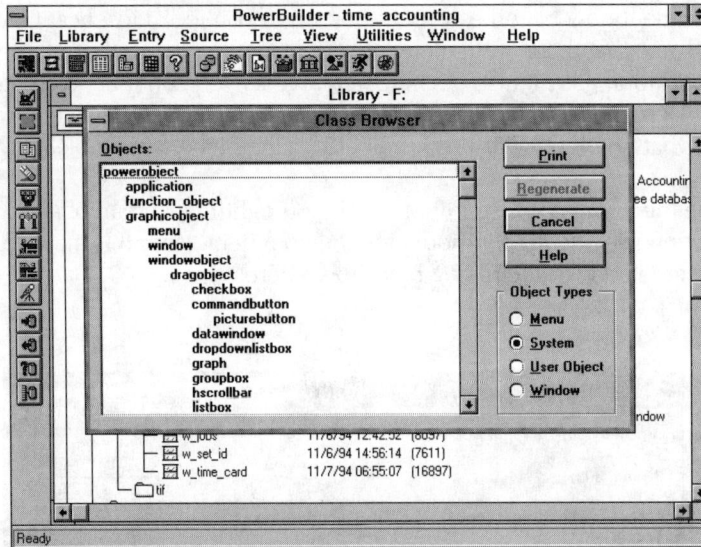

FIGURE 12-2. *The class hierarchy for the objects shows the inheritance of each object*

To the left of each object is an icon depicting which type of object the item represents. If you want to only look at specific types of objects, select Include from the View menu, and you will see the dialog box shown here:

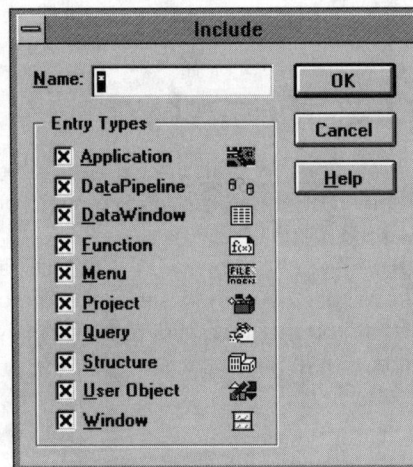

This also shows you the different icons used to depict each type of object.

Once you have looked through the hierarchy of the library and the class hierarchy, you may be ready to look at the specific objects.

Looking at the Objects

If you select a library from the directory display, you can browse (with the right-click menu) through all the information about the objects in that library. The display of information looks like that shown in Figure 12-3.

This is a very quick way to search for specific information in your libraries. Quickly, you can select the type or types of objects you wish to view (Application, DataWindow, Enumerated, Function, Menu, Standard, Structure, System, User Object, and Window), the type of information you need for each object (attributes or functions), and the format of the information selected.

Looking at the PowerBuilder examples, you might start to find objects that you can use in your own applications. This is a perfect use for the Library painter;

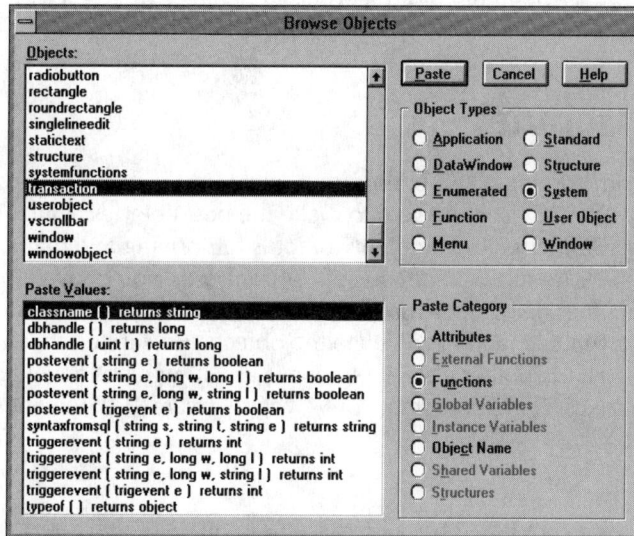

FIGURE 12-3. *Browsing the object information is quite informative*

create a new library, and copy the objects you want from the existing libraries. The Copy Library Entries dialog box, shown here, is very simple and straightforward:

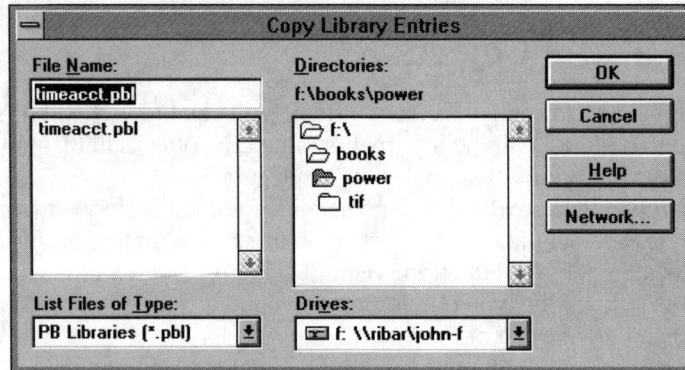

Simply select the name of the library that is to receive the copy of the object. PowerBuilder takes care of the rest. Of course, copying isn't the only thing you can do with objects.

Building Libraries

When you begin working with libraries, you might find yourself organizing them all of the time. After all, isn't the goal to make the best libraries available?

Well, PowerBuilder gives you plenty of tools for moving and managing your application objects (of all sorts, of course). Not only can you copy an object from one place to another (leaving the original intact), you can also move it (not leaving the original copy intact), and even delete the objects. Be careful, though. If you delete an object, and another object references it, you will no longer be able to access *either* object. Therefore, delete only when you are 100 percent sure the object is unused.

Working with Other People's Libraries

Now we get to the best part—trying to work together with other people without destroying each other's files (not to mention their sanity). One way to protect everyone is by using the Check-in and Check-out facility in PowerBuilder.

When you are ready to work on an object in a library, you simply select the Check-out option using the appropriate PowerBar button, or using the menus. If the object is available (meaning that no one else has checked it out previously, and kept it checked out), then you will be asked for the name of the working, or development, library. The object will be placed in that library, and the original is marked as being checked out. Now, no one else can get the file until you check it back in.

If you need an object and it is checked out, or you aren't sure which objects you have checked out, use the Check Status button and you will see a list of the files that are checked out, either for yourself or for everyone, as shown in Figure 12-4.

Remember to check the files back in when you are finished, so that other people may be able to use them.

By the way, there are also several excellent commercial version control packages available, some of which work quite nicely with PowerBuilder. While the PowerBuilder Check-in and Check-out facility is useful, the commercial add-on packages are much more robust, and provide greater security for your files and your development teams.

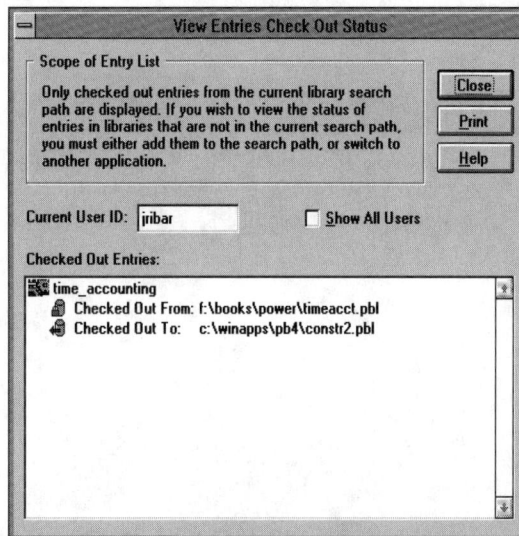

FIGURE 12-4. *The View Entries Check Out Status dialog box lets you know which files you have checked out*

Putting the Whole Package Together

There you have it. A complete application. A full help system. A library of reusable components, ready for your next project. You have it all, and are ready to pass it out to the users. Where do you go next?

In the next chapter, you'll learn how to put your application together in a way that it can be distributed.

CHAPTER 13

Creating the Final Release

You've spent long hard hours building a fantastic application. You've meticulously crafted the ultimate database, taking everyone into consideration in the design of your user interface, and you've written mounds of help for the novice as well as special tips for advanced users. Everything is ready. But now, how do you give this application to everyone to enjoy?

Hold tight. In this chapter, you'll learn about creating executable files (EXEs) for yourself and for distribution, and you'll learn about the different methods that are available.

Creating a Release for Yourself or Your Office

As you were developing your new application, you probably thought about the people who would be using it. Perhaps it will just be you, yourself. Or a few associates at the office, your buddies in the bowling league, or the new mothers support group. Any way you slice it, it's time to move the application out of PowerBuilder and into its new life as an executable program.

You have no doubt tried running your application while you were in the midst of development. After all, what good is a program that won't run? Clicking the Run icon in the PowerBar works wonderfully for testing your application at any time. But if you don't generate an executable form of your program, you'll have to get into PowerBuilder each time you want to run the application. And all your users will also have to get into PowerBuilder; this means that they will all have to own copies of PowerBuilder. This would make Powersoft happy, to be sure, but might make for a much smaller audience for your application.

Therefore, once you think you're ready to give a copy of your program away, or you are ready to use it without the PowerBuilder safety net running, you'll need to generate an executable version of your program. In the next few sections, you'll learn about creating an application for yourself, or someone with whom you share a computer or network. Later in the chapter, we'll talk about more complex executables, and why they are necessary.

Creating an EXE

There is a very simple way to create an executable from your application. Simply select the application object in the Application painter, and choose Create Executable from the File menu. That's it! You'll need to enter the name and location where you want the program created, naturally, but there aren't many other options. The Create Executable window is shown in Figure 13-1.

If you simply choose OK, the entire application and the libraries listed in the Dynamic Libraries portion of the dialog will be combined into your very own first EXE file. This file can be given to anyone you like. No other files are needed. No hidden fees. Nothing else.

Of course, there might be reasons why you'd want to do things differently. For instance, if several libraries show up in a lot of your applications, you might be better off generating dynamic versions of these libraries (covered in the next section, "Using Dynamic Libraries").

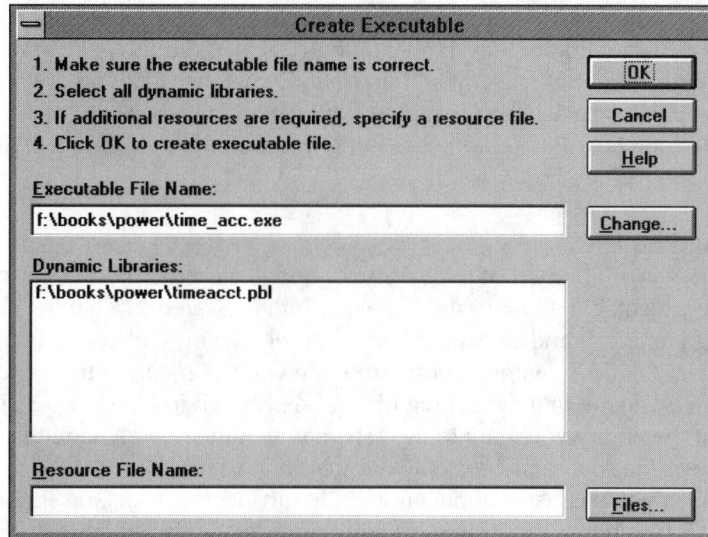

FIGURE 13-1. *Creating a simple executable requires few decisions*

Also, if your EXE file gets too big (say, over 1.5MB or so), the program will be hard to put on floppies (for passing out to your friends), and it will start to slow down in execution speed. After all, PowerBuilder needs to search that one huge file for all the objects in your application.

How do dynamic libraries help? And how hard is it to create them? The following section will answer these questions.

Using Dynamic Libraries

To break your application down a bit, start by choosing one or more of the dynamic libraries listed in the Create Executable dialog box (refer back to Figure 13-1). If you select any of these libraries (by highlighting them), PowerBuilder will not include them in your executable file. This means that you will need to create dynamic libraries for each of these libraries selected. These PBD files, as the PowerBuilder dynamic libraries are called, are only loaded by the application when it actually runs.

Of course, when you give someone your application now, your disk must include the dynamic library files. How are these created, you might ask? In the next section, "Generating PBD Files," you'll find out. Remember that you only need to create PBDs if you selected one or more of the dynamic libraries in the Create Executable dialog box. If you did not select any of the libraries, they will all be included in the EXE file itself.

Generating PBD Files

Creating a dynamic library (PBD) file for your application is almost as simple as creating the executable. Go into the Library painter (covered in Chapter 12, "Using and Sharing Libraries") and select the library for which you will generate a PBD file.

Now, select Build Dynamic Library from the Utilities menu of the Library painter. When you are in the resulting dialog box (shown in Figure 13-2), just give the name of the library you want to use. The name of the new dynamic library will be the same as the source file, except with the PBD extension.

Now when you pass your application on to prospective users, be sure to give them the EXE file and all the related PBD files. These all need to be in a directory along the DOS PATH, or in the Windows or Windows System directories; otherwise, Windows will not be able to find the PBD files when your executable starts running.

So, given the hassle of distributing all the files, having to make sure you don't miss any of them and that you put them into the right places, why would you not just create a single EXE file, as we demonstrated at the beginning of this chapter?

Good Reasons to Use PBDs

One reason not to use a single large EXE file is because of the sheer size of it all. When you progress from personal databases into real-life applications, your EXE will begin to take on a life of its own. It will seem to eat everything in sight, taking on megabytes of storage as it grows. As mentioned earlier, anything over the size of a floppy is too big for a couple of reasons. First, you need an alternative distribution method if you can't fit your application onto floppy disks. And second, the bigger the EXE file is, the longer it will take for your application to find all the objects it needs.

Another reason for keeping your libraries separate is for bug fixes and enhancements. If you only need to send a single, smaller library file to someone with a change, it is much simpler than sending the entire application again and again. This is also true for adding new modules or functions to your application.

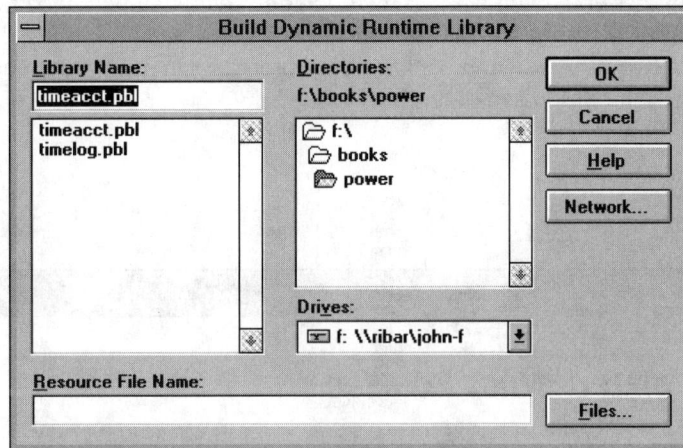

FIGURE 13-2. *The Build Dynamic Runtime Library dialog box*

A third reason to break your application up is for sharing common code and/or objects. If you have a library of common objects that you use on every project, you can save a lot of disk space by using the same PBD file for each project. You and your users only need one copy on the hard drive, no matter how many different applications might be using the objects at any given time.

Creating Applications for Distribution

Even with all the good reasons just listed, building a complex executable for distribution can be a lot of work. Of course, PowerBuilder has a special painter for this task too; if you decide to break your application up into smaller pieces, look first to the Project painter.

The Project Painter

The Project painter is fairly straightforward to use. When you create or load a project, you will see the screen in Figure 13-3. From this simple dialog box, you can select the files that will be required for your application, including PBD files, and any resources you might want to include (fonts, etc.) that will need to be installed before your program can run.

There are two ways you can package your program when you are ready to distribute; these are discussed next.

Project Painter—What You See

PainterBar Icon

Build Creates a new executable file from the options specified.

Main Window Options

Executable File Name The name and path of the EXE file to create.

Resource File Name The name and path of the PBR file containing resources to be used in the application.

Prompt For Overwrite When checked, files will not be overwritten without confirmation.

Regenerate All Objects When checked, the PBL files will be recompiled before the EXE file is created.

Library The names of the libraries to be used or referenced when creating the EXE file.

PBD When checked, the PBL file will be converted to a dynamic library rather than directly included in the EXE file.

PBD Resource File Name The name and path of the PBR file containing resources to be used when creating the dynamic library.

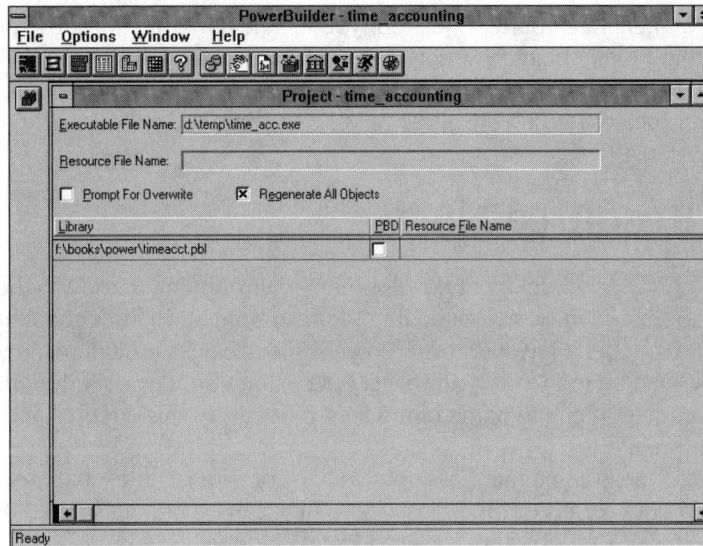

FIGURE 13-3. *Simple options for generating an executable*

The All-in-One EXE

As mentioned at the start of this chapter, the simplest way to distribute your application is to package the whole thing, including libraries, resources (graphic bitmaps, fonts, and much, much more), and everything else you'll need, into the simple but versatile EXE file. This is ideal for smaller, personal applications, where you don't need to be too careful, and nothing is too large.

An EXE with Dynamic Libraries

Once the file starts to get too big (a good rule of thumb is to keep files below a maximum of 800K to 1.5MB in size), you should consider breaking down your application by using dynamic libraries, which were discussed in the section, "Using Dynamic Libraries," earlier in this chapter.

When you generate your application, you list the dynamic libraries you might be using in the Project painter. When the user wants to start this new application, the external files containing the libraries need to be located, and so need to be in the right path (otherwise PowerBuilder or your application will crash).

Using Resource Files

PowerBuilder is a very intelligent development environment. It knows when you associate a toolbar icon with a menu item, for example, to include the icon when it creates an executable. However, even PowerBuilder has its limitations. If you dynamically load an icon from within a script or function, PowerBuilder does not attempt to predetermine the name of the icon it needs. In this circumstance you need a resource file.

A *resource file* is a text file that contains a list of external files that are referenced in your scripts or functions. These files can be bitmap images (BMP and RLE files), icons (ICO files), fonts, or even DataWindows.

To make sure that the EXE or PBD file you create has all the resources it needs, add the name of the resource file next to the EXE or PBD file in the Project painter.

On with the Show

One of the biggest features of PowerBuilder is its all-in-one approach to application building. But what if there are other features you feel would help your work that aren't part of the Enterprise package? Believe it or not, Powersoft has a great deal of support from outside companies, which provide additional products that work very well with the PowerBuilder Enterprise package.

You've already learned about RoboHelp (in Chapter 11, "Adding Help for Your Users"), a tool to assist you in creating help files for your PowerBuilder applications. RoboHelp is not designed specifically for use with PowerBuilder, but in the next chapter, you'll learn about a product that is.

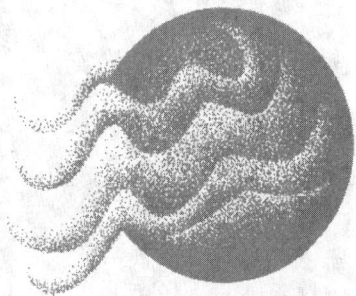

CHAPTER 14

Database Design with ERwin/ERX for PowerBuilder

You've been introduced to one of the most complete client-server programs ever created for the personal computer. PowerBuilder has the capabilities you need for nearly any type of database application you might want, and possibly even more.

But PowerBuilder isn't everything that everyone might want. In Chapter 11, "Adding Help for Your Users," for instance, you learned about RoboHelp, and other tools to aid in creating help files for your PowerBuilder applications. PowerBuilder gave you the hooks (ways to use outside tools), and you saw how to take advantage with RoboHelp.

There are other parts of the design process that can also be done a little better (or at least with more detail) than in PowerBuilder. One of these areas is in the database design itself. ERwin/ERX is a general database design tool, which Powersoft has customized to create ERwin/ERX for PowerBuilder.

In this chapter, you'll learn more about this tool, and about entity-relationship diagrams in general.

Entities and Relationships

You may remember how the Database painter was used in Chapter 5, "Building Your Database," to draw the database design for your application. The drawing looked like Figure 14-1, and showed the different tables, with the keys marked, and the foreign keys attached. This was a good view of your data, and how the relationships connected the tables together.

But there is a lot more information that is needed for a database design. Some of it is probably in your head, and other parts are on pieces of paper all over your office. ERwin helps to bring all the elements of design together in one package, and then integrates directly into your PowerBuilder configuration.

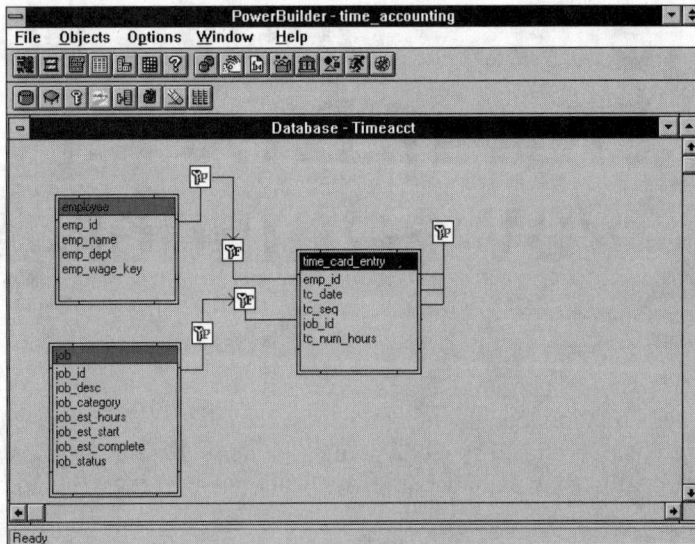

FIGURE 14-1. *A simple database design from PowerBuilder's Database painter*

Before we go any further, let's define some terms. An *entity* is an object that is self-contained, that maintains some internal data, and that can be looked at as a storage place for data. In entity-relationship diagrams, entities generally represent the data files, or tables, in your design.

The *relationship*, then, is how the entities are tied together. In the Database painter, you were able to show how fields from one table were tied to those from another. In ERD (entity-relationship diagram) terminology, a relationship gives much more information. For instance, we know that a time card has an employee number associated with it. We also know that the employee number is a foreign key into the employee table. With an ERD, we can also note that the relationship between these two objects is "lists work for" (see Figure 14-2).

The complete drawing in Figure 14-2 can be read as "A time card lists work for an employee." This is the beginning of an entity-relationship diagram. This type of diagramming technique is very useful in database design. It is also extremely useful in database documentation, such as when you are trying to explain the whole thing to your boss or client.

The Client Side

ER*win* would be a very nice tool without any hooks into PowerBuilder. There are numerous capabilities for designing your database structures, how the tables and

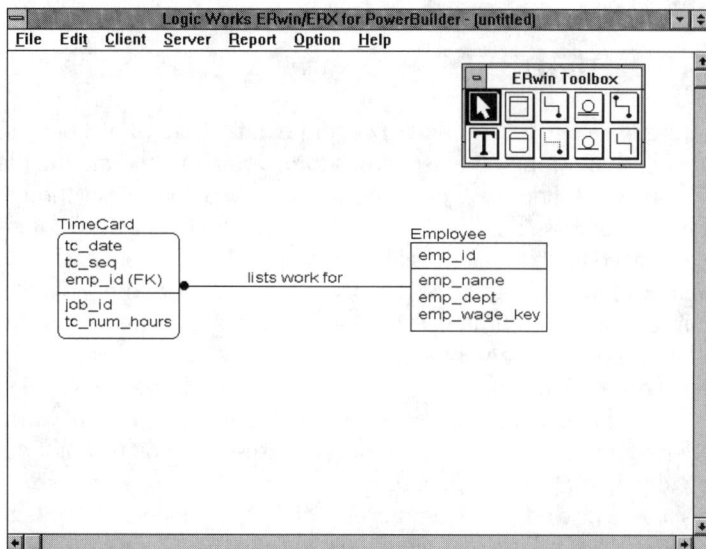

FIGURE 14-2. *Relationships are more meaningful with ERDs*

fields interact, and how the data should look. But with the PowerBuilder connection, you have even more power at your fingertips. You can directly edit the extended attributes for your tables. This can also be done in the Database painter, but with ER*win*, you can design and develop the database in the same tool.

This is, by the way, considered part of the Client design. After all, your computer is the client, communicating with a server for the information it needs. And the client is the part that is most integrated with PowerBuilder. That is why it needs to have all the same tools that the Enterprise series has (i.e., extended attributes, etc.).

The other side of the design is for the server side.

ER*win* and Your Database Server

One place where ER*win* really stands out over PowerBuilder is in the design and development of database server connectivity. While PowerBuilder does have support for multiple database servers, it's not always such a good idea to pick a database that is not very well known.

Using ER*win*, you can develop the server side of the database, connecting to any SQL server of your choice. Then you develop the client side for PowerBuilder, and voilà, and complete client-server solution.

Adding New Life to Your Existing Databases

Another feature of ER*win* is its ability to generate data descriptions of existing data files. This means that through the use of this tool, you can generate the files you need to allow PowerBuilder to access one of your old databases as though it were created with the Database painter. You can develop the client side of the database, adding the enhanced attributes and making a completely new front end for your data.

As a small test, look at Figure 14-3. This is the time accounting database as we designed it in Chapter 5, "Building Your Database." It was generated from the PowerBuilder files, without any other changes. But with a little massage, we can make a thing of beauty and a much nicer documentation tool, as shown in Figure 14-4. This is what you should show your boss. This is also what you should strive for when you design and then document your databases. It is much simpler to remember with a good piece of paper!

ER*win* is a very powerful tool, and is especially useful since it is integrated with PowerBuilder. Imagine taking that old database from the mainframe, the one that hasn't been changed for years, and adding a new set of menus, data entry screens, reports, and viewers, without any help but the ER*win* tool.

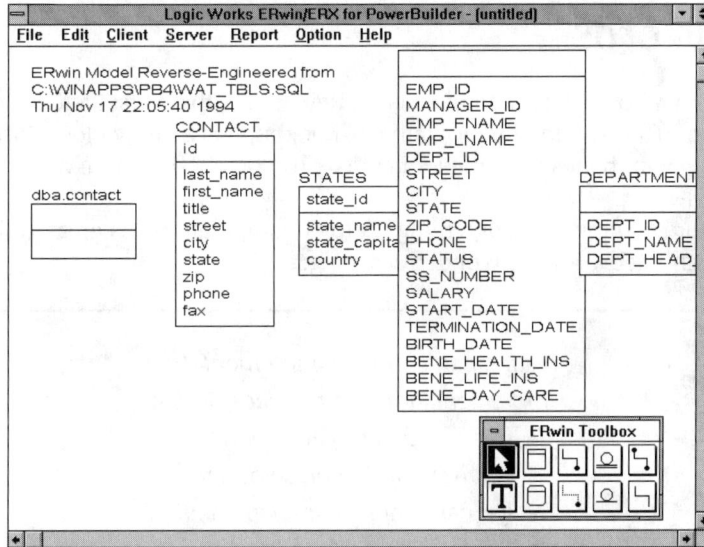

FIGURE 14-3.   *This is an ER diagram without any manipulation*

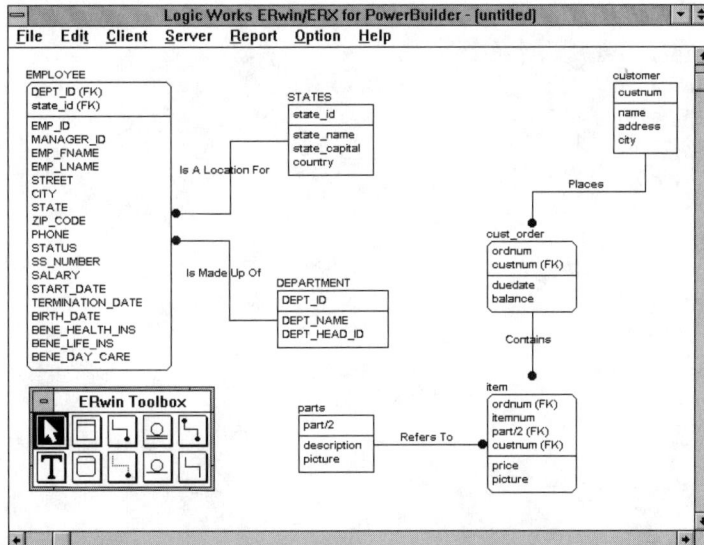

FIGURE 14-4.   *Look at the difference a few touches can make*

Final Words

You can be a hero, just by utilizing a great new tool with a versatile development environment. This isn't totally programmer-free, but it is awfully close. Just think of the power in your hands (provided, of course, by somebody who *is* a programmer...).

Make sure you think through things before manipulating this great tool. Kevin Weeks is attributed with this wonderful saying:

> *Testing can't replace implementation*
> *Implementation can't replace design*
> *Design can't replace analysis*
> *Analysis can't replace design*
> *Design can't replace implementation*
> *Implementation can't replace testing.*

It all goes hand in hand. As you begin to develop your own applications with PowerBuilder, keep in mind the great power at your fingertips and use it wisely.

CHAPTER 15

Testing and Debugging for a Perfect Finish

So, you have the perfect application completed. You've followed the ideas in this book, looked at all the manuals Powersoft gave you, learned the script language well, gone to user interface design classes, and put together what looks like the ultimate application.

So off you go to market. That's all you need to do, right? That depends. Yes, you need to create some help for the users, and you probably did that back in Chapter 11, "Adding Help for Your Users." You also need to create an executable version of the program (which is covered in Chapter 13, "Creating the Final Release"). But what have you forgotten?

If this is your first project, or the first large project for you and the team, there is a good chance that you only lightly did the testing and debugging necessary to create a professional quality program. Let's see what is involved here, and what help you can get from PowerBuilder.

Testing

There are a lot of different ways to do testing. Almost as many different ways as there are people who do the testing. There are dozens of books that tell great detailed stories about how to test and not to test. There are even programs specifically written to automate the testing process; they keep repeating a sequence of steps to find out whether your application will continue without a hitch. But in all of this, how do you know what to test, or how long to test?

There are several phases of testing that you may want to pursue with your applications. The sections which follow will cover these phases in more detail.

Unit Testing

Unit testing is what the programmer does with his or her own code when they believe it is finished. This is the testing you do at your desk, trying to see whether the menus look right, whether the dialog boxes are laid out correctly, and whether the printed reports end up on your printer or on the network backup tape.

Unit testing is the testing that takes place throughout your application's development. It tests one piece of your program at a time, without (necessarily) a lot of regard for other parts of the application. If you are working with several people on the project, the unit tests are done by the programmers themselves, possibly before the entire project is even brought together.

Integration Testing

The second level of testing is called *integration testing*, because this is where you start to bring the pieces of the project together. Whether you are working alone or with a project team, this is the point where you take all the pieces that were tested individually in the privacy of your own office and subject them to the rigors of interfacing with all the other "unit-tested" modules. This test is meant to be sure that all the pieces of your puzzle fit together.

Unit testing and integration testing are all done in-house, however. Your client should not be part of these tests, because the level of surety that your application is perfect may be less than perfect!

Alpha and Beta Testing

Once you are feeling more confident about your software, you may begin an *Alpha* and then a *Beta* test. These tests are the first time that an actual end user should get access to the program. And not just any end user, but one you can trust to try things and let you know what they found.

Testers are not much use to you if they won't let you know about the bugs they find. Also, testers who expect the software to be perfect in the Alpha or Beta releases are not fit to be working with your software. After all, you already know there are bugs; you just want to find out where they are so you can fix them.

Release or Release Candidate

The last version you do before it goes to the general public is the *Release Candidate*. For this phase of the testing, you should let using some "normal" users work with your software, the ones who aren't specially prepared and are more likely to do things incorrectly, hopefully finding any bugs in this last shot before stardom.

When you have fixed all the bugs you know about and are satisfied that the program is bug-free, or at least that it seems bug-free, you are ready for a *Release*. This is the actual software that is delivered to the stores, hopefully in time to make you money for the holidays.

What if They Find Bugs?

The whole purpose of testing, in all its phases, is to find anything that might go wrong and to fix it before the software goes out the door as a Release. But as the bug reports come in (if they do), make sure to categorize them, you spend your time on the things that need the most attention. Here is a suggested list of bug levels, in the order that they should be fixed:

1. The worst type of bugs are those that mangle, lose, or misplace your data. What good is a program that keeps the wrong data, or loses it altogether? If you hear about these types of bugs, drop everything and fix them immediately. Warn all your testers, so they won't lose anything important.

2. Another bug that has a big "byte" is the kind that causes your application to crash. These types often create the mangled data noted in Number 1 of this list, but might cause other problems, too. These require immediate attention. If at all possible, let everyone know how to work around the problem until you can fix it.

3. Bugs that appear when a function doesn't do what is expected is next on the list. If you ask for a report of time card entries, and get an employee list instead, you might get annoyed, but you shouldn't lose data (or sleep!) over it. Fix these next, however, so your users can try to do the things they think the program allows.

4. If you have any functions that don't work at all, fix them next. Make sure all your menus and buttons do something. And, if at all possible, make them work the same way in each window you create; consistency is very important for users!

5. Cosmetic changes do not require a lot of attention in the earliest stages, but become very important as you get closer to the time when the product will be marketed. So keep track of these changes—they should be simple to perform, and you can do them one afternoon when you are too full after lunch.

6. Programs that don't do what was expected, or that do it differently than expected, are not necessarily filled with bugs, as far as the programmer is concerned. Nevertheless, the customer is always right, so you might have to make changes anyway. Save these for last, however, because adding totally new functionality has the highest chance of adding the bugs in Numbers 1 through 5 above, which starts your testing and fixing all over again.

As your testers come up with problems, whether or not they are bugs, write them all down. Those that don't make it to the bug list, might make for good tutorial topics. Often, "bugs" are just misunderstandings about how the program is to work.

Now, if you have a bug list in front of you, how do you find those silly problems so they can be solved? Read on to find out more.

Debugging

It is fairly simple to start the debugging process within PowerBuilder. Simply select your application in the Application painter, and then Debug from the File menu to start the process. This will bring up a window that looks like Figure 15-1.

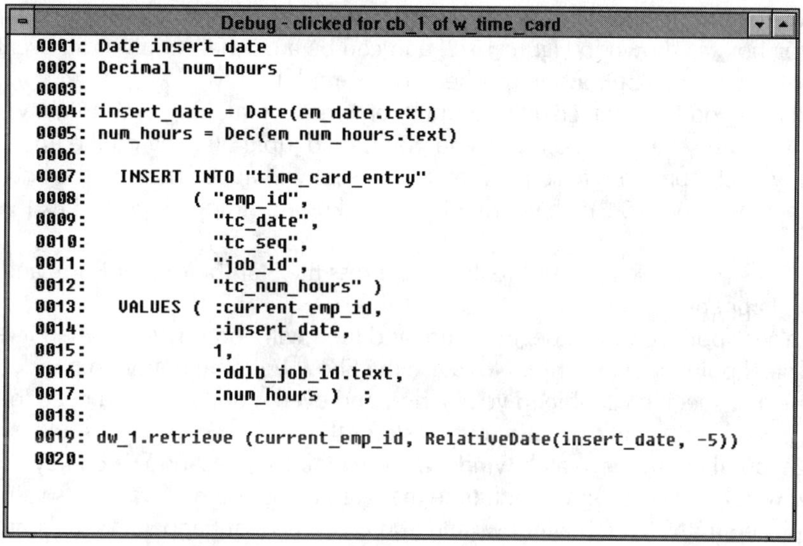

```
┌─────────────────────────────────────────────────────────────────┐
│ ─         Debug - clicked for cb_1 of w_time_card         ▼  ▲   │
├─────────────────────────────────────────────────────────────────┤
│ 0001: Date insert_date                                            │
│ 0002: Decimal num_hours                                           │
│ 0003:                                                             │
│ 0004: insert_date = Date(em_date.text)                            │
│ 0005: num_hours = Dec(em_num_hours.text)                          │
│ 0006:                                                             │
│ 0007:    INSERT INTO "time_card_entry"                            │
│ 0008:           ( "emp_id",                                       │
│ 0009:             "tc_date",                                      │
│ 0010:             "tc_seq",                                       │
│ 0011:             "job_id",                                       │
│ 0012:             "tc_num_hours" )                                │
│ 0013:    VALUES ( :current_emp_id,                                │
│ 0014:             :insert_date,                                   │
│ 0015:             1,                                              │
│ 0016:             :ddlb_job_id.text,                              │
│ 0017:             :num_hours )  ;                                 │
│ 0018:                                                             │
│ 0019: dw_1.retrieve (current_emp_id, RelativeDate(insert_date, -5))│
│ 0020:                                                             │
└─────────────────────────────────────────────────────────────────┘
```

FIGURE 15-1.   *The Debug window without any bugs*

The first thing you need to do is select a script that you want to keep an eye on (you can pick as many as you like, actually, but set them up one at a time,

Debug Painter– What You See

PainterBar Icons

Start	Starts the application running.
Step	Used to step though a script one line at a time.
Select	Allows you to choose a script to watch or debug.
Edit Stop	Used to modify stops that are already in place.
Show	Toggles whether the Watch window will be displayed.
Add	Adds another variable to be watched in the Watch window.
Remove	Removes a variable from the Watch window.
Show	Toggles whether the Variable window is opened, showing all the variables in a single window.

following this general discussion). This script is selected from the Select Script dialog box, as shown in Figure 15-2, and can be a normal script, or an event script (what to do when buttons are pushed, for example).

Once you have selected the script, there are several things you might want to do. You can set a breakpoint, or stop point, by double-clicking on the line where you want the program to stop. A small stop sign will appear next to the line in the script (see Figure 15-3). To get rid of the breakpoint, simply double-click the line again.

Once you have set your breakpoints, press the Start button (or Run), and see what happens.

Your application will begin to run, and then will abruptly stop when it reaches the breakpoint in your script. Now, use the Show Variable button to check the value of a specific variable in your script, and even modify it if you need to.

If you don't want to continuously ask for the same variables over and over, you might put them in the Watch window. Here, you use the Add Watch key to add a new watch variable. Now, each time that variable gets a new value, its value will be placed in the Watch window, and you can see what happens as the watch variable takes on new watched values.

Using breakpoints, variable displays, watched variables, and by stepping through the scripts in your application, you should be able to find, analyze, and fix any possible problems within a short time.

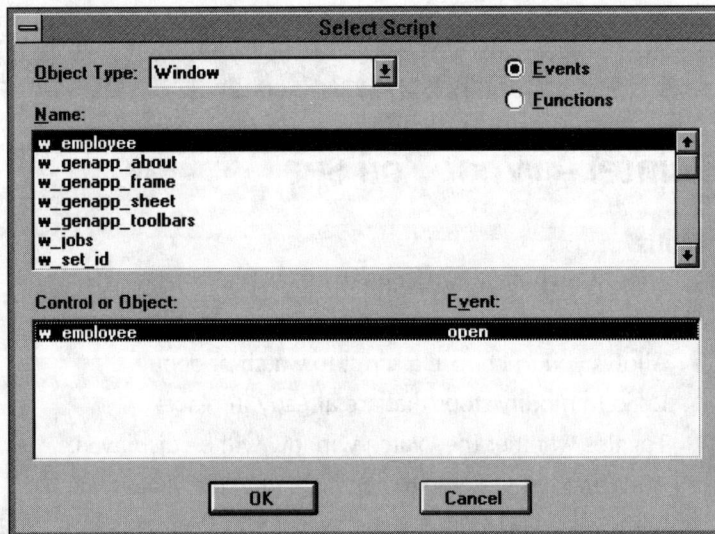

FIGURE 15-2. *Selecting a script is very straightforward*

```
┌─────────────────────────────────────────────────────────┐
│ ─        Debug - clicked for cb_1 of w_time_card    ▼ ▲  │
├─────────────────────────────────────────────────────────┤
│   0001: Date insert_date                                 │
│   0002: Decimal num_hours                                │
│   0003:                                                  │
│   0004: insert_date = Date(em_date.text)                 │
│🛑 0005: num_hours = Dec(em_num_hours.text)               │
│   0006:                                                  │
│   0007:    INSERT INTO "time_card_entry"                 │
│   0008:         ( "emp_id",                              │
│   0009:           "tc_date",                             │
│   0010:           "tc_seq",                              │
│   0011:           "job_id",                              │
│   0012:           "tc_num_hours" )                       │
│   0013:    VALUES ( :current_emp_id,                     │
│   0014:            :insert_date,                         │
│   0015:            1,                                    │
│   0016:            :ddlb_job_id.text,                    │
│🛑 0017:            :num_hours )  ;                        │
│   0018:                                                  │
│🛑 0019: dw_1.retrieve (current_emp_id, RelativeDate(insert_date, -5))│
│   0020:                                                  │
│                                                          │
│                                                          │
└─────────────────────────────────────────────────────────┘
```

FIGURE 15-3.   *Adding too many breakpoints makes your script look like a driver's education course*

Now Release It

That's it. If you've done all the things we talked about in this chapter, made a conscientious effort to look for and eliminate all your bugs, then the program should be ready. Send it out, and be relaxed; there is no need to think anything will go wrong. After all, you did the testing. All will be well in "Powerland."

A P P E N D I X **A**

PowerScript Function Quick Reference

This appendix lists the PowerScript functions, with short descriptions and syntax listings. For complete information on each function, refer to your PowerBuilder Function Reference manual, supplied with your software.

Refer to Chapter 9, "Defining How the Program Acts," for an introduction to the use of PowerScripts. All the functions in this appendix can be used in your PowerScripts. A brief glance through here will give you a good idea what is available, and will serve as a quick reference when you get more proficient at programming scripts.

The following conventions are followed in this appendix:

■ Items enclosed in curly braces {} are optional.

■ Return variable types are shown at the beginning of each function call, surrounded by square brackets []. For many functions, a return type of [*integer*] is used to signify whether the function succeeded (1 was returned) or failed (-1 was returned). For other functions, these integer values have different meanings, and most are noted.

Abs

This function returns the absolute value of the number passed as a parameter.

Syntax

```
[type of n] Abs( n )
```

AcceptText

This function is used to access the text value of a currently selected editing field. The data is first passed to the validation routine.

Syntax

```
[integer] datawindowname.AcceptText()
```

AddItem

This function adds a new item into a ListBox or DropDownListBox. The list is sorted if necessary. Otherwise, the item is added to the end of the list. The item is passed into this function as a string.

Syntax

```
[integer] listboxname.AddItem( item )
```

ArrangeSheets

This function arranges the sheets in an MDI frame, according to the arrangement type passed in as a parameter; possible values are Cascade!, Layer!, and Tile!.

Syntax

```
[integer] mdiframe.ArrangeSheets( arrangeType )
```

Asc

This function returns the ASCII value of a character, or of the first character in a string variable.

Syntax

```
[integer] Asc( string )
```

Beep

This function beeps the computer speaker the number of times specified as the parameter.

Syntax

```
[integer] Beep( )
```

Blob

This function converts a string of text into a *blob* (binary large object). The blob variable is returned.

Syntax

```
[blobvariable] Blob( string )
```

BlobEdit

This function is used to copy data into a blob variable at a specified location. If the function succeeds, the location for the next insertion is returned.

Syntax

```
[long] BlobEdit( blobvariable, position, data )
```

BlobMid

This function pulls a section of data out of the center of a blob, and returns it. If no data is available, an empty blob is returned.

Syntax

```
[blobvariable] BlobMid( data, position {, length} )
```

Cancel

This function is used to cancel the execution of a pipeline object. This should only be called when the Start or Repair scripts are running.

Syntax

```
[integer] pipelineobject.Cancel()
```

CanUndo

This function returns TRUE if the previous edit for a specific editing field can be cancelled (undone). FALSE is returned if the previous edit cannot be undone.

Syntax

```
[Boolean] editname.CanUndo()
```

Ceiling

This function returns the smallest whole number that is at least as big as the parameter passed into the function. The return value is the same type of variable as *n*.

Syntax

```
[datatype_of_n] Ceiling( n )
```

ChangeMenu

This function is used to change the menu being used in a specific window. If the *position* parameter is used, the list of open sheets is added to the menu specified by *position*, if the window is an MDI frame window.

Syntax

```
[integer] windowname.ChangeMenu( menuname {, position} )
```

Char

This function returns the first character of a blob or a string. It is also used to return the character version of a number, when a number is passed as a parameter.

Syntax

```
[char] Char( data )
```

Check

This function is used to place a check mark next to a menu item. If the menu is already checked, then the mark is toggled on each successive call to Check.

Syntax

```
[integer] menuitem.Check()
```

ClassName

This function returns a string variable with the class name of the item referenced. An empty string is returned if any error occurs.

Syntax

```
[string] controlname.ClassName
```

Clear

This function is used to delete, or clear, data from an edit line. The information is not stored in the clipboard, and therefore cannot be retrieved once cleared.

Syntax

```
[integer] editname.Clear()
```

ClearValues

This function deletes all the values associated with the specified column in the DataWindow referenced in the function call.

Syntax

```
[integer] datawindowname.ClearValues( column )
```

Clipboard

This function is used to retrieve information from the clipboard. It can also be used to place information onto the clipboard, if the *string* parameter is specified. Returns the current contents of the clipboard, or an empty string if the clipboard is empty or contains non-text information.

Syntax

```
[string] Clipboard( { string } )
```

Close

This function removes the referenced DataWindow from the screen, and calls the Close and CloseQuery event scripts, if they exist.

Syntax

```
[integer] Close( windowname )
```

CloseChannel

This function closes a DDE channel, as specified in the *handle* parameter, in the active window. If the *windowhandle* is specified, the DDE channel in that window will be closed instead.

Syntax

```
[integer] CloseChannel( handle {, windowhandle } )
```

CloseUserObject

This function removes the user object specified from the screen. The scripts for the Destructor event are also executed.

Syntax

```
[integer] CloseUserObject( userobjectname )
```

CloseWithReturn

This function removes the referenced window from view, but also returns the information placed into the *returnvalue* name.

Syntax

```
[integer] CloseWithReturn( windowname, returnvalue )
```

CommandParm

This function is used to access the command line used to start the application, if available. If the command line is available, it is returned as a string, otherwise an empty string is sent.

Syntax

```
[string] CommandParm()
```

ConnectToNewObject

This function is used to create a new OLE object, and connect to it.

Syntax

```
[integer] oleobject.ConnectToNewObject( classname )
```

ConnectToObject

This set of functions is used to connect OLE objects, using a variety of methods.

Syntax

```
[integer] oleobject.ConnectToObject( filename )
[integer] oleobject.ConnectToObject( filename, classname )
[integer] oleobject.ConnectToObject( classname )
```

Copy

This function copies text from an edit control to the clipboard. The number of characters placed onto the clipboard is returned.

Syntax

```
[integer] editname.Copy()
```

Cos

This function is used to calculate the cosine of a number. The parameter should be an angle, specified in radians.

Syntax

```
[double] Cos( n )
```

Count

This function returns the number of rows in a specified column of a DataWindow. If the group is specified, the number of rows in the column that are also in the group, is returned.

Syntax

```
[long] Count( column { for group } )
```

CPU

This function lets you know the number of milliseconds of CPU time that have passed since the current application began.

Syntax

```
[long] Cpu()
```

CrosstabAvg

This function is used to calculate the average of all values in a specific expression. This can only be used in a Crosstab DataWindow.

Syntax

```
[double] CrosstabAvg( n )
```

CrosstabCount

This function is used to determine the count of all values in a specific expression. This can only be used in a Crosstab DataWindow.

Syntax

`[long] CrosstabCount( n )`

CrosstabDialog

This function is used to present the Crosstab dialog box to the user, allowing a modification of the crosstab style setup.

Syntax

`[integer] datawindowname.CrosstabDialog()`

CrosstabMax

This function is used to calculate the maximum of all values in a specific expression. This can only be used in a Crosstab DataWindow.

Syntax

`[long] CrosstabMax( n )`

Cut

This function deletes any text in an edit control that is currently selected. The information that is cut is then placed onto the clipboard, for possible later retrieval.

Syntax

`[integer] editname.Cut()`

Date

This group of functions returns a date, based on the variable passed as a parameter. Each format of the Date function uses a different parameter type, but always returns a date. If the parameter is not valid, a return value of 0000-00-00 is produced.

Syntax

```
[date] Date( datetime )
[date] Date( string )
[date] Date( year, month, day )
```

DateTime

This function returns a datetime variable for a specified date, and optional time. If the time is omitted, midnight is used.

Syntax

```
[datetime] DateTime( date {, time} )
```

Day

This function returns the day portion of a date. The return value is in the range of 1 through 31.

Syntax

```
[integer] Day( date )
```

DayName

This function returns the name of the day, as specified in the date parameter.

Syntax

```
[string] DayName( date )
```

DayNumber

This function returns the number of the day of the week of the day portion of the date parameter. Sunday is returned as 1, Monday is 2, etc.

Syntax

```
[integer] DayNumber( date )
```

DaysAfter

This function is used to determine the number of days between two dates; that is, the number of days after *date1* that *date2* occurs. The return value can be positive, negative, or 0 (if the dates are the same).

Syntax

```
[long] DaysAfter( date1, date2 )
```

DBCancel

This function is used to cancel any retrieval that might be in progress in a DataWindow.

Syntax

```
[integer] datawindowname.DBCancel()
```

DBErrorCode

This function is used to determine the database error that occurred in a specified DataWindow. Zero is returned if no errors have occurred.

Syntax

```
[long] datawindowname.DBErrorCode()
```

DBErrorMessage

This function performs the same task as DBErrorCode, except that the text of the database error is returned. If there was no error, an empty string is returned.

Syntax

[*string*] *datawindowname*.DBErrorMessage()

DBHandle

This function returns the handle for your database. This handle is used for all interface tasks. If you are not connected, a 0 will be returned.

Syntax

[*long*] DBHandle(*transactionobject*)

Dec

This function returns a value that represents the number portrayed in a string or blob.

Syntax

[*decimal*] Dec(*string*)

DeletedCount

This function returns the number of rows in a DataWindow that have been deleted, but have not been updated in the associated database. If no rows have been deleted, or if they have all been updated in the database, a 0 is returned.

Syntax

[*long*] *datawindowname*.DeletedCount()

DeleteItem

This function is used to delete an item from a ListBox or DropDownListBox. You specify the position of the item that is to be deleted.

Syntax

```
[integer] listboxname.DeleteItem( position )
```

DeleteRow

This function deletes a row from a DataWindow. The row is not actually deleted from the database until a call is made to the Update function. If *row* is specified as 0, the current row is deleted.

Syntax

```
[integer] datawindowname.DeleteRow( row )
```

DirList

This function fills a ListBox or DropDownListBox with the files matching the specific file name specification given. The path is not required, but may be included. The file type represents the value or combination of the file types requested, from the following list of possibilities:

- 0 Read/write files
- 1 Read-only files
- 2 Hidden files
- 4 System files

- 16 Subdirectories
- 32 Archive (modified) files
- 16384 Drives
- 32768 Exclude the read/write files

If you want to display the current drive and directory, specify a statictext control variable to receive the information.

Syntax

```
[Boolean] listboxname.DirList( filespec, filetype {, statictext } )
```

DirSelect

This function is used to retrieve a file selection from a ListBox filled with the DirList function. TRUE is returned if the returned item is a drive or directory that can be expanded further, and FALSE if the item is strictly a file name.

Syntax

```
[Boolean] listboxname.DirSelect( selection )
```

Disable

This function is used to disable a menu item. This causes the menu item to be grayed, and no longer allowed as a selection.

Syntax

```
[integer] menuitem.Disable()
```

DisconnectObject

This function is used to release the OLE connection for an object.

Syntax

```
[integer] oleobject.DisconnectObject()
```

Double

This function converts the contents of a string into a *double* numeric value.

Syntax

```
[double] Double( string )
```

Drag

This function is used to begin, end, or cancel the dragging of a control. The *dragmode* should be specified as Begin!, Cancel!, or End!, relating to what function is to be performed.

Syntax

```
[integer] control.Drag( dragmode )
```

DraggedObject

This function returns the item that is currently being dragged, if any. To determine the type of object being dragged, use the TypeOf function.

Syntax

```
[dragobject] DraggedObject()
```

Draw

This function is used to draw a picture in a parent window at the specified location.

Syntax

```
[integer] picture.Draw( xlocation, ylocation )
```

dwCreate

This function creates a DataWindow object. If you specify the *errorbuffer*, any error messages will be placed there upon the functions return.

Syntax

```
[integer] datawindowname.dwCreate( syntax {, errorbuffer } )
```

dwDescribe

This function is used to determine the makeup of a DataWindow. It returns information about the structure of the DataWindow, based on the *syntax*, or request that is made.

Syntax

[*string*] *datawindowname*.dwDescribe(*syntax*)

dwFind

This function is used to find specific conditions in a DataWindow, before a database update is processed. It is especially useful in finding out-of-range conditions. The search can be contained between the rows specified in *start* and *end*. The first row that matches the condition is returned, or 0 if no rows match.

Syntax

[*long*] *datawindowname*.dwFind(*expression, start, end*)

dwFindGroupChange

This function is used to find data breaks in the DataWindow. Starting at the row specified, the DataWindow is searched for the next row in which a break occurs for the level specified. The row number is then returned, or 0 is returned if no breaks are found.

Syntax

[*long*] *datawindowname*.dwFindGroupChange(*row, level*)

dwFindRequired

This function is used to make sure that required fields are filled, prior to final database updating. The first row with a required field having a null value, is returned in the *row* parameter. If *updateonly* is TRUE, only the changed rows are checked; otherwise, all rows are verified.

Syntax

```
[integer] datawindowname.dwFindRequired( dwbuffer, row,
colnumber, colname, &updateonly )
```

dwGetBandAtPointer

This function is used to determine where the pointer is in a DataWindow. The function returns the band, followed by a tab character, and the row within the band, where the pointer is located.

Syntax

```
[string] datawindowname.dwGetBandAtPointer()
```

dwGetChild

This function stores a reference to the child window with the given name, in the *dwchildvariable* parameter.

Syntax

```
[integer] datawindowname.dwGetChild( name, dwchildvariable )
```

dwGetItemStatus

This function is used to determine the current status of a row in a DataWindow. One of the following values are returned: NotModified!, DataModified!, New!, or NewModified!. The *dwbuffer* is passed as PRIMARY!, DELETE!, or FILTER!.

Syntax

```
[dwitemstatus] datawindowname.dwGetItemStatus( row, column,
dwbuffer )
```

dwGetNextModified

This function returns the first row that was modified, that follows the starting row specified. The *dwbuffer* is passed as PRIMARY!, DELETE!, or FILTER!.

Syntax

[*long*] *datawindowname*.dwGetNextModified(*row, dwbuffer*)

dwGetObjectAtPointer

This function returns the name of the object under the pointer, followed by a tab character, and the row. An empty string is returned if an error occurs.

Syntax

[*string*] *datawindowname*.dwGetObjectAtPointer()

dwGetSQLPreview

This function is used to view the current SQL statement in effect for a DataWindow. This should only be called in a dbError script, or the SQLPreview event.

Syntax

[*string*] *datawindowname*.dwGetSQLPreview()

dwGetUpdateStatus

This function is used to determine the current status of an update. This can only be called in the DBError script, or in an SQLPreview event triggered by an update. The *dwbuffer* is passed as PRIMARY!, DELETE!, or FILTER!.

Syntax

[*integer*] *datawindowname*.dwGetUpdateStatus(*row, dwbuffer*)

dwGroupCalc

This function is used to regenerate the breaks in grouping levels in a DataWindow.

Syntax

```
[integer] datawindowname.dwGroupCalc()
```

dwModify

This function is used to create and destroy objects, as well as to modify the attributes for an existing object. This function returns an empty string if successful, or an error message if it fails.

Syntax

```
[string] datawindowname.dwModify( modstring )
```

dwOLEActivate

This function actives OLE for the row and column specified, using the *verb* parameter.

Syntax

```
[integer] datawindowname.dwOLEActivate( row, column, verb )
```

dwResetUpdate

This function is used to reset the update flags for a DataWindow.

Syntax

```
[integer] datawindowname.dwResetUpdate()
```

dwSetItemStatus

This function forces a specific item to have the specified status. The *dwbuffer* is specified as PRIMARY!, DELETE!, or FILTER!. The *status* is specified as NotModified!, DataModified!, New!, or NewModified!.

Syntax

```
[integer] datawindowname.dwSetItemStatus( row, column, dwbuffer, status )
```

dwSetPosition

This function is used to place a graphic object into a DataWindow, in the band, and at the location specified.

Syntax

```
[integer] datawindowname.dwSetPosition( objectname, band, bringtofront )
```

dwSetSQLPreview

This function is used to set the SQL statement for a DataWindow. It should only be used in the SQLPreview event script.

Syntax

```
[integer] datawindowname.dwSetSQLPreview( sqlsyntax )
```

dwShareData

This function allows data to be shared between primary and secondary DataWindow controls. Only the data is shared, so formatting may be different in each window.

Syntax

`[integer] dwprimary.dwShareData( dwsecondary )`

dwShareDataOff

This function turns off data sharing for a DataWindow, reversing the effects of the dwShareData function.

Syntax

`[integer] datawindowname.dwShareDataOff()`

dwSyntaxFromSQL

This function returns the source code required to build a DataWindow with the SQL statement passed in the *sqlselect* parameter.

Syntax

`[string] dwSyntaxFromSQL( transaction, sqlselect, presentation, err )`

Enable

This function is used to enable a menu item, and make it available for selection by the user of your application.

Syntax

`[integer] menuitem.Enable()`

EventParmDouble

This function is used to retrieve numeric parameters from VBX and custom controls. The value of the parameter specified by *parameter* is returned in *parmvariable*.

Syntax

```
[integer] vbxuserobject.EventParmDouble( parameter, parmvariable )
```

EventParmString

This function is used to retrieve text parameters from VBX and custom controls. The value of the parameter specified by *parameter* is returned in *parmvariable*.

Syntax

```
[integer] vbxuserobject.EventParmString( parameter, parmvariable )
```

ExecRemote

This set of functions is used to start DDE applications. If you use the second format of this function, you should use the OpenChannel function first.

Syntax

```
[integer] ExecRemote( command, applicationname, topicname )
[integer] ExecRemote( command, handle {, windowhandle} )
```

Exp

This function returns the value of e raised to the *n*'th power (exponentiation).

Syntax

```
[double] Exp( n )
```

Fact

This function returns the factorial value for *n*.

Syntax

```
[double] Fact( n )
```

FileClose

This function closes the file with the number specified. This number is assigned when the file is created.

Syntax

```
[integer] FileClose( filenumber )
```

FileDelete

This function removes the file with the name specified. The function returns TRUE if successful, and FALSE otherwise.

Syntax

```
[Boolean] FileDelete( filename )
```

FileExists

This function returns TRUE if the named file exists. Otherwise, FALSE is returned.

Syntax

```
[Boolean] FileExists( filename )
```

FileLength

This function returns the size of the file specified, or -1 if the file does not exist.

Syntax

```
[long] FileLength( filename )
```

FileOpen

This function is used to open files for use by your application. *filemode* is specified as LineMode! or StreamMode!. *fileaccess* is specified as Read! or Write!. *filelock* may use LockReadWrite!, LockRead!, LockWrite!, or Shared!. *writemode* may be ether Append! or Replace!. The integer return value is the handle for the file opened, or -1 if an error occurs.

Syntax

```
[integer] FileOpen( filename {, filemode {, fileaccess {,
filelock {, writemode }}}} )
```

FileRead

This function is used to read information from a disk file. This function can read 32,768 characters each time. If an End of File condition occurs, -100 is returned; otherwise, this function returns the number of characters actually read.

Syntax

```
[integer] FileRead( filenumber, variable )
```

FileSeek

This function is used to position the file pointer to a specific location in the data file. The *position* for placement is based on the *origin* parameter, which has one of the following values: FromBeginning!, FromCurrent!, or FromEnd!.

Syntax

```
[long] FileSeek( filenumber, position, origin )
```

FileWrite

This function is used to write information into a data file, at the current pointer location. The function returns the number of characters written, or -1 if an error occurred.

Syntax

```
[integer] FileWrite( filenumber, variable )
```

Fill

This function is used to create a string variable made up of a specific character or group of characters, repeated until a specified total string length has been reached.

Syntax

```
[string] Fill( string, n )
```

Filter

This function displays rows in a DataWindow that match the current filtering criteria specified for the window.

Syntax

```
[integer] datawindowname.Filter()
```

FilteredCount

This function returns the count of the rows that do not match the filter currently in effect for the DataWindow, that is, the number of rows not being displayed because of the filter.

Syntax

```
[integer] datawindowname.FilteredCount()
```

FindItem

This function is used to locate an item in a ListBox that starts with the text given. You may specify where in the list to start searching by using the *index* parameter.

Syntax

```
[integer] listboxname.FindItem( text, index )
```

GetActiveSheet

This function returns the currently active sheet in an MDI frame window.

Syntax

```
[window] mdiframewindow.GetActiveSheet()
```

GetBorderStyle

This function returns the border style that is associated with a DataWindow. The possible return values are Box!, NoBorder!, ShadowBox!, and Underline! If this function fails, it returns NULL.

Syntax

```
[border] datawindowname.GetBorderStyle( column )
```

GetClickedColumn

This function returns the column number for the currently selected column, or 0 if no column is selected.

Syntax

```
[integer] datawindowname.GetClickedColumn()
```

GetClickedRow

This function returns the row number for the currently selected row, or 0 if no row has been selected.

Syntax

```
[integer] datawindowname.GetClickedRow()
```

GetColumn

This function is used to determine the currently selected column in the DataWindow. If no column is current, 0 is returned.

Syntax

```
[integer] datawindowname.GetColumn()
```

GetColumnName

This function returns the name of the currently selected column. If no column is selected, an empty string is returned.

Syntax

```
[string] datawindowname.GetColumnName()
```

GetCommandDDE

This function retrieves a command from a DDE client application, and places it in the *string* parameter.

Syntax

```
[integer] GetCommandDDE( string )
```

GetCommandDDEOrigin

This function returns the source of the DDE command request, placing the application name in the *application* parameter.

Syntax

`[integer] GetCommandDDEOrigin( application )`

GetData

This set of functions is used to retrieve raw data from the edit controls.

Syntax

`[integer] controlname.GetData( date )`
`[integer] controlname.GetData( datetime )`
`[integer] controlname.GetData( decimal )`
`[integer] controlname.GetData( double )`
`[integer] controlname.GetData( string )`
`[integer] controlname.GetData( time )`

GetDataDDE

This function is used to retrieve data from a DDE application, and place it into the *string* parameter.

Syntax

`[integer] GetDataDDE( string )`

GetDataDDEOrigin

This function returns the source of the DDE data, placing the application name in the *application* parameter.

Syntax

`[integer] GetDataDDEOrigin( application, topicstring, itemstring )`

GetDynamicDate

This function should only be used in certain dynamic SQL scripts. It is used to retrieve the date from the *index* parameter of the *DynamicDescriptionArea*.

Syntax

```
[date] GetDynamicDate( DynamicDescriptionArea, index )
```

GetDynamicDateTime

This function should only be used in certain dynamic SQL scripts. It is used to retrieve the date and time from the *index* parameter of the *DynamicDescriptionArea*.

Syntax

```
[datetime] GetDynamicDateTime( DynamicDescriptionArea, index )
```

GetDynamicNumber

This function should only be used in certain dynamic SQL scripts. It is used to retrieve numbers from the *index* parameter of the *DynamicDescriptionArea*. The return value is based on the request.

Syntax

```
[numerictype] GetDynamicNumber( DynamicDescriptionArea, index )
```

GetDynamicString

This function should only be used in certain dynamic SQL scripts. It is used to retrieve string values from the *index* parameter of the *DynamicDescriptionArea*.

Syntax

```
[string] GetDynamicString( DynamicDescriptionArea, index )
```

GetDynamicTime

This function should only be used in certain dynamic SQL scripts. It is used to retrieve the time from the *index* parameter of the *DynamicDescriptionArea*.

Syntax

```
[time] GetDynamicTime( DynamicDescriptionArea, index )
```

GetEnvironment

This function is used to retrieve different pieces of information from the environment of the computer running your application. The *environ* parameter is an object with many pieces of information, including the following: PBType, PBMajorRevision, PBMinorRevision, PBFixesRevision, OSType, OSMajorRevision, OSMinorRevision, OSFixesRevision, CPUType, ScreenWidth, ScreenHeight, and NumberOfColors.

Syntax

```
[integer] GetEnvironment( environ )
```

GetFileOpenName

This function is used to display the File Open dialog box (a Windows common dialog box), and allow the user to select a file name from the dialog box. The *title* is placed at the top of the dialog box. *pathname* and *filename* are used to store the returned values. If *extension* is provided, only files with that extension will be shown. Returns 1 if a selection was made.

Syntax

```
[integer] GetFileOpenName( title, pathname, filename {, extension
{, filter }} )
```

GetFileSaveName

This function is used to display the File Save dialog box (a Windows common dialog), and allow the user to select a file name from the dialog box. The *title* is placed at the top of the dialog box. *filename* is the default file name, and *newfile* is used to store the selected file name. If *extension* is provided, only files with that extension will be shown. Returns 1 if a selection was made.

Syntax

```
[integer] GetFileSaveName( title, filename, newfile {, extension
{, filter }} )
```

GetFirstSheet

This function is used to retrieve the top sheet in an MDI frame window. If no sheet is displayed, an invalid value will be returned, so use IsValid to determine whether there is a first sheet available.

Syntax

```
[window] window.GetFirstSheet()
```

GetFocus

This function is used to find the control that has current focus. If no object has the focus, NULL is returned.

Syntax

```
[graphicobject] GetFocus()
```

GetFormat

This function is used to determine the current format of a column. This can then be restored with SetFormat.

Syntax

[*string*] *datawindowname*.GetFormat(*column*)

GetItemDate

This function is used to retrieve the date information from a specified location in a control. The *dwbuffer* is specified as PRIMARY!, DELETE!, or FILTER!. If *originalvalue* is TRUE, the original information will be returned, otherwise the current data will be used.

Syntax

[*date*] *datawindowname*.GetItemDate(*row, column* {, *dwbuffer* {, *originalvalue* }})

GetItemDateTime

This function is used to retrieve the date and time information from a specified location in a control. The *dwbuffer* is specified as PRIMARY!, DELETE!, or FILTER!. If *originalvalue* is TRUE, the original information will be returned, otherwise the current data will be used.

Syntax

[*datetime*] *datawindowname*.GetItemDateTime(*row, column* {, *dwbuffer* {, *originalvalue* }})

GetItemDecimal

This function is used to retrieve decimal information from a specified location in a control. The *dwbuffer* is specified as PRIMARY!, DELETE!, or FILTER!. If *originalvalue* is TRUE, the original information will be returned, otherwise the current data will be used.

Syntax

[*decimal*] *datawindowname*.GetItemDecimal(*row, column* {, *dwbuffer* {, *originalvalue* }})

GetItemNumber

This function is used to retrieve numeric information from a specified location. The *dwbuffer* is specified as PRIMARY!, DELETE!, or FILTER!. If *originalvalue* is TRUE, the original information will be returned, otherwise the current data will be used. The return value is determined by the type of the column specified.

Syntax

```
[numerictype] datawindowname.GetItemNumber( row, column {,
dwbuffer {, originalvalue }} )
```

GetItemString

This function is used to retrieve string information from a specified location. The *dwbuffer* is specified as PRIMARY!, DELETE!, or FILTER!. If *originalvalue* is TRUE, the original information will be returned, otherwise the current data will be used.

Syntax

```
[string] datawindowname.GetItemString( row, column {, dwbuffer {,
originalvalue }} )
```

GetItemTime

This function is used to retrieve the time information from a specified location. The *dwbuffer* is specified as PRIMARY!, DELETE!, or FILTER!. If *originalvalue* is TRUE, the original information will be returned, otherwise the current data will be used.

Syntax

```
[Time] datawindowname.GetItemTime( row, column {, dwbuffer {,
originalvalue }} )
```

GetMessageText

This function is used to retrieve the message text for a specified DataWindow. This is only valid for Crosstab windows, and returns an empty string if there are no messages pending.

Syntax

```
[string] datawindowcontrol.GetMessageText()
```

GetNextSheet

This function is used to return the next sheet in an MDI frame window. The next window is the window following *window2* in front-to-back order.

Syntax

```
[window] window.GetNextSheet( window2 )
```

GetRemote

This set of functions is used to retrieve data from another application, from a specific location within that application's data space. The second format requires the use of the OpenChannel function before GetRemote can be called.

Syntax

```
[integer] GetRemote( location, target, application, topicname )
[integer] GetRemote( location, target, handle {, windowhandle } )
```

GetRow

This function is used to determine the current row that is in use in a DataWindow. Zero is returned if no row is current.

Syntax

```
[long] datawindowname.GetRow()
```

GetSelectedRow

This function determines the first row that is currently selected, starting from the *row* specified.

Syntax

`[long] datawindowname.GetSelectedRow( row )`

GetSQLSelect

This function is used to retrieve the currently active SQL statement for a DataWindow. If there is an error, an empty string is returned.

Syntax

`[string] datawindowname.GetSQLSelect()`

GetText

This function returns the current row and column selected, as a string variable.

Syntax

`[string] datawindowname.GetText()`

GetTrans

This function is used to retrieve the current transaction object and save it into the *transaction* variable.

Syntax

`[integer] datawindowname.GetTrans( transaction )`

GetValidate

This function is used to retrieve the current validation rule. Since this function returns a string value, the information may be stored for later use with SetValidate.

Syntax

```
[string] datawindowname.GetValidate( column )
```

GetValue

This function returns the value of a specific item in the DataWindow. You specify the column you are interested in, as well as the index (which determines the offset into the value list, or the edit style). If the column does not have a value list or a style code table, an empty string is returned.

Syntax

```
[string] datawindowname.GetValue( column, index )
```

grAddCategory

This function is used to add a category to a graph. If successful, it returns the number assigned to the category. If it is a duplicate category, the existing category's number is returned. A return value of -1 means that the addition could not be made.

Syntax

```
[integer] controlname.grAddCategory( categoryname )
```

grAddData

This set of functions is used to add values to a series that is in use by a graph.

Syntax

```
[integer] controlname.grAddData( seriesnumber, datavalue {,
categorylabel } )
[integer] controlname.grAddData( seriesnumber, xvalue , yvalue )
```

grAddSeries

This function is used to add a series of data to a graph. It returns the number assigned to the series if all goes well; otherwise, -1 is returned.

Syntax

```
[integer] controlname.grAddSeries( seriesname )
```

grCategoryCount

This function is used to determine the number of categories that are currently active in a graph. This count is returned unless there is an error, in which case -1 is returned. In the case of a DataWindow, *graphcontrol* is used to specify the actual name of the graph to use.

Syntax

```
[integer] controlname.grCategoryCount( {graphcontrol} )
```

grCategoryName

This function is used to determine the name of a category, as specified in the *categorynumber* parameter. An empty string is returned if an error occurs.

Syntax

```
[string] controlname.grCategoryName( { graphcontrol, }
categorynumber )
```

grClipboard

This function copies the graph related to the *controlname* to the clipboard. If *controlname* is a DataWindow, the graph referred to by *graphcontrol* will be copied.

Syntax

```
[integer] controlname.grClipboard( {graphcontrol} )
```

grDataCount

This function is used to determine the number of data points that are active in a series within a specified graph. If *controlname* is a DataWindow, the graph referred to by *graphcontrol* will be counted. If an error occurs, -1 is returned.

Syntax

```
[integer] controlname.grDataCount( {graphcontrol,} seriesname )
```

grDataStyle

This function is used to retrieve certain details about the presentation style used for a specific graph. If *controlname* is a DataWindow, the graph referred to by *graphcontrol* will be used. The valid *colortype*s are Background!, Foreground!, LineColor!, and Shade!.

Syntax

```
[integer] controlname.grDataStyle( {graphcontrol,} seriesnumber,
datapointnumber, colortype, colorvariable )
[integer] controlname.grDataStyle( {graphcontrol,} seriesnumber,
datapointnumber, fillpatternvariable )
[integer] controlname.grDataStyle( {graphcontrol,} seriesnumber,
datapointnumber, linestylevariable )
[integer] controlname.grDataStyle( {graphcontrol,} seriesnumber,
datapointnumber, symboltypevariable )
```

grDeleteCategory

This function is used to remove an entire category (including data) from a graph.

Syntax

```
[integer] controlname.grDeleteCategory( categoryname )
```

grDeleteData

This function is used to remove a specific point of data from a series in a graph.

Syntax

```
[integer] controlname.grDeleteData( seriesnumber, datapointnumber )
```

grDeleteSeries

This function is used to remove an entire series of data from a graph.

Syntax

```
[integer] controlname.grDeleteSeries( seriesname )
```

grFindCategory

This function helps determine the number associated with a specific named category. This function returns -1 if the specified category name does not exist. If *controlname* is a DataWindow, the graph referred to by *graphcontrol* will be used.

Syntax

```
[integer] controlname.grFindCategory( {graphcontrol,}
categoryname )
```

grFindSeries

This function helps determine the number associated with a specific series in a graph. This function returns -1 if the specified series name does not exist. If *controlname* is a DataWindow, the graph referred to by *graphcontrol* will be used.

Syntax

```
[integer] controlname.grFindSeries( {graphcontrol,} seriesname )
```

grGetData

This function is used to retrieve specific points of data from a graph. If *controlname* is a DataWindow, the graph referred to by *graphcontrol* will be used. *datatype* should be xValue! or yValue!.

Syntax

```
[double] controlname.grGetData( {graphcontrol,} seriesnumber,
datapoint {,datatype} )
```

grImportClipboard

This function copies the contents of the clipboard into a control. The clipboard data must have tabs between columns. This function returns the number of rows that were imported, or a negative number if errors occurred.

Syntax

```
[long] controlname.grImportClipboard( {startrow {, endrow
{,startcolumn }}} )
```

grImportFile

This function imports a data file into a control. The data in the file must be separated by tab characters for each column. This function returns the number of rows that were imported, or a negative number if errors occurred.

Syntax

```
[long] controlname.grImportFile( filename {, startrow {, endrow
{,startcolumn }}} )
```

grImportString

This function reads information from a string, and places it into a control. The data within the string must be delimited with tabs. To start new data points, use a carriage return character. This function returns the number of data points actually found in the string, or a negative number if an error occurred.

Syntax

```
[integer] controlname.grImportString( string {, startrow {,
endrow {,startcolumn }}} )
```

grInsertCategory

This function inserts a new category into a graph, before another category that already exists in the graph (denoted by the *categorynumber* parameter). The number of the new category is returned if successful. If the category duplicates one which already exists, the original category's number is returned.

Syntax

```
[integer] controlname.grInsertCategory( categoryname,
categorynumber )
```

grInsertData

This function is used to add values to a series that is in use by a graph, at a specific location (specified by *datapoint*).

Syntax

```
[integer] controlname.grInsertData( seriesnumber, datapoint,
datavalue {, categorylabel } )
```

grInsertSeries

This function is used to add a series of data to a graph in a specific location (specified by *seriesnumber*). The function returns the number assigned to the series if all goes well; otherwise, -1 is returned.

Syntax

```
[integer] controlname.grInsertSeries( seriesname, seriesnumber )
```

grModifyData

This series of functions is used to modify data in a graph.

Syntax

```
[integer] controlname.grModifyData( seriesnumber, datapoint,
datavalue {, categorylabel} )
[integer] controlname.grModifyData( seriesnumber, datapoint,
xvalue, yvalue )
```

grObjectAtPointer

This function determines where the mouse is pointing (the number of the series and the data point). If the user clicks in a series, *datapoint* is returned as 0. If the user clicks in a category, 0 is stored in *seriesnumber*. If *controlname* is a DataWindow, the graph referred to by *graphcontrol* will be used.

Syntax

```
[grobjecttype] controlname.grObjectAtPointer( {graphcontrol,}
seriesnumber, datavalue )
```

grReset

This function removes all the data from the associated graph, restoring it for a new application. The *graphresettype* takes one of the following values: All!, Category!, Data!, or Series!.

Syntax

```
[integer] controlname.grReset( graphresettype )
```

grResetDataColors

This function resets the color for specific data, restoring it to the default value for the application. If *controlname* is a DataWindow, the graph referred to by *graphcontrol* will be used.

Syntax

```
[integer] controlname.grResetDataColors( {graphcontrol,}
seriesnumber, datapointnumber )
```

grSaveAs

This function is used to save a control into a file, in a specific file format. The *saveastype* parameter can take one of these values: CSV!, Clipboard!, dBASE2!, dBASE3!, DIF!, Excel!, SQLInsert!, SYLK!, Text!, WKS!, or WK1!. If *controlname* is a DataWindow, the graph referred to by *graphcontrol* will be used. If *colheading* is TRUE, the column headings will be saved at the beginning of the file.

Syntax

```
[integer] controlname.grSaveAs( {graphcontrol,} {filename {,
saveastype {, colheading }}} )
```

grSeriesCount

This function returns the number of series that are found within a graph. If *controlname* is a DataWindow, the graph referred to by *graphcontrol* will be used.

Syntax

```
[integer] controlname.grSeriesCount( {graphcontrol} )
```

grSeriesName

This function returns the name of a series, specified by the number assigned to that series. If *controlname* is a DataWindow, the graph referred to by *graphcontrol* will be used.

Syntax

```
[string] controlname.grSeriesName( {graphcontrol,} seriesnumber )
```

grSeriesStyle

This set of functions is used to determine the style of how series are presented within the graph in question. If *controlname* is a DataWindow, the graph referred to by *graphcontrol* will be used. The valid *colortype*s are Background!, Foreground!, LineColor!, and Shade!.

Syntax

```
[integer] controlname.grSeriesStyle( {graphcontrol,} seriesname,
colortype, colorvariable )
[integer] controlname.grSeriesStyle( {graphcontrol,} seriesname,
fillpatternvariable )
[integer] controlname.grSeriesStyle( {graphcontrol,} seriesname,
linestylevariable )
[integer] controlname.grSeriesStyle( {graphcontrol,} seriesname,
symboltypevariable )
[integer] controlname.grSeriesStyle( {graphcontrol,} seriesname,
overlayindicator )
```

grSetDataStyle

This set of functions is used to specify the styles that should be used for data within a graph. If *controlname* is a DataWindow, the graph referred to by *graphcontrol* will be used. The valid *colortype*s are Background!, Foreground!, LineColor!, and Shade!. The *fillpattern* parameter may be Bdiagonal!, Diamond!, Fdiagonal!, Horizontal!, Solid!, Square!, or Vertical!. The *linestyle* parameter may be Continuous!, Dash!, DashDot!, DashDotDot!, Dot!, or Transparent!. The *symbol* parameter may be NoSymbol!, SymbolHollowBox!, SymbolX!, SymbolStar!, SymbolHollowUpArrow!, SymbolHollowCircle!, SymbolHollowDiamond!,

SymbolSolidDownArrow!, SymbolSolidUpArrow!, SymbolSolidCircle!, SymbolSolidDiamond!, SymbolPlus!, SymbolHollowDownArrow!, or SymbolSolidBox!.

Syntax

```
[integer] controlname.grSetDataStyle( {graphcontrol,} seriesname,
datapointnumber, colortype, color )
[integer] controlname.grSetDataStyle( {graphcontrol,} seriesname,
datapointnumber, fillpattern )
[integer] controlname.grSetDataStyle( {graphcontrol,} seriesname,
datapointnumber, linestyle )
[integer] controlname.grSetDataStyle( {graphcontrol,} seriesname,
datapointnumber, symbol )
```

grSetSeriesStyle

This set of functions is used to specify the styles that should be used for series within a graph. If *controlname* is a DataWindow, the graph referred to by *graphcontrol* will be used. The valid *colortypes* are Background!, Foreground!, LineColor!, and Shade!. The *fillpattern* parameter may be Bdiagonal!, Diamond!, Fdiagonal!, Horizontal!, Solid!, Square!, or Vertical!. The *linestyle* parameter may be Continuous!, Dash!, DashDot!, DashDotDot!, Dot!, or Transparent!. The *symbol* parameter may be NoSymbol!, SymbolHollowBox!, SymbolX!, SymbolStar!, SymbolHollowUpArrow!, SymbolHollowCircle!, SymbolHollowDiamond!, SymbolSolidDownArrow!, SymbolSolidUpArrow!, SymbolSolidCircle!, SymbolSolidDiamond!, SymbolPlus!, SymbolHollowDownArrow!, or SymbolSolidBox!. The *overlaystyle* parameter is TRUE if you want the overlay style to be set, and FALSE otherwise.

Syntax

```
[integer] controlname.grSetSeriesStyle( {graphcontrol,}
seriesname, colortype, color )
[integer] controlname.grSetSeriesStyle( {graphcontrol,}
seriesname, fillpattern )
[integer] controlname.grSetSeriesStyle( {graphcontrol,}
seriesname, linestyle )
[integer] controlname.grSetSeriesStyle( {graphcontrol,}
seriesname, symbol )
```

```
[integer] controlname.grSetSeriesStyle( {graphcontrol,}
seriesname, overlaystyle )
```

Handle

This function returns the handle of a specific object. This handle is used for making calls directly to Windows API functions, or for use with the Send function. If *previous* is TRUE, you will get the handle for the previous instance; 0 will be returned if the object is an application and there are no previous instances of the application.

Syntax

```
[integer] Handle( objectname {, previous } )
```

Hide

This function is used to toggle the hidden state of an object. In other words, if the object currently appears on the screen, it will be hidden; if the object is already hidden, it will be made visible.

Syntax

```
[integer] objectname.Hide()
```

Hour

This function returns the hour portion of a time, as an integer between 0 and 23.

Syntax

```
[integer] Hour( time )
```

Idle

This function causes an Application Idle event to be triggered after *n* seconds of inactivity. This timing restarts after any user activity (keyboard or mouse). It returns 1 if the timer can be started, and -1 if there was an error.

Syntax

```
[integer] Idle( n )
```

ImportClipboard

This function copies the clipboard from *startrow, startcolumn* to *endrow, endcolumn*, into the DataWindow starting at location *dwstartcolumn*. The number of rows imported is returned. If there is an error, a negative number is returned.

Syntax

```
[long] datawindowname.ImportClipboard( { startrow {, endrow {,
startcolumn {, endcolumn {, dwstartcolumn }}}}} )
```

ImportFile

This function reads the contents of the specified data file, from *startrow, startcolumn* to *endrow, endcolumn*, into the DataWindow starting at location *dwstartcolumn*. The number of rows imported is returned. If there is an error, a negative number is returned. The data types and column order in the file must match the DataWindow.

Syntax

```
[long] datawindowname.ImportFile( filename {, startrow {, endrow
{, startcolumn {, endcolumn {, dwstartcolumn }}}}} )
```

ImportString

This function reads the contents of the specified string, from *startrow, startcolumn* to *endrow, endcolumn*, into the DataWindow starting at location *dwstartcolumn*. The number of rows imported is returned. If there is an error, a negative number is returned. The data types and column order in the string must match the DataWindow.

Syntax

```
[long] datawindowname.ImportString( string {, startrow {, endrow
{, startcolumn {, endcolumn {, dwstartcolumn }}}}} )
```

InsertItem

This function is used to insert an item into a ListBox or DropDownListBox, at a location before the item number specified in *index*. The position into which the item is actually placed is returned, with -1 signifying an error.

Syntax

```
[integer] listboxname.InsertItem( item, index )
```

InsertRow

This function inserts a row into a DataWindow. The row is inserted into the position previous to the row specified in the *row* parameter. If successful, the position where the row was inserted is returned; otherwise, a -1 is returned.

Syntax

```
[long] datawindowname.InsertRow( row )
```

Int

This function returns the integer portion of a number; that is, the largest whole number that is less than or equal to the parameter.

Syntax

```
[type_of_n] Int( n )
```

Integer

This function returns the integer that is represented by a string.

Syntax

```
[integer] Integer( string )
```

IntHigh

This function returns the value stored in the high-order word of a long number, or -1 if an error occurs.

Syntax

```
[unsigned_int] IntHigh( long )
```

IntLow

This function returns the value stored in the low-order word of a long number, or -1 if an error occurs.

Syntax

```
[unsigned_int] IntLow( long )
```

IsDate

This function returns a TRUE value if the string parameter is in the format of a valid date, and a FALSE otherwise.

Syntax

```
[Boolean] IsDate( string )
```

IsNull

This function returns a TRUE value if the parameter is currently NULL, and a FALSE otherwise. This function works on variables of any data type, but not with arrays.

Syntax

```
[Boolean] IsNull( any_type )
```

IsNumber

This function returns a TRUE value if the string parameter forms a valid number, and returns a FALSE otherwise.

Syntax

```
[Boolean] IsNumber( string )
```

IsRowModified

This function returns a TRUE value if the current row has been modified.

Syntax

```
[Boolean] datawindowname.IsRowModified()
```

IsRowNew

This function returns a TRUE value if the current row has been recently created.

Syntax

```
[Boolean] datawindowname.IsRowNew()
```

IsSelected

This function determines whether a clicked row has been selected, and is called from the Clicked event script.

Syntax

```
[Boolean] datawindowname.IsSelected( row )
```

IsTime

This function returns a TRUE value if the string parameter is in the format of a valid time, and a FALSE otherwise.

Syntax

```
[Boolean] IsTime( string )
```

IsValid

This function is used to determine whether a window is open; that is, whether it is valid to perform processing with that window.

Syntax

```
[Boolean] IsValid( objectname )
```

KeyDown

This function returns a TRUE value if a specific key is being held down on the keyboard, and a FALSE otherwise.

Syntax

```
[Boolean] KeyDown( keycode )
```

Large

This function returns the *n*'th largest number for a given range or group selection, and matching optional criteria expressions. *return_exp* is the name of the column to return when the *n*'th largest value is found. *range* may be one of the following: All, Crosstab, Graph, GroupNbr, or Page. If DISTINCT is used, only the largest distinct values are located (i.e., no duplications).

Syntax

```
[type_of_large] Large( return_exp, large_exp, n { FOR range {
DISTINCT {express1 {, express2 {, ...}}}}} )
```

Left

This function returns the leftmost portion of a string, including a given number of characters. An empty string is returned if an error occurs.

Syntax

```
[string] Left( string, number_of_chars )
```

LeftTrim

This function returns the string that is passed as a parameter, but with any spaces trimmed (removed) from the left of the string (the start of the string).

Syntax

```
[string] LeftTrim( string )
```

Len

This function returns the length of a string, that is the number of characters that it contains.

Syntax

```
[integer] Len( string )
```

LibraryCreate

This function is used to create a library file, adding an optional comment if specified.

Syntax

```
[integer] LibraryCreate( libraryname {, comment} )
```

LibraryDelete

This function is used to either delete a complete library, or to delete a specific object from a library.

Syntax

```
[integer] LibraryDelete( libraryname {, objectname, objecttype} )
```

LibraryDirectory

This function is used to retrieve a listing of all the objects maintained in a specific library. The returned value is a string listing all the objects in the library, giving name, date/time, and comments, all separated by tab characters. The objects are separated by carriage return characters. *objecttype* may be one of the following: DirAll!, DirApplication!, DirDataWindow!, DirFunction!, DirMenu!, DirStructure!, DirUserObject!, or DirWindow!.

Syntax

```
[string] LibraryDirectory( libraryname, objecttype )
```

LibraryExport

This function is used to export an object from a library. Upon success, the syntax required to create the object is returned. Otherwise, the error message is returned. *objecttype* is one of the following: ExportApplication!, ExportDataWindow!, ExportFunction!, ExportMenu!, ExportStructure!, ExportUserObject!, or ExportWindow!.

Syntax

```
[string] LibraryExport( libraryname, objectname, objecttype )
```

LibraryImport

This function is used to import an object into a library, or in other words, to add it to the library.

Syntax

```
[integer] LibraryImport( libraryname, objectname, objecttype,
syntax, errors {, comment} )
```

LineCount

This function returns the number of lines in an edit control.

Syntax

```
[integer] editcontrol.LineCount()
```

LineLength

This function returns the length of the line upon which the cursor rests in an edit control.

Syntax

```
[integer] editname.LineLength()
```

Log

This function is used to determine the natural logarithm of a number.

Syntax

```
[double] Log( n )
```

LogTen

This function is used to determine the decimal logarithm of a number.

Syntax

```
[double] LogTen( n )
```

Long

This set of functions returns a long number, created from separate low and high words, or from the contents of a string.

Syntax

```
[long] Long( lowword, highword )
[long] Long( string )
```

Lower

This function converts a string into all lowercase letters.

Syntax

```
[string] Lower( string )
```

LowerBound

This function returns the lower bound of an array, that is, the lowest index that can be used. If specified, the lowest bound for a specific dimension will be returned.

Syntax

```
[integer] LowerBound( array {, dimension} )
```

mailAddress

This function is used to update the mailRecipient array for a mail message. It returns one of the following: mailReturnSuccess!, mailReturnFailure!, mailReturnInsufficientMemory!, or mailReturnUserAbort!.

Syntax

```
[mailReturnCode] mailsession.mailAddress( {mailmessage} )
```

mailDeleteMessage

This function is used to delete a mail message. It returns one of the following: mailReturnSuccess!, mailReturnFailure!, mailReturnInsufficientMemory!, or mailReturnUserAbort!.

Syntax

```
[mailReturnCode] mailsession.mailDeleteMessage( messageid )
```

mailGetMessages

This function is used to retrieve mail messages, populating the messageID array of *mailsession*. It returns one of the following: mailReturnSuccess!, mailReturnFailure!, mailReturnInsufficientMemory!, mailReturnUserAbort!, or mailReturnNoMessages!.

Syntax

```
[mailReturnCode] mailsession.mailGetMessages( {returnreadonly} )
```

mailHandle

This function is used to determine the handle of a specific mail session.

Syntax

```
[unsigned_long] mailsession.mailHandle()
```

mailLogoff

This function is used to log off of a mail server, or a mail session. It returns one of the following: mailReturnSuccess!, mailReturnFailure!, or mailReturnInsufficientMemory!.

Syntax

```
[mailReturnCode] mailsession.mailLogoff()
```

mailLogon

This function is used to log onto a mail server, or a mail session. It returns one of the following: mailReturnSuccess!, mailReturnFailure!, mailReturnInsufficientMemory!, mailReturnLoginFailure!, mailReturnTooManySessions!, or mailReturnUserAbort!. *logonoption* may be one of the following: mailNewSession!, mailDownLoad!, or mailNewSessionWithDownLoad!.

Syntax

```
[mailReturnCode] mailsession.mailLogon( {userid, password} {,
logonoption} )
```

mailReadMessage

This function is used to read specific mail messages. *mailreadoption* is one of the following: mailEntireMessage, mailEnvelopeOnly!, mailBodyAsFile!, or mailSuppressAttach!. This function returns one of the following values: mailReturnSuccess!, mailReturnFailure!, or mailReturnInsufficientMemory!. If *mark* is TRUE, the message will be noted as having been read.

Syntax

```
[mailReturnCode] mailsession.mailReadMessage( messageid,
mailmessage, mailreadoption, mark )
```

mailRecipientDetails

This function is used to retrieve the recipient information for a specific mail message. It returns one of the following codes: mailReturnSuccess!, mailReturnFailure!, mailReturnInsufficientMemory! mailUnknownReturnRecipient!, mailReturnUserAbort!.

Syntax

```
[mailReturnCode] mailsession.mailRecipientDetails( mailrecipient
{, allowupdates} )
```

mailResolveRecipient

This function is used to resolve the name of a recipient. If *allowupdates* is TRUE, you will be allowed to edit the recipient information.

Syntax

```
[mailReturnCode] mailsession.mailResolveRecipient( recipientname
{, allowupdates} )
```

mailSend

This function is used to send a message through a mail session. It returns one of the following: mailReturnSuccess!, mailReturnFailure!, mailReturnInsufficientMemory!, mailReturnLogFailure!, mailReturnUserAbort!, mailReturnDiskFull!, mailReturnTooManySessions!, mailReturnTooManyFiles!, mailReturnTooManyRecipients!, mailReturnUnknownRecipient!, or mailReturnAttachmentNotFound!.

Syntax

```
[mailReturnCode] mailsession.mailSend( {mailmessage} )
```

Match

This function is used to determine whether a given string matches a specified string pattern.

Syntax

`[Boolean] Match( string, pattern )`

Max

This function returns the greater (or maximum) of two numbers.

Syntax

`[number] Max( x, y )`

Median

This function returns the median value for a column or expression that you specify. *range* may be one of the following: All, Crosstab, Graph, GroupNbr, or Page.

Syntax

`[number] Median( number_expression {FOR range {DISTINCT {express1 {, express2 {, ...}}}}} )`

MessageBox

This function is used to display a message on the screen, in a small window. The *title* is placed at the top of the window, and the *text* is displayed within the window. *icon* may be one of the following: Information!, StopSign!, Exclamation!, Question!, or None!. *button* may be one of the following: OK!, OKCancel!, YesNo!, YesNoCancel!, RetryCancel!, or AbortRetryIgnore!. *default* is the button you want to be the default (1 is the first button, etc.). The selected button is returned.

Syntax

```
[integer] MessageBox( title, text {, icon {, button {, default}}}
)
```

Mid

This function is used to pull out a section of a string. If a length is specified, that will be the number of characters retrieved; otherwise, the rest of the original string will be retrieved.

Syntax

```
[string] Mid( string, start {, length} )
```

Min

This function returns the lesser (or minimum) of two numbers.

Syntax

```
[number] Min( x, y )
```

Minute

This function returns the minute portion of a given time.

Syntax

```
[integer] Minute( time )
```

Mod

This function returns the modulus, or remainder, found when dividing x by y.

Syntax

```
[number] Mod( x, y )
```

Mode

This function returns the mode, or most common, value for a column or expression that you specify. *range* may be one of the following: All, Crosstab, Graph, GroupNbr, or Page.

Syntax

```
[number] Mode( number_expression {FOR range {DISTINCT {express1
{, express2 {, ...}}}}} )
```

ModifiedCount

This function returns the number of rows in a specific DataWindow that have been modified.

Syntax

```
[long] datawindowname.ModifiedCount()
```

Month

This function returns the month portion (1 through 12) of a given date.

Syntax

```
[integer] Month( date )
```

Move

This function is used to move an object on the screen.

Syntax

```
[integer] objectname.Move( x, y )
```

Now

This function returns the current system time.

Syntax

```
[time] Now()
```

Open

This set of functions is used to open a window.

Syntax

```
[integer] Open( windowname {, parent} )
[integer] Open( window_var, window_type {, parent} )
```

OpenChannel

This function is used to open a DDE channel to a specific application.

Syntax

```
[integer] OpenChannel( application, topicname {, windowhandle} )
```

OpenSheet

This function is used to open a new sheet in an MDI frame window. The *arrangeopen* parameter may be one of the following: Cascaded!, Layered!, or Original!.

Syntax

```
[integer] OpenSheet( sheet {, windowname}, mdiframe {, position
{,arrangeopen}} )
```

OpenSheetWithParm

This function is used to open a new sheet in an MDI frame window. The *arrangeopen* parameter may be one of the following: Cascaded!, Layered!, or Original!.

Syntax

```
[integer] OpenSheetWithParm( sheet_refvar, parameter {,
windowname}, mdiframe {, position {,arrangeopen}} )
```

OpenUserObject

This set of functions is used to retrieve and display a user object. If *x* and *y* are specified, the object will be placed at a specific location.

Syntax

```
[integer] OpenUserObject( userobjectname {, x, y} )
[integer] OpenUserObject( userobject_var, userobject_type {, x,
y} )
```

OpenUserObjectWithParm

This set of functions is used to retrieve and display a user object. If *x* and *y* are specified, the object will be placed at a specific location.

Syntax

```
[integer] OpenUserObjectWithParm( userobjectname, parameter {, x,
y} )
[integer] OpenUserObjectWithParm( userobject_var, parameter,
userobject_type {, x, y} )
```

OpenWithParm

This set of functions is used to open windows.

Syntax

```
[integer] OpenWithParm( windowname, parameter {, parent} )
[integer] OpenWithParm( windowname, parameter, windowtype {,
parent} )
```

PageAcross

This function determines which page the cursor is currently within, as a count across the horizontal plane.

Syntax

```
[integer] datawindowname.PageAcross()
```

PageCountAcross

This function determines the number of pages of width that a DataWindow or report occupies.

Syntax

```
[integer] datawindowname.PageCountAcross()
```

ParentWindow

This function returns the handle of the parent window of a given window.

Syntax

```
[object] windowname.ParentWindow()
```

Paste

This function is used to paste (insert) the contents of the clipboard into an edit control.

Syntax

[*integer*] *editname*.Paste()

Pi

This function returns a number that is calculated by multiplying pi by the given parameter.

Syntax

[*double*] Pi(*n*)

PixelsToUnits

This function converts a number of pixels into the equivalent number of PowerBuilder units. *type* may be specified as XPixelsToUnits!, or YPixelsToUnits!.

Syntax

[*integer*] PixelsToUnits(*pixels*, *type*)

PointerX

This function returns the number of PowerBuilder units that separate the left edge of an object from the pointer.

Syntax

[*integer*] *objectname*.PointerX()

PointerY

This function returns the number of PowerBuilder units that separate the top of an object from the pointer.

Syntax

[*integer*] *objectname*.PointerY()

PopMenu

This function is used to display a pop-up menu at a specified location.

Syntax

[*integer*] *menuitem*.PopMenu(*xlocation*, *ylocation*)

Pos

This function is used to determine whether one string is within another string. If so, the starting position of the match is returned, otherwise -1 is returned. If *start* is specified, the search will begin at that position within the string.

Syntax

[*long*] Pos(*string*, *search_string* {, *start*})

Position

This function returns the position of the cursor within an edit control. The first position is 1.

Syntax

[*integer*] *editname*.Position()

Post

This function is used to place a message into a window's queue.

Syntax

```
[Boolean] Post( handle, message_number, word, long )
```

PostEvent

This function is used to place a message into an object's queue.

Syntax

```
[Boolean] objectname.PostEvent( event )
```

Print

This set of functions is used to print various items to the currently selected printer. If *canceldialog* is TRUE, a dialog box will be displayed to allow the cancellation of printing.

Syntax

```
[integer] objectname.Print( printjobnumber, x, y {, width {,
height}} )
[integer] datawindowname.Print( {canceldialog} )
[integer] Print( printjobnumber, string )
[integer] Print( printjobnumber, string, tab )
[integer] Print( printjobnumber, tab, string )
[integer] Print( printjobnumber, tab1, string, tab2 )
```

PrintBitmap

This function is used to print a bitmap image. As part of this process, the location and final size of the bitmap (in PowerBuilder units) may be specified.

Syntax

```
[integer] PrintBitmap( printjobnumber, bitmap, x, y, width,
height )
```

PrintCancel

This set of functions is used to cancel print jobs.

Syntax

```
[integer] PrintCancel( printjob_id )
[integer] datawindowname.PrintCancel()
```

PrintClose

This function is used to complete a print job, sending the final page to the printer.

Syntax

```
[integer] PrintClose( printjobnumber )
```

PrintDataWindow

This function prints a specific DataWindow.

Syntax

```
[integer] PrintDataWindow( printjob_id, datawindowname )
```

PrintDefineFont

This function is used to specify the font to be used for printing. *fontpitch* may be Default!, Fixed!, or Variable!. *fontfamily* is one of the following: AnyFont!, Decorative!, Modern!, Roman!, Script!, or Swiss!. If *italic* or *underline* is TRUE, the appropriate item will be applied.

Syntax

```
[integer] PrintDefineFont( printjobnumber, fontnumber, facename,
height, weight, fontpitch, fontfamily, italic, underline )
```

PrintLine

This function draws a line on the printed page, between the coordinates given.

Syntax

```
[integer] PrintLine( printjobnumber, x1, y1, x2, y2, thickness )
```

PrintOpen

This function begins the printing process. It returns the *printjobnumber* used by most printing functions, or -1 if the function failed. You may give an optional name to the print job.

Syntax

```
[integer] PrintOpen( {jobname} )
```

PrintOval

This function is used to place an oval shape on the printed page. The coordinates and size refer to the rectangle (invisible) which represents the boundary of the oval shape drawn.

Syntax

```
[integer] PrintOval( printjobnumber, x, y, width, height,
thickness )
```

PrintPage

This function sends the current page to the printer, and sets up another page for continued print functions.

Syntax

```
[integer] PrintPage( printjobnumber )
```

PrintRect

This function draws a rectangle on the printed page, between the coordinates given.

Syntax

```
[integer] PrintRect( printjobnumber, x, y, width, height,
thickness )
```

PrintRoundRect

This function draws a rounded rectangle on the printed page, between the coordinates given.

Syntax

```
[integer] PrintRoundRect( printjobnumber, x, y, width, height,
xradius, yradius, thickness )
```

PrintSend

This function sends a string to the printer, at the current print location. If you specify *zerochar*, then that character will be used to denote the end of the string.

Syntax

```
[integer] PrintSend( printjobnumber, string {, zerochar} )
```

PrintScreen

This function is used to send the current screen image to the printer. You may specify the location on the screen where the image is to start, and the size of the image.

Syntax

```
[integer] PrintScreen( printjobnumber, x, y {, width {, height}} )
```

PrintSetFont

This function is used to select a font for printing, and is used in conjunction with PrintDefineFont. Upon success, this function returns the character height of the font selected.

Syntax

```
[integer] PrintSetFont( printjobnumber, fontnumber )
```

PrintSetSpacing

This function is used to set the line spacing for a print job. The parameter is multiplied by the current font height to determine the line spacing.

Syntax

```
[integer] PrintSetSpacing( printjobnumber, spacingfactor )
```

PrintSetup

This function calls the Windows Printer Setup dialog box, as installed for the current default printer, and allows editing of the setup information.

Syntax

```
[integer] PrintSetup()
```

PrintText

This function is used to place text on the printed page, starting at a given coordinate. If desired, a font may also be selected.

Syntax

```
[integer] PrintText( printjobnumber, string, x, y {, fontnumber} )
```

PrintWidth

This function is used to determine the size of a string for printing, using the current default font and size.

Syntax

```
[integer] PrintWidth( printjobnumber, string )
```

PrintX

This function returns the current X (vertical) location on the printed page for the print job specified.

Syntax

```
[integer] PrintX( printjobnumber )
```

PrintY

This function returns the current Y (horizontal) location on the printed page for the print job specified.

Syntax

```
[integer] PrintY( printjobnumber )
```

ProfileInt

This function is used to read integer information from a profile file, commonly named with the extension INI. The default value is returned if the file or specified section/key combination is not found.

Syntax

```
[integer] ProfileInt( filename, section, key, default )
```

ProfileString

This function is used to read string information from a profile file, commonly named with the extension INI. The default value is returned if the file or specified section/key combination is not found.

Syntax

```
[string] ProfileString( filename, section, key, default )
```

Rand

This function returns a random whole number between one and the number specified.

Syntax

```
[number] Rand( n )
```

Randomize

This function starts the random number generator, and should be called before the first call to Rand. The *seed* can be zero (in which case the sequence will not be repeatable), or a number of your choice. Using the same *seed* will generate the same sequence of random numbers.

Syntax

```
[integer] Randomize( seed )
```

Real

This function looks at a string or blob, and returns the real number stored there.

Syntax

[*real*] Real(*string_or_blob*)

RelativeDate

This function is used to determine what date is a given number of days away from another. The number of days specified may be positive or negative.

Syntax

[*date*] RelativeDate(*date, days*)

RelativeTime

This function is used to determine what time is a given number of seconds away from another. The number of seconds specified may be positive or negative.

Syntax

[*time*] RelativeTime(*time, seconds*)

Repair

This function is called after DataWindow errors are fixed, to reconnect to the database and make necessary updates.

Syntax

[*integer*] *pipelineobject*.Repair(*destinationtransaction*)

Replace

This function replaces a sequence of characters in one string, starting at a given location and for a specific number of characters, with a different sequence.

Syntax

```
[string] Replace( string, start, size, replacement )
```

ReplaceText

This function is used to replace the selected text in an edit control with the parameter passed to this function.

Syntax

```
[integer] editname.ReplaceText( string )
```

ReselectRow

This function is used to reread the database, perform any updates that are needed, and redisplay the row specified.

Syntax

```
[integer] datawindowname.ReselectRow( row )
```

Reset

This set of functions is used to clear objects of the information they contain.

Syntax

```
[integer] datawindowname.Reset()
[integer] listboxname.Reset()
```

ResetTransObject

This function disallows the use of transactions with an object.

Syntax

```
[integer] datawindowname.ResetTransObject()
```

Resize

This function is used to change the size of a graphic object or an edit control.

Syntax

```
[integer] objectname.Resize( width, height )
```

RespondRemote

This function determines whether the command or data received from a remote DDE connection was acceptable.

Syntax

```
[integer] RespondRemote( Boolean )
```

Restart

This function stops all processing within an application, closes all windows (without processing the Close scripts), and disconnects from the database. Then, the application Open script is started to restart the application.

Syntax

```
[integer] Restart()
```

Retrieve

This function forces a DataWindow to read data from the database, based on the current setup of the DataWindow. Any arguments passed to this function are used in the SQL statement for the window.

Syntax

```
[long] datawindowname.Retrieve( { argument, argument, ... } )
```

RGB

This function provides the long number that represents a specific combination of red, green, and blue coloring.

Syntax

```
[long] RGB( red, green, blue )
```

Right

This function retrieves the rightmost portion of a string, for the length (number of characters) specified.

Syntax

```
[string] Right( string, length )
```

RightTrim

This function is used to cut any extraneous spaces from the right end of a string.

Syntax

```
[string] RightTrim( string )
```

Round

This function is used to round numbers to the closest number. You may select the number of decimal places to use when rounding.

Syntax

```
[decimal] Round( number, places )
```

RowCount

This function returns the number of rows that are available in a DataWindow.

Syntax

```
[long] datawindowname.RowCount()
```

RowHeight

This function returns the height of the current row of a DataWindow.

Syntax

```
[integer] datawindowname.RowHeight()
```

RowsCopy

This function is used to copy rows from one DataWindow into another. *copybuffer* and *targetbuffer* may have the values Primary!, Delete!, or Filter!.

Syntax

```
[integer] datawindowname.RowsCopy( startrow, endrow, copybuffer,
targetdw, beforerow, targetbuffer )
```

RowsDiscard

This function is used to delete rows from a DataWindow. *buffer* may have the value Primary!, Delete!, or Filter!

Syntax

```
[integer] datawindowname.RowsDiscard( startrow, endrow, buffer )
```

RowsMove

This function is used to move rows from one DataWindow into another. *movebuffer* and *targetbuffer* may have the values Primary!, Delete!, or Filter!.

Syntax

```
[integer] datawindowname.RowsMove( startrow, endrow, movebuffer,
targetdw, beforerow, targetbuffer )
```

Run

This function is used to run an external program. *windowstate* may have the value Maximized!, Minimized!, or Normal!.

Syntax

```
[integer] Run( string {, windowstate} )
```

SaveAs

This function is used to save the DataWindow specified. *saveastype* may be specified as one of the following: CSV!, Clipboard!, dBASE2!, dBASE3!, DIF!, Excel!, SQLInsert!, SYLK!, Text!, WKS!, or WK1!. If *colheading* is TRUE, the column headings will be saved as the first item in the file. If you do not supply the file name and type, PowerBuilder will prompt you for the information.

Syntax

```
[integer] datawindowname.SaveAs( { filename, saveastype,
colheading } )
```

Scroll

This function is used to scroll an edit control in the direction specified, and by the number of rows given. A positive number of rows moves down, while a negative number moves up.

Syntax

```
[integer] editname.Scroll( number )
```

ScrollNextPage

This function moves the DataWindow down one page of data.

Syntax

```
[integer] datawindowname.ScrollNextPage()
```

ScrollNextRow

This function moves the DataWindow down one row of data.

Syntax

```
[integer] datawindowname.ScrollNextRow()
```

ScrollPriorPage

This function moves the DataWindow up one page of data.

Syntax

```
[integer] datawindowname.ScrollPriorPage()
```

ScrollPriorRow

This function move the DataWindow up one row of data.

Syntax

```
[integer] datawindowname.ScrollPriorRow()
```

ScrollToRow

This function moves the DataWindow to a specific row of data.

Syntax

```
[integer] datawindowname.ScrollToRow( row )
```

Second

This function returns the seconds portion of a time value.

Syntax

```
[integer] Second( time )
```

SecondsAfter

This function is used to determine the number of seconds between two times; or in other words, how many seconds after *time1* that *time2* occurs.

Syntax

```
[long] SecondsAfter( time1, time2 )
```

SelectedIndex

This function returns the index of the item that is currently selected in a ListBox. If nothing is selected, -1 is returned.

Syntax

```
[integer] listboxname.SelectedIndex()
```

SelectedItem

This function returns the item that is currently selected in a ListBox. If nothing is selected, an empty string is returned.

Syntax

`[string] listboxname.SelectedItem()`

SelectedLength

This function is used to determine the number of characters that are currently selected in an edit box.

Syntax

`[integer] editname.SelectedLength()`

SelectedLine

This function returns the number of the line in the edit control where the cursor is located.

Syntax

`[integer] editname.SelectedLine()`

SelectedStart

This function returns the location of the first character selected in the edit control.

Syntax

`[integer] editname.SelectedStart()`

SelectedText

This function returns the text that is selected in the edit control.

Syntax

```
[string] editname.SelectedText()
```

SelectItem

This set of functions is used to select items in a ListBox.

Syntax

```
[integer] listboxname.SelectItem( item, index )
[integer] listboxname.SelectItem( itemnumber )
```

SelectRow

This function is used to select a specific row in a DataWindow. If *Boolean* is TRUE, the row is selected; otherwise, it is deselected.

Syntax

```
[integer] datawindowname.SelectRow( row, Boolean )
```

SelectText

This function is used to select text in an edit control.

Syntax

```
[integer] editname.SelectText( start, length )
```

Send

This function is used to pass a message to a specific window.

Syntax

```
[long] Send( handle, message_number, lowword, long )
```

SetActionCode

This function is used to set the value of an action code for the specific DataWindow.

Syntax

```
[integer] datawindowname.SetActionCode( code )
```

SetBorderStyle

This function is used to change the border style selected for a DataWindow column. *borderstyle* may be one of the following: Box!, Noborder!, ShadowBox!, or Underline!.

Syntax

```
[integer] datawindowname.SetBorderStyle( column, borderstyle )
```

SetColumn

This function is used to make a specific column of a DataWindow active. It does not scroll the window.

Syntax

```
[integer] datawindowname.SetColumn( column )
```

SetDataDDE

This function is used to send data to a DDE application.

Syntax

```
[integer] SetDataDDE( string {, application, topic, item } )
```

SetDetailHeight

This function is used to change the detail height in a DataWindow, for the rows specified.

Syntax

```
[integer] datawindowname.SetDetailHeight( startrow, endrow,
height )
```

SetDynamicParm

This function changes the item at the specified index in the *DynamicDescriptionArea* to the value given.

Syntax

```
[integer] SetDynamicParm( DynamicDescriptionArea, index, value )
```

SetFilter

This function is used to modify the filter criteria for the DataWindow.

Syntax

```
[integer] datawindowname.SetFilter( format )
```

SetFocus

This function is used to set the focus on a specific item.

Syntax

```
[integer] objectname.SetFocus()
```

SetFormat

This function is used to define the format of a specific column in the DataWindow.

Syntax

```
[integer] datawindownameSetFormat( column, format )
```

SetItem

This function is used to change the value of a specific item in the DataWindow.

Syntax

```
[integer] datawindowname.SetItem( row, column, value )
```

SetMask

This function is used to define the mask that is to be used for an edit control. The following values may be used for *maskdatatype*: DateMask!, DateTimeMask!, DecimalMask!, NumericMask!, StringMask!, or TimeMask!.

Syntax

```
[integer] editmaskname.SetMask( maskdatatype, mask )
```

SetMicroHelp

This function defines the MicroHelp for a window to the specified text.

Syntax

```
[integer] windowname.SetMicroHelp( string )
```

SetNull

This function sets a specific variable to have a NULL value.

Syntax

```
[integer] SetNull( any_variable )
```

SetPicture

This function is used to create a new bitmap for the specific control, using the bitmap supplied.

Syntax

```
[integer] control.SetPicture( bitmap )
```

SetPointer

This function changes the appearance of the pointer. *type* may be any one of the following: Arrow!, Cross!, Beam!, HourGlass!, Size!, SizeNS!, SizeNESW!, SizeWE!, SizeNWSE!, or UpArrow!.

Syntax

```
[old_pointer_type] SetPointer( type )
```

SetPosition

This function specifies a location for the object. The *position* can be given as Behind!, NotTopMost!, ToTop!, ToBottom!, or TopMost!.

Syntax

```
[integer] objectname.SetPosition( position {, precedingobject} )
```

SetProfileString

This function is used to change values in a profile (or INI) file.

Syntax

```
[integer] SetProfileString( filename, section, key, value )
```

SetRedraw

This function is used to control whether an object should be redrawn automatically after each time it changes.

Syntax

```
[integer] objectname.SetRedraw( Boolean )
```

SetRemote

This set of functions is used to change values on remote applications.

Syntax

```
[integer] SetRemote( location, value, application, topicname )
[integer] SetRemote( location, value, handle {, windowhandle} )
```

SetRow

This function is used to select a specific row in the DataWindow.

Syntax

```
[integer] datawindowname.SetRow( row )
```

SetRowFocusIndicator

This function is used to change the indicator for the item having focus. The possible values for *focusindicator* are Off!, FocusRect!, Hand!, or Picture control.

Syntax

```
[integer] datawindowname.SetRowFocusIndicator( focusindicator {,
xlocation ylocation} )
```

SetSort

This function changes the sorting criteria for a DataWindow. The *format* is A for Ascending, D for Descending, or NULL if you want PowerBuilder to prompt you when the script runs.

Syntax

```
[integer] datawindowname.SetSort( format )
```

SetSQLSelect

This function is used to change the SQL Select statement for a DataWindow.

Syntax

```
[integer] datawindowname.SetSQLSelect( statement )
```

SetState

This function changes the state of a specific item in a ListBox. If *state* is TRUE, the item is selected; otherwise, it is deselected.

Syntax

```
[integer] listboxname.SetState( index, state )
```

SetTabOrder

This function is used to change the tab sequence for a column in a DataWindow.

Syntax

```
[integer] datawindowname.SetTabOrder( column, tabnumber )
```

SetText

This function changes the text that is in the current row and column in a DataWindow.

Syntax

```
[integer] datawindowname.SetText( text )
```

SetTop

This function is used to bring a specific entry in a ListBox to the top of the list box display; that is, the item is placed at the top of the window.

Syntax

```
[integer] listboxname.SetTop( index )
```

SetTrans

This function changes the internal transaction object for a DataWindow, replacing it with the transaction parameter.

Syntax

```
[integer] datawindowname.SetTrans( transaction )
```

SetTransObject

This function changes the internal transaction object for a DataWindow, replacing it with the programmer-specified transaction parameter.

Syntax

```
[integer] datawindowname.SetTransObject( transaction )
```

SetValidate

This function changes the validation rule for a specific column in a DataWindow.

Syntax

```
[integer] datawindowname.SetValidate( column, rule )
```

SetValue

This function changes the value of an item in a specified column to the given value.

Syntax

```
[integer] datawindowname.SetValue( column, index, value )
```

Show

This function is used to place an object on the screen if it is not already displayed, or to bring it to the topmost position if it is already on the screen.

Syntax

```
[integer] objectname.Show()
```

ShowHelp

This function is used to call the Windows Help system with a specific topic. The valid *helpcommand* values are Index!, Keyword!, and Topic!.

Syntax

`[integer] ShowHelp( helpfile, helpcommand {, typeid} )`

Sign

This function returns a 1 if the parameter is positive, 0 if it is zero, and -1 if it is negative.

Syntax

`[integer] Sign( n )`

SignalError

This function is used to provide a system error event for Windows, at the application level.

Syntax

`[integer] SignalError()`

Sin

This function calculates the sine value of an angle, which must be specified in radians.

Syntax

`[double] Sin( n )`

Small

This function returns the *n*'th smallest number for a given range or group selection, and matching optional criteria expressions. *return_exp* is the name of the column to return when the *n*'th smallest value is found. *range* may be one of the following: All, Crosstab, Graph, GroupNbr, or Page. If DISTINCT is used, only the smallest distinct values are located (i.e., no duplications).

Syntax

```
[type_of_small] Small( return_exp, small_exp, n { FOR range {
DISTINCT {express1 {, express2 {, ...}}}}} )
```

Sort

This function causes a DataWindow to be sorted, based on the current criteria set up for the window.

Syntax

```
[integer] datawindowname.Sort()
```

Space

This function is used to assign values to variables that are totally made up of *n* space characters.

Syntax

```
[string] Space( n )
```

Sqrt

This function returns the square root of a number.

Syntax

```
[double] Sqrt( n )
```

Start

This function is used to begin execution of a pipeline object, using the transaction, window, and arguments specified.

Syntax

```
[integer] pipelineobject.Start( sourcetransaction,
destinationtransaction, errordatawindow {, argn } )
```

StartHotLink

This function establishes a hot link with an application so that when data changes in the application, a notification is sent to PowerBuilder.

Syntax

```
[integer] StartHotLink( location, application, topic )
```

StartServerDDE

This function is used to start the application specified as a DDE server.

Syntax

```
[integer] StartServerDDE( { windowname ,} application, topic {,
item} )
```

State

This function returns the state of an item in a ListBox. A return value of 1 means the item is selected; 0 means it is not highlighted.

Syntax

```
[integer] listboxname.State( index )
```

StopHotLink

This function stops the hot link connection started with the StartHotLink function.

Syntax

```
[integer] StopHotLink( location, application, topic )
```

StopServerDDE

This function stops the application from being a DDE server.

Syntax

```
[integer] StopServerDDE( { windowname ,} application, topic )
```

String

This set of functions is used to create string values from different pieces of information.

Syntax

```
[string] String( date {, format} )
[string] String( datetime {, format} )
[string] String( number {, format} )
[string] String( string, textpattern )
[string] String( time {, format} )
```

Tan

This function calculates the tangent for an angle, specified in radians.

Syntax

```
[double] Tan( n )
```

Text

This function retrieves the text for a specific item in a ListBox.

Syntax

```
[string] listboxname.Text( index )
```

TextLine

This function returns the text on the cursor line in an edit control.

Syntax

```
[string] editname.TextLine()
```

Time

This set of functions is used to return the time specified in one of several formats.

Syntax

```
[time] Time( datetime )
[time] Time( hour, minute, second {, microsecond} )
[time] Time( string )
```

Timer

This function is used to trigger an event after a specified number of seconds, and to continue this action until the delay time is set to 0.

Syntax

```
[integer] Timer( number {, windowname} )
```

Today

This function returns the current system date.

Syntax

[*date*] Today()

Top

This function returns the index number of the top element displayed in a ListBox.

Syntax

[*integer*] *listboxname*.Top()

TotalItems

This function returns the total number of items in a ListBox.

Syntax

[*integer*] *listboxname*.TotalItems()

TotalSelected

This function is used to determine the number of items in a ListBox which are currently selected.

Syntax

[*integer*] *listboxname*.TotalSelected()

TriggerEvent

This function is used to trigger any specified event for any object that has events associated with it.

Syntax

```
[integer] objectname.TriggerEvent( event {, word, long} )
```

Trim

This function removes all leading and trailing spaces from a string.

Syntax

```
[string] Trim( string )
```

Truncate

This function is used to drop off trailing decimal places on a number. No rounding is performed.

Syntax

```
[number] Truncate( n, number_of_places )
```

TypeOf

This function returns the type of a specific object.

Syntax

```
[object] objectname.TypeOf()
```

Uncheck

This function removes the check mark from a menu selection.

Syntax

```
[integer] menuitem.Uncheck()
```

Undo

This function reverses the last change that was made in an edit control.

Syntax

`[integer] editname.Undo()`

UnitsToPixels

This function converts a number of PowerBuilder units into the equivalent number of pixels. *type* may be XUnitsToPixels! or YUnitsToPixels!.

Syntax

`[integer] UnitsToPixels( units, type )`

Update

This function is used to make the actual changes to the database that have been made in the DataWindow.

Syntax

`[integer] datawindowname.Update( {accept {, resetflag}} )`

Upper

This function changes all the characters in a string to uppercase.

Syntax

`[string] Upper( string )`

UpperBound

This function determines the upper bound of an array. If there are multiple dimensions in the array, the dimension can be specified.

Syntax

```
[integer] UpperBound( array {, n} )
```

WorkSpaceHeight

This function returns the height of the work space area.

Syntax

```
[integer] windowname.WorkSpaceHeight()
```

WorkSpaceWidth

This function returns the width of the work space area.

Syntax

```
[integer] windowname.WorkSpaceWidth()
```

WorkSpaceX

This function returns the current X location of the work space in relation to the left edge of the physical screen.

Syntax

```
[integer] windowname.WorkSpaceX()
```

WorkSpaceY

This function returns the current Y location of the work space in relation to the top edge of the physical screen.

Syntax

```
[integer] windowname.WorkSpaceY()
```

Year

This function is used to determine the year portion of a date.

Syntax

```
[integer] Year( date )
```

Yield

This function allows other graphic objects to have control as needed, including non-PowerBuilder objects.

Syntax

```
[Boolean] Yield()
```

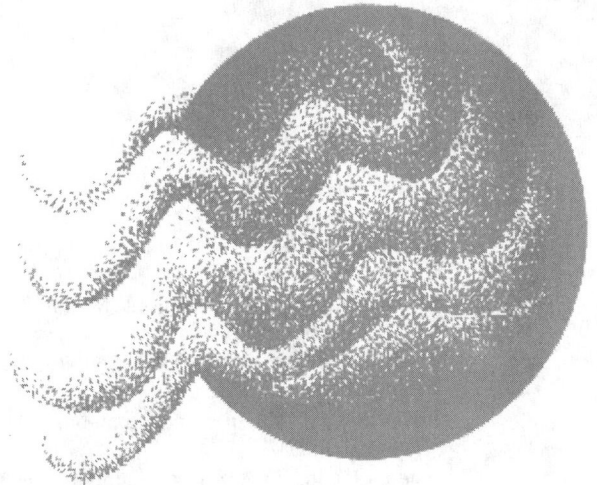

Index

Symbols

& (ampersand)
    defining menu accelerators, 70-71
    in PowerScript code, 113
▶ (arrow symbol), in cascaded menus, 71
* (asterisk), for PowerScript comments, 115-116
$ (dollar sign), Help topic tag, 158, 160
- (hyphen), defining menu separators, 70
(number sign), Help topic tag, 158, 160
/ (slash), for PowerScript comments, 115-117

A

Abs function, 206
Accelerators, creating for menus, 70-71
AcceptText function, 206
AddItem function, 206
Algorithms, in PowerScript, 114-115
Alpha testing, 199

Ampersand (&)
    defining menu accelerators, 70-71
    in PowerScript code, 113
Application painter
    creating applications, 40-46
    creating executable files, 180
    Debug window, 200-203
    overview of, 3, 6, 7
    PainterBar icons, 46
Applications, 37-46, 179-186
    adding Help systems to, 162-163
    adding windows to, 100-101
    application objects, 40
    creating, 6-7, 40-46
    creating releases, 179-186, 199
      creating executable files (.EXE), 180-181, 182, 185-186
      creating for distribution, 183-186
      creating for yourself or your office, 180-183
      dynamic libraries and, 181-183, 185-186
      Project painter and, 183-185
      Release Candidates and Releases, 199
      resource files and, 186
    defined, 12

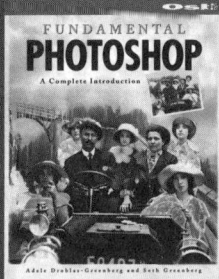

MAKE THE RIGHT
Connection

IT'S WHAT YOU KNOW THAT COUNTS.
WITH INNOVATIVE BOOKS FROM LAN TIMES
AND OSBORNE/MCGRAW-HILL, YOU'LL BE
THE ONE IN DEMAND.

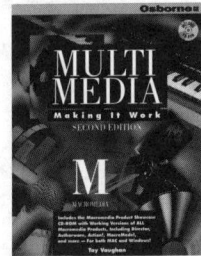

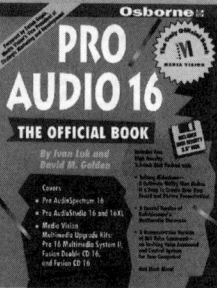

Yo Unix!

Think
Fast
PASSING
LANE AHEAD

What's the quickest route to tech support? Osborne's new Certified Tech Support series. Developed in conjunction with Corporate Software Inc., one of the largest providers of tech support fielding more than 200,000 calls a month, Osborne delivers the most authoritative question & answer books available anywhere. Speed up your computing and stay in the lead with answers to the most frequently asked end-user questions— from the simple to the arcane. And watch for more books int the series.

LOTUS NOTES
ANSWERS:
Certified Tech Support

From the Data Banks of Corporate Software, One of the World's Largest Providers of Tech Support, Answers to the Most Frequently Asked Questions...From the Simple to the Arcane.

Polly Kornblith

Lotus Notes Answere: Certified Tech Support
by Polly Russell Kornblith
$16.95
ISBN: 0-07-882045-6

The Internet Yellow Pages
by Harley Hahn and Rick Stout
$27.95
ISBN: 0-07-882023-5

Sound Blaster: The Official Book, Second Edition
by Peter M. Ridge, David Golden, Ivan Luk, Scott Sindorf, and Richard Heimlich. Includes 3.5-Inch Disk.
$34.95
ISBN: 0-07-882000-6

Osborne Windows Programming Series
by Herbert Schildt Chris H. Pappas, and William H. Murray, Ill.
Vol. I - Programming Fundamentals $39.95
ISBN: 0-07-881990-3
Vol. 2 - General Purpose API Functions $49.95
ISBN: 0-07-881991-1
Vol. 3 - Special Purpose API Functions $49.95

The Microsoft Access Handbook
by Mary Campbell
$27.95
ISBN: 0-07-882014-6

ORDER BOOKS DIRECTLY FROM OSBORNE/McGRAW-HILL

For a complete catalog of Osborne's books, call 510-549-6600 or write to us at 2600 Tenth Street, Berkeley, CA 94710

Call Toll-Free: 1-800-822-8158
24 hours a day, 7 days a week in U.S. and Canada

Mail this order form to:
McGraw-Hill, Inc.
Blue Ridge Summit, PA 17294-0840

Fax this order form to:
717-794-5291

EMAIL
7007.1531@COMPUSERVE.COM
COMPUSERVE GO MH

Ship to:

Name _____

Company _____

Address _____

City / State / Zip _____

Daytime Telephone: _____
(We'll contact you if there's a question about your order.)

ISBN #	BOOK TITLE	Quantity	Price	Total
0-07-88				
0-07-88				
0-07-88				
0-07-88				
0-07-88				
0-07-88				
0-07-88				
0-07-88				
0-07-88				
0-07-88				
0-07-88				
0-07-88				
0-07-88				
0-07-88				
	Shipping & Handling Charge from Chart Below			
	Subtotal			
	Please Add Applicable State & Local Sales Tax			
	TOTAL			

Shipping & Handling Charges

Order Amount	U.S.	Outside U.S.
Less than $15	$3.45	$5.25
$15.00 - $24.99	$3.95	$5.95
$25.00 - $49.99	$4.95	$6.95
$50.00 - and up	$5.95	$7.95

Occasionally we allow other selected companies to use our mailing list. If you would prefer that we not include you in these extra mailings, please check here: ☐

METHOD OF PAYMENT

☐ Check or money order enclosed (payable to Osborne/McGraw-Hill)

☐ AMERICAN EXPRESS   ☐ DISCOVER   ☐ MasterCard   ☐ VISA

Account No. ☐☐☐☐☐☐☐☐☐☐☐☐☐☐☐

Expiration Date _____

Signature _____

In a hurry? Call 1-800-822-8158 anytime, day or night, or visit your local bookstore.

Thank you for your order

Code BC640SL